Critiquing THE *Critics* OF JOSEPH SMITH

AF807713

Critiquing THE *Critics* OF JOSEPH SMITH

Hartt Wixom

CFI

Springville, Utah

© 2005 Hartt Wixom

All rights reserved.

No part of this book may be reproduced in any form whatsoever, whether by graphic, visual, electronic, film, microfilm, tape recording, or any other means, without prior written permission of the author, except in the case of brief passages embodied in critical reviews and articles.

ISBN: 1-55517-834-0
v.1

Published by CFI,
an imprint of Cedar Fort, Inc.
925 N. Main, Springville, Utah 84663
www.cedarfort.com

Distributed by:

CEDAR FORT

Cover design by Nicole Williams
Cover design © 2005 by Lyle Mortimer

Printed in the United States of America
10 9 8 7 6 5 4 3 2 1

Printed on acid-free paper

Contents

Acknowledgments

The compilation and writing of this book required the resources and assistance of many people. I especially appreciate my wife, Judene, for her labor of love, encouragement, tireless efforts, and technical expertise in editing and aligning both text and endnotes.

I thank Rafael Del Vecchio and Wade Wixom for providing much technical assistance and insight, and I appreciate Elder Vaughn J. Featherstone for providing valuable feedback.

I also wish to thank those entities that provided library manuscripts, both pro and con, concerning Joseph Smith's announced message of renewed revelation. They include the Foundation for Ancient Research and Mormon Studies (FARMS), the L. Tom Perry Special Collections in the Harold B. Lee Library at Brigham Young University, and the Archives Division of the Family and Church History Department of The Church of Jesus Christ of Latter-day Saints.

In addition, I appreciate the diaries and letters of many, in and out of the LDS Church, who were willing to share unpublished records, rich in historical insight and enlightenment.

Finally, I wish to thank Orson Foulger for his assistance and encouragement and for access to his vast private library.

Preface

This work examines historical objectivity. The author is well aware of the perils of such an enterprise. Facts, dates, and places are often agreed upon, but interpretations and conclusions from them often are not. For example, some may not agree with the selection of Fawn Brodie as a prototype representative of anti-Mormon writers.

She may not be. But she is certainly the most decorated. From that viewpoint, owing to her many awards for "detached objectivity," she draws the most attention. There is no way, of course, to critique every critic who attempts to defrock Joseph Smith or discredit the Latter-day Saints. But no critic of Joseph Smith can be found who has put forth the research effort of Mrs. Brodie. Hence, she represents the best of the worst that can be said about Smith and becomes the focus of this book.

Many continue to use Brodie's vein of thought, if not her precise words, that Joseph Smith must have written the Book of Mormon by himself. Yet they do not offer a plausible explanation of how the book came to be written by an unlearned teenaged boy. The result is refusal to face reality.

Other authors have done the same about other facets of Latter-day Saint Church history. Irving Wallace insisted that he was the proper non-Mormon (or anti-Mormon) author to write about "Ann," who as the celebrated twenty-seventh wife of Brigham Young grew tired of polygamy and the Mormon Church. The reason? Wallace knew nothing of Mormonism upon his arrival in Salt Lake City to write his book *The Twenty-Seventh Wife*. For the Latter-day Saints, he also knew little of the Church when he left. For non-Latter-day Saints, Wallace gave the world the inside lowdown because he was harsh.

The *World Book Encyclopedia* says Thomas Jefferson was the framer of our nation's Declaration of Independence, the founder of a major university, and a leader who took our country from the gloom of servitude to the glory of self-government.

But a television program I watched recently, using the same data as the encyclopedia, depicted the third president of the United States as a fornicator so inept in personal affairs that he went bankrupt and had to auction off his loyal slaves. Which history is correct? Perhaps both. It simply depends on the chosen highlighted facts and how they are interpreted.

Writing history can be wrought with peril. It will always be so.

Introduction

Meet Bill Jensen. He is in his early twenties, is of average height and weight, and has a girlfriend named Karla Jones. Bill has finished two years of college and has lived across much of the United States because his father frequently changed jobs. He has heard of the Mormon religion from someone he met but remembers little of it. Bill also has an Uncle James, who is an atheist and intends to remain one.

Karla is in her first year of college and is undecided as to which religion to join. She has an Aunt Marge, who has a master's degree in United States history. Marge doesn't belong to any religion but says she sometimes reads the Bible.

Bill cannot decide which church is right but has decided to get and study a book on The Church of Jesus Christ of Latter-day Saints. His Uncle James, who used to be an investigative newspaper reporter for the *New York Times,* tells him to avoid all religions, in particular Mormonism. "This cult was despised from the beginning in western New York. You should read the things said about the Mormons in the eastern libraries!"

Bill checks out a book his uncle recommends from the local library titled *No Man Knows My History,* written in 1971 by Fawn Brodie. She is a former Mormon and an expert on the subject. The book agrees with many of the things Bill's uncle has told him. As he reads, Bill is not only convinced Mormonism is false but also that there is no true religion. James assures Bill, "You've got it right there, my boy."

Meanwhile, Karla begins to study with Bill and Marge and

has some questions. She checks out the footnotes and begins to write down comparisons between Brodie's book and other books on the same subject. After a few chapters of Brodie's book, she declares to Bill: "I can't make up my mind about this Joseph Smith. They all say something different about him. Look at this chart I've made. Who do you think all these people are talking about?

"He 'drank like a sailor and swore like a pirate.'

"He 'was a tender and affectionate husband and parent . . . a warm and sympathizing friend.'

"He was a 'lazy, good-for-nothing lout . . . not given to exercising his muscles in any practical way.'

"And then someone wrote, 'I feel like shouting hallelujah, all the time, when I think that I ever knew Joseph Smith, the Prophet.'"

Bill replied, "I don't know. Four different people?"

"No," Karla replied. "They're all talking about Joseph Smith, founder of the Mormon religion. And they all claimed to know him well. The authors are, in order, Illinois governor Thomas Ford, John Bernhisel, the *Detroit Post-Times,* and Brigham Young."

Bill observed, "Writing a biography about religious figures seems to be a challenge different from your normal history. It hardly seems to be an exact science."

Karla agreed. "I've got the *History of the Church* here by Joseph Smith," she said. "It says that the United Order of the Mormons was similar to conventional communism only in that all participants placed their material goods in common possession. There would 'be no poor among them.' And this seems important: distribution by a fair and impartial bishop named Edward Partridge provided that the goods were equally shared. The Church members didn't have to live under the rule—they could choose."

Marge pitched in now, reading a reference from *History of the Church* 1:365: "It says here that a Church member, one Titus Billings, consecrated his worldly surplus 'of my own free will and accord.'"

Karla replied, "But on pages 121–22 in *No Man Knows My*

History, Brodie says, 'When the mixture of communists and non-communists became too troublesome, Joseph sent word to Missouri that unless a man joined the order, he should be denied membership in the Church.'"

Bill piped in. "Yet strangely, a footnote to her statement refers us to the *History of the Church,* volume 1, page 365—the same reference we just read that said a man could choose whether he wanted to live in the united order."

"It would seem that she contradicts herself," Karla said. "But what did the critics think of Brodie's book?"

"She won tons of national awards from various magazine and newspaper publications for 'detached objectivity,'" Marge replied. "She receives special praise for finding an answer to the Book of Mormon without all the spiritual stuff. It's here on the back flyleaf of *No Man Knows My History.*"

"I found another book in the library titled *Reconsidering No Man Knows My History,*" said Karla. "It says on page 60 that a retired Brigham Young University professor states that Brodie 'is still the most influential and referenced' anti-Mormon writer of them all. There must be a reason."

"With all those awards from such prominent magazines and newspapers," Bill mused, "she must truly have told it like it was."

"But it does become confusing at times," Karla added. "All these contradictions! I don't know what to believe."

Thus it has been for many who have begun a search for reason and truth on a subject that just will not go away. Some simply reject the Mormon claim. But on the logic that if we want to learn about the African jungle, we must examine it firsthand, the following volume is offered.

1
Joseph Smith, the "Impostor"

When Fawn McKay Brodie's *No Man Knows My History* appeared on bookshelves in 1945 (with an update in 1971), it created a firestorm of controversy. For many reasons, it still does.

As the niece of LDS Church president David O. McKay and daughter of Thomas McKay, an assistant to the Quorum of the Twelve, Brodie unleashed a bombshell of exhaustive research. Her book spelled out reasons for more than five hundred pages why Joseph Smith, revered as the first prophet of The Church of Jesus Christ of Latter-day Saints, had to be an impostor. Even many LDS historians hailed her work as the most extensive ever published on the prophet from Palmyra.

Some non-Mormon advisers tried to convince Brodie that Smith was not an outright charlatan but was sincerely deluded into thinking himself in communion with God. But Brodie's Smith emerges as a conscious deceiver. In the reissue of her book in 1971, Brodie asserts in her preface that she has even more evidence why she can justify declaring to all thinking students of religious history that Joseph Smith was a fraud.

Marvin S. Hill, professor emeritus at LDS Church-owned Brigham Young University, said this of Brodie's effort: "It quickly became the standard life of Joseph Smith and the most influential book on early Mormonism, a status it has retained."[1]

Sydney E. Ahlstrom of Yale University termed it a "sympathetic and insightful account that is unequaled in portraying the life of the Mormon prophet."[2]

Hill then adds this critical challenge to historians, "That Brodie's work has gone so long without effective challenge or criticism is peculiar."[3]

Mormons protested that it was not written in the "right spirit," but non-Mormons loved it because Brodie had, for them, debunked the Mormon "fable." It didn't hurt either that she managed to inveigh a certain benign sympathy for Smith. For example, she pictured him as such a charismatic man that he was able to gather a large following of converts seeking insight into the mysteries of godliness. Brodie's Smith takes on the air of a rather likable impostor.

But for Mormons, unlike the remainder of the world, it was little solace if Smith was, as Brodie molded him, charming and benevolent. If he was not divinely directed, forget it. The Mormons wanted a divine link, not a well-meaning daydreamer or deceiver.

It is to this charge—that Smith was a knowing mountebank—that we focus attention. Does Brodie (or anyone) provide evidence of a masquerade standing up to the test of objective scrutiny? A dozen or so newspapers and magazines say she did and showered her with more accolades for detached and scrupulous objectivity than for any other chronicler of LDS history.[4] In other words, she represented the best of the anti-Mormon authors in debunking Joseph Smith. It follows that if you refute Brodie successfully you have, in effect, defused a host of serious arguments against Mormondom's prophet.

It was such lavish praise of Brodie that first attracted this author to study her work and evaluate it on the basis of academic and journalistic truth-seeking standards, those that would or should have been applied by the publications heaping the praise. Having completed a master's thesis in journalistic standards of objectivity[5] and further post-graduate work in the field of history, coupled with forty-five years of active experience in newspaper investigative reporting, I was attracted to her scholarship, or at least to a full analysis of it.

I was also intrigued independently by the life of Joseph Smith after long study of both Latter-day Saint and non-Latter-day Saint sources, and after visiting Palmyra, New York, and Nauvoo a number of times to learn more about the background, life setting, and historicity of Joseph Smith.

None of the above, of course, can once and for all prove anyone right or wrong in evaluating Smith as pretender or prophet. In order to accept his teachings as meaningful (or otherwise), we would need to implement in our own lives what he taught and assess its validity. But perhaps we can answer this question: "Has Fawn Brodie (or anyone) successfully exposed Joseph Smith to be a false prophet?"

Of course, members of The Church of Jesus Christ of Latter-day Saints may feel they have put the Book of Mormon to an adequate test by applying Alma 32:28 (dare to experiment by planting and nourishing a spiritual seed) and Moroni 10:4 (prayer and testimony). Some members may comfortably, or perhaps even smugly or ignorantly, feel they can skip all anti-Mormon rhetoric. After all, Book of Mormon teachings, intertwined with those of the Bible and other accepted scriptures, would seem to have found efficacy in the daily lives of more than twelve million Mormons of record facing life's dilemmas, along with millions of others during the past 170 years. That is apparently why so many joined and remained members.

But Latter-day Saints must embrace a sobering thought if they are to be effective missionaries and proponents of Joseph Smith's teachings. Many sincere non-Mormons, influential and intellectual leaders in universities and centers of communications the world over, believe Fawn Brodie did it. They believe she explained in entertaining fashion how Joseph Smith could fool so many of his followers for so long. Her book, rich in prose and imagery, still in print after selling dozens of editions since 1945, leans a long shadow toward anyone seeking an understanding of early LDS Church beginnings. Brodie's Joseph Smith stands in the way.

Indeed, probably no one painted in word pictures as eloquently as she the difficulties, setbacks, and even triumphs experienced by Mormondom's prophet. She begins by speaking of the embarrassment in Sharon, Windsor County, Vermont, that the Mormon prophet, an "infamous impostor," was born there: "the dreamy town . . . where he [Joseph Smith] was born has long since abandoned hope of being known for anything else."[6] Hers was not a dull account of the Mormon prophet's life. As an example, after describing Joseph's martyrdom, she writes this hauntingly poignant line, "leaving Carthage forlorn and silent with its dead."

History consists, of course, of more than comely sentences. Very early in her volume, Brodie was cautioned to pay more attention to fine points of accuracy. Non-Mormon advisers such as Dale Morgan warned of depicting Joseph as a knowing fraud—an impostor, perhaps, suggested Morgan, but not one fully aware of what he was doing. Morgan opined that the deliberate fraud approach did not explain how Smith could influence so many followers to make so many sacrifices for their peculiar belief.[7]

Morgan and others also pointed out that letters written in private to family members, including the Prophet's wife, Emma, provided insight into a Joseph Smith who was a loving father, husband, and church leader. The letters also pointed out that he was a man who believed thoroughly in his announced mission as a prophet and cared deeply about the welfare of his followers.[8]

But Brodie had a point. Joseph Smith claimed much more than inspiration. He was not a Luther or Gautama merely seeking reform. Smith claimed visions, three in one night, leading to a restoration of the early Christian church—far more than a mere reformation. The Mormon leader seemed always aware of the extraordinary claims he made. He proposed no middle ground, nor indeed did there seem to be any. It would seem he was either courageous prophet or articulate "bunko" artist.

Yet while Brodie claimed to expose Joseph Smith, the research shared with her brother, Thomas, who had just returned from an LDS mission, convinced Thomas all the more of Joseph's prophetic calling.[9] Why would this be so? In the pages ahead, let us reason together the conspicuous phenomena of polarized religious conviction.

At the same time there is irony. One of Brodie's "crushing blows" to Mormonism, she claimed, was that Joseph could not even convince his own family members he had received a vision. Nor could Brodie convince her own family members he had not.

Some Mormons accused Brodie of being emotionally biased. Didn't she stray from the teachings of a loving and devoted family (her father and her uncle) dedicated to bringing her up *correctly?* Didn't she feel that her family's religion placed too many restrictions on her, thus compelling her to write a book denouncing them?

Yes and no. I praise Brodie for her independent search for truth. Growing up in Mormon country, I have heard a plethora of faith-promoting rumors—not all are about doctrine. Some are merely provincial virtues, such as the account of the son who, as he is dying, reaches up with the name of a deceased relative on his lips. Yet those who were actually there say he simply went into a coma and died.

In the LDS Church (as in other churches), blind faith is too often substituted for researchable knowledge. Or obedience is rendered to ecclesiastical authority without checking the conscience. The latter occurred in 1857, when Mormons in southern Utah killed immigrants on the orders of two LDS stake presidents.[10] Loyalty in that case was misdirected to people, rather than directed to principle.

It would appear on the surface that Brodie's purpose in launching her monumental *No Man Knows My History* was more than merely seeking liberation from a family lifestyle. She sought to explore for herself truth she felt did not sit well with her astute intellectual curiosity. So she went to work.

Thus, I applaud her announced search for truth. But that is not the question. The question is, did she find it?

Growing up in an LDS environment, she might have heard the Church make some declarations indefensible on a logical rationale.

As an example, the book *What of the Mormons?* lists the Church as author and contains this statement: "Indications point to the fact that as a rule the children of polygamous marriages were superior physically and mentally."[11]

What indications, fact, or rule? Based on what study and how large a sample? And what do LDS children not born of polygamous unions think of such a claim?

The above declaration on superior children born of polygamy, written in 1947, came two years after Brodie's first edition of *No Man Knows My History*. It was, in time, however, to be considered for her revised edition begun in 1971.

Here's another example of what might be labeled provincial folklore: Hole-in-the-Rock expedition leaders of 1879–80 seeking a route to San Juan County, Utah, are held up for praise. Or, in other words, they faithfully and dutifully completed a difficult Church assignment. They reached their destination in southeastern Utah as programmed and succeeded months later in settling there—but only after risking lives to dig holes in cliffs and lower wagons across the great abyss of the Colorado River.[12]

With less stubborn faith (or blind loyalty to ecclesiastical injunction) might they have retreated, crossed the gorgeless Green and Colorado rivers farther north (say, near today's towns of Green River and Moab), and settled San Juan County much sooner?

Brodie was not alive at that time, but it would not be too far amiss to say that if she had been, she would have announced: "This is nonsense. Put me down as a dissenter if you wish and lacking faith in your orders as a church leader, but Brother Jones, I've looked at the map, and I'm going around the other way. It is much safer and saner, and I can get there in far less time. See you there."

In other words, Brodie tacked up her own sail across the stern of the good ship *Religion*. It matters little if she rocks the boat so long as she isolates truth. She owes allegiance to nothing else.

Nor does anyone.

We cannot become encumbered with loyalties when writing

history as chambers of commerce do in pronouncing the virtues of their hometowns.

Almost immediately following the publication of her biography on Smith, Brodie was the recipient of knee-jerk criticism from a number of Church members who hadn't studied the book on its merits. No scientific analysis was made of her work. She was simply wrong, according to these faithful.

Much of this criticism is mentioned in reviews of Brodie's work titled *Reconsidering No Man Knows My History*, published in 1996. One of her cousins refers to her as Mrs. Jew (her husband Bernard was from a Jewish family) and states that she is "not convinced of the things she has written."[13] Others called her naughty and predicted a life of punishment. Some warned her not to venture into their neighborhood.[14] These are most unfortunate in that they have nothing at all to do with the truth or error of her work. None of these critics appear to have spent much time within the covers of *No Man*. They simply oppose it because she goes against conventional wisdom of the area's dominant church.

Others debated whether Brodie was an atheist. Her brother, Thomas, said he never knew her to have any faith in a divine power. Her frequent debunking of New Testament miracles reinforces his observation. We have, for example, this in *No Man*: "the primitive church with all its naive realism, oversimplified ethics, and antiquated theology."[15]

No record exists of her attaching the slightest credibility to religious philosophy. There are occasional outbursts of "Oh, my God," but they are clearly not meant to suggest piety. Her husband, Bernard, is also pictured as one not believing in deity, despite a Jewish background.[16] It is well known that Bernard influenced Brodie's *No Man* epic, for she discloses as much within her acknowledgment. The matter is discussed even further in *Reconsidering*.[17]

But it would seem an injustice for Brodie's uncle, or anyone, to describe her as simply a "straying pony" that "found a hole in the fence and partook of poisoned grain."[18] Her writings don't indicate a naughty-girl syndrome, one displaying deviance for its own sake or preferring the life of an undisciplined libertine. She seems to have a mind searching for answers that at least meets one absolute, preconceived condition: there must be no supernatural. However, it must be examined as to whether that condition is honest in light of the evidence. It makes for an awkward conflict, for Smith claimed almost nothing throughout his thirty-eight years, if not direct divine guidance.

I believe that Brodie, while showing some restraint toward an upset family, was also wrong in saying her uncle personally orchestrated her excommunication because he "felt keenly the need for self-protection" or wanted to get rid of her "in the most dramatic possible fashion."[19] Any church must make it plain that the doctrinal teachings of known dissidents do not reflect the true teachings of that particular church. After Brodie was no longer a member of the LDS Church, she was free to teach anything she wanted. Or, if so moved, to form her own sect. Churches throughout the ages, whatever the denomination, have routinely divorced such dissenters from their doctrine.

Thus, it seems folly that one of Brodie's uncles would declare the Mormon Church "to be in error" for separating one of its most scholarly members, as he (perhaps naively) put it, for "creative writing."[20]

If Joseph Smith was not a prophet, as Brodie charges, the LDS Church has little if any purpose for existing or being organized in the first place. Members might as well disperse into other Christian faiths—Protestant or Catholic—if there is nothing new in the faith taught by Smith.

A social organization? Possibly. But that is not what Smith, or Mormonism, claimed.

But a number of Brodie's advisers, including Morgan, appear uncomfortable with an either/or approach. They want a compromise best described as sincere fraud. Some critics in *Reconsidering* clearly want to place a man-made halo on the head of a deluded non-prophet. But Smith's claims were not compromising. He said he was told all the churches were wrong and that God wanted him to be an instrument in restoring Christ's original, true church. That leaves little room for compromise. Are those who want a compromise, such as Morgan, simply unwilling to face the hard facts of either/or?

Some writers have hinted that Juanita Brooks was in jeopardy of losing her Church membership, as did Brodie, for railing against Church authorities in her *Mountain Meadows Massacre*. But that was a different matter entirely. Brooks never questioned the doctrines of her church or claimed to replace them as Brodie did. Brooks's position was simply that a few authorities, imperfect human beings, acted unwisely in ordering and trying to cover up a tragedy, which was the theme of her *Mountain Meadows Massacre*. It should be added that Brooks lauded Brodie for taking authorities to task. But Brooks differed from Brodie in that Brooks declared that she firmly believed in the restoration of the early Christian church via Joseph Smith.[21] Brodie did not.

Certainly Brodie's academic credentials were impressive. She was a dean team's dream, a relentless scholar, graduating from high school at age fourteen and from the University of Utah at eighteen. By twenty-one she had a master's degree from the University of Chicago and later taught history at UCLA until her death in 1981.

We are left with this: Brodie researched relentlessly in the field of LDS history, especially the anti-references. She amassed the most exhaustive and complete (up to her time) research in the history of The Church of Jesus Christ of Latter-day Saints. As most will agree, hers was no shallow effort. She appeared to exhume every affidavit and every legal document ever published about Mormondom's prophet.

Now that we have Brodie's background, let us examine where it led her.

Let us examine her charges thoroughly, giving her every possible opportunity to prove Joseph Smith an impostor.

Let us do so minus any of the alleged hocus-pocus of faith, testimony, and spirit that she denounces.

Let us give her every benefit of a doubt that *No Man Knows*

My History deserves the appellation of detached objectivity, for which she won so many awards.

Let us find out once and for all to what extent Fawn Brodie has added meaningful scholarship to the search for historical truth pertaining to Joseph Smith, founder of Mormonism.

Let us find out if she deserves continued honors as the author of the one of the most insightful accounts to the life of Joseph Smith. Despite her academic credentials, and giving her all credit for an honest search to find religious truth, let us find out if she continues to be without effective challenge.

2
Red Flags

It could be said that Brodie displayed more writing talent than the usual didactic skills of the teaching profession, and is credited by many as producing the most readable biography of Joseph Smith. But red flags start popping up.

To Marvin Hill's statement that it is peculiar Brodie's book has gone so long (1996) without effective challenge or criticism, Mormons respond by saying that from page one Brodie never allowed the remotest possibility that Smith's mission could have been sincere. Hill himself said, "Her book is not entirely adequate because it did not consider Smith to be religiously motivated."[1] Yet the allusion remains that no LDS historian has taken the bulk of Brodie's allegations to examine them one by one. This is exactly what is proposed herein, to examine the main points she sets forth, and those championed by other anti-Mormon writers, seeking to expose Joseph Smith.

The reader unfamiliar with ecclesiastical history should also realize from the outset that it is the norm, not the exception, for religious biographies to attract highly polarized viewpoints. Indeed, Brodie's work might have been more scholarly if she had pointed out this anomaly for those claiming divine inspiration. It has been true in treatises written about Jesus Christ, Mohammed, and nearly all who have claimed supernatural events in their lives. Thus, it was nothing extraordinary when those who lauded the Smith family prior to the early 1820s suddenly had nothing good to say about it following Joseph's announced communion with divine sources. It has been the same for many religious leaders.

The Apostle Paul received similar treatment following his claim to a vision, as we shall see later. Thus, it would weigh more equitably toward objectivity if both sides of any ecclesiastical claim are presented. This Brodie did not do. In her preface, she announced that she wanted to find truth, but she also announced that she had already decided that Smith was a charlatan. This, of course, placed an added burden on Brodie to prove her one-sided assessments.

If and when Brodie does provide counterarguments, her negative conclusions usually receive headline treatment, while the counterargument is often reduced to a footnote. Worse, some footnotes referenced to the index are tilted, as in the entry "Brotherton, Martha, *slandered* by Mormon pamphlet, 307n".[2] Martha can say what she wants about the church she disfavors, but when the Church tries to defend itself, the same is termed slander.

It is also true that much of LDS history has been glossed over, perhaps to mislead or perhaps because it is simply out of the LDS comfort zone. If it isn't faith promoting, it may be labeled irrelevant by some Church leaders.

The historian has no responsibility to build faith. That is the job of the Sunday School teacher. If faith is built in recording history, it must be a byproduct of ferreting out truth. It would seem the old phrase heard by some LDS members to "forget that discussion because it is not necessary to your salvation" does a disservice in the crusade to find all residue of truth in history's petri dish. We must isolate truth; the reader can then decide where that truth fits and how to use it.

It is also possible that LDS historians do not explore some of Brodie's claims because they simply don't want to probe into unseemly allegations. One such allegation was whether Oliver Cowdery really accused Joseph Smith of having a "nasty affair" with an "orphan girl."[3] But if Brodie's book is to be fairly analyzed, it is time to roll up the sleeves and examine all her research, particularly the interpretations and conclusions. Glossing over history without delving into the burrs and thistles of the human experience only paves the way for energetic writers such as Brodie to command center stage for the half century she has. History, like nature, abhors a vacuum.

On that stage, *No Man Knows My History* drew high accolades from many sources Americans had come to respect. The *Book of the Month Club News* said, "The first satisfactory explanation of the extraordinary power of Smith . . . an excellent biography."[4] *The New York Times* opined, "Scholarly, comprehensive, judicial . . . a masterly job of thorough research . . . scrupulously objective."[5] *The New York Herald Tribune* (Bernard DeVoto) called it the "first honest and intelligent biography of Joseph Smith. . . . She has written as a detached, modern intelligent, grounded in naturalism, rejecting the supernatural."[6] *Time* magazine further applauded Brodie for her "admirable detachment."[7]

Wilson Follett, Knopf Publishing House, added this as an editor: "[The book will be taken] as the final authority on Joseph Smith by everyone except those speaking for the official point of view by the Mormon hierarchy."[8] Rich praise. In addition, the front flyleaf of *No Man* promises much: "The reader is made to know him [Joseph Smith] fully." A lofty promise, indeed! But it would be unfair to hold Brodie to this latter statement, for in the concluding remarks of her preface, she openly invites more research. In addition, most flyleaf promotions are written by publishers, not authors.

None of the above critics giving out their accolades for objectivity, however, claimed to have read much LDS history or to know details of the life of Joseph Smith, with the possible exception of Utah-born DeVoto. Brodie saved critics the trouble of researching for themselves, or at least those critics who were content to take her word as authoritative. To be fair, Brodie's scholarship does appear exhaustive, probing more deeply into the life of Joseph Smith than anyone had theretofore done. Her text, flowing smoothly, is also highly readable.

But despite eloquent rhetoric, did Brodie distort data,

consciously or unconsciously, or slant preconceived ideas toward how she perceived things ought to be, to the point of distortion?

A friend of mine, now a famous author, wrote a beautiful book titled *The Last Valentine*. It begins, "Caroline's heart beat wildly as she entered the revolving doors . . . soldiers, their wives and girlfriends filled the hallways. That old feeling came back to her. It was as if she felt him close to her, as if he were there, leaving her again. The feeling of desperation had consumed her one year earlier as she held onto her husband's arm . . . the last touch of his strength before sending him to the hostilities raging in the Pacific."[9]

I was with James M. Pratt years ago in a private tutoring session when he penned these words. Bewitching. But pure fiction. Historical fiction. Arthur Conan Doyle did it so effectively with his Sherlock Holmes series, according to his publishers, that even today when tourists go to London, many want to see the detective's fictional apartment at 221B Baker Street.

As for Brodie's own historical effort, I had personally expected to be much enlightened, considering the many accolades accumulated for detached objectivity. In the beginning, it appeared that she could and would thoroughly defuse the founding prophet of The Church of Jesus Christ of Latter-day Saints.

But point by point, as will be documented in subsequent chapters, I was alerted to the suspicion that for all her exhaustive research, she repeatedly slips in indefensible opinion as fact. She bases fact on reliable sources at times, but sentences such as, "There is no record of her anger except in the dubious gossip"[10] do little to engender trust. I was surprised to find multiple speculations founded on little more than sheer determination to force a point, such as one instance where she alleges that Smith made unwanted romantic advances. Brodie says, "Nancy [Rigdon] threatened to scream until the whole town came running unless he [Joseph] let her go home."[11] No responsible historian could let this bombshell go without some sort of reference or footnote. There is none. Yet if the whole town might come running, surely there were many witnesses to this sexually suggestive affront. How is it Brodie doesn't furnish any? In addition, Brodie is playing games with us here. She doesn't say Nancy did scream. She says Nancy threatened to scream. How does Brodie know this?

The reader continues to search, for there are times when Brodie dislodges fascinating details about the Mormon prophet, especially the initial romantic liaison between Joseph and Emma. Still, the conclusions often found are unlinked to the material presented. Many carry no connection at all to Smith's claims of prophethood. If no link to this false-prophet premise exists, why bother making the assertions? Does she simply want to show us how much time she has spent in obscure archives?

Brodie also includes strange statements that make the reader wonder how much she actually knows about the traumatic Missouri epoch. For instance, "At no time in Joseph Smith's career was he more at peace with the world than the three years following Zion's Camp."[12] Even a cursory reading of Joseph's *History of the Church* indicates that the campaign to redeem Zion was becoming more precarious. Events are leading to expulsion of the Saints from the last bastion of Zion at Far West. Persecution was also growing so rampant in Kirtland that Brigham Young and other Church leaders fled for their lives. But this is being at peace?

Brodie has an even stranger statement declaring that the high council in Kirtland was bent on banishing liquor even "more than adultery."[13] Open sex was a favorite theme of Brodie's *No Man*, often primarily for what appears to be shock value. But if she wants the reader to believe Mormondom of that period had nothing on Hollywood when it comes to a libertine sexual lifestyle, she offers no evidence other than polygamy, which if practiced at this time, was not widespread. It seems she'd rather titillate than tell the truth—or at least attempt to substantiate her claims.

But let us try to discern her logic. Brodie refers to *History of the Church* 1:167 to prove that Smith freely imbibed liquor despite preaching against it in the Doctrine and Covenants. But section 89, verses 6–7, which Brodie identifies as the best-known scripture in Mormondom, describes the drink used by early Church members as "pure wine of the grape of the vine, of your own make. And, again, strong drinks are not for the belly." Maybe Smith broke the rule against alcoholic drinks, but no proof exists here that he imbibed liquor. Brodie states it as known fact.

Because she lived twenty years among the Mormons, Brodie asserts she is unusually qualified to write their history. She seems to feel she has Mormonism by the throat. Many LDS historians have lived a half century among the Mormons without claiming to be unusually qualified to write their history. In fact, millions of people have lived their whole lives among the Mormons without making such a brash claim. How does time alone assure objectivity? During her twenty years exactly what did she observe?

Forced links also mislead the unwary reader. For example, in her preface Brodie says, "Joseph's conception of perfection was by no means exclusively spiritual."[14] She then quotes 2 Nephi 2:25: "And men are, that they might have joy." Joy for Smith, she says, meant "creating for himself the nucleus of an American empire."[15] How does she know what he did was bent only on building his own empire? Where is any supporting evidence other than her own subjective conclusion? Maybe he did get people angry at him, or maybe he tried to be of service to his constituents. It is recorded fact that many men, such as Willard Richards, John Taylor, Hyrum Smith, Lyman Wight, Orrin Porter Rockwell, and many others, felt a close allegiance to Joseph. Many were willing to follow him to his death. You don't get this from intelligent men if someone is trying to lord it over them.

Brodie makes much of Smith's money digging. She is certain that prophets do not go hunting for hidden treasure in lost Spanish silver mines, as Joseph did in his late teens. Her chapter 2 is labeled "Treasures in the Earth " and ends with this parting shot: "In the next five years Joseph climbed out of the world of magic into a world of religion."[16] So, he didn't have religion in mind until climbing out of his world of magic? It wasn't there when he claimed the first vision or visits by an angelic messenger?

Smith admitted looking for buried treasure in his official autobiography. So did his mother, Lucy Mack, but she has a much different viewpoint than does Brodie. In her *History of Joseph Smith*, Lucy Mack says, "Joseph endeavored to divert him [Josiah Stoal, or Stowell] from his vain pursuit but he was inflexible in his purpose and offered high wages. . . . After laboring for the old gentleman for about a month, without success, Joseph prevailed upon him to cease his operations."[17]

For Brodie, Joseph just couldn't be a prophet of God if he looked for buried treasure. Yet the Apostle Peter lied about Jesus three times in order to save his skin. The Apostle Paul was an accomplice to killing, holding coats of those who persecuted Christians. According to Acts 8:3, Paul also entered houses of Christians, committing them to prison. We might ask, what's the big deal here with Smith? He tried to make money that the family desperately needed by hiring out to a treasure hunter? Certainly it proved to be poor public relations. Yet what is so far from biblical injunction in deity calling on people with human weakness to serve the Christian cause? Brodie may have little respect for Bible scripture, but if she is going to judge who God can select as a prophet, she should know something about what has been written on the subject.

In addition, despite Brodie's labored premise, it is clear that Smith's money digging had little to do with his life's overall direction. Some indications exist that treasure hunting was a respected profession back in the 1820s among New Englanders.[18]

Brodie expresses surprise that Stoal should continue to back Joseph even when his protégé can't produce treasure. One reason that has never been fully explored by non-Mormon historians is that Stoal might have been willing to employ the young man to learn more about his religious views. One historian even says Stoal was later baptized into the church Joseph founded.[19]

It appears that when Stoal backed Joseph at the 1830 South Bainbridge trial (Brodie expresses surprise at this), Stoal saw the lad as someone who spoke the truth and conducted himself with integrity.[20] This is important, for Brodie later brings up negative affidavits from neighbors about Smith's character. Joseph never did convince his father-in-law, Isaac Hale, that he was what he claimed, but the same does not pronounce Joseph a deceiver or fraud. The number of people not eulogized by in-laws must be legion.

Hale complained that Joseph had stolen his daughter. But even if Joseph was dishonest, Emma was twenty-three, not a minor and certainly old enough to make up her own mind. And while Emma differed with Joseph on several matters, no record exists that she ever doubted Joseph's calling. Even Brodie admits as much.[21] This is singular, indeed, for she was privy to many things her husband did in the name of prophethood, never withdrawing her support. Does she know all her husband is thinking? No. But Brodie seems to, as we shall see.

Another interesting note: It was in 1823–24 when Stoal heard that the Smith boy had supernatural abilities. So, even though Joseph didn't write a history about the first vision until 1831, apparently either he or his family talked about it long before then. (See also chapter 6.) This is important because Brodie makes much of the fact that Joseph did not write about the first vision until 1838. However, she changed that date to 1831 in her revised edition of 1971.

It is interesting too that at one time, as the Smiths were about to lose their farm under an act of chicanery, a Mr. Robinson and others went about Palmyra and vicinity circulating a petition attesting to the family's good character. Sixty signatures were obtained in an hour.[22] The reader should keep this in mind as Brodie paints Joseph and his family members as ne'er-do-wells with a lowly reputation among neighbors.

My own half century of experience and background in investigative reporting, as well as a master's thesis in public credibility thresholds dealing with pursuit of truth via the written word,[23] indicates that Brodie leans heavily toward selective objectivity. This is not the objectivity explained in the *American Heritage Dictionary:* "Uninfluenced by emotion, surmise, or personal prejudice; based on observable phenomena; presented factually."

Truly, a history entirely devoid of emotion would be both dull and impossible. The author must necessarily use some color to flesh in skeletal remains, but we must be careful that the applied varnish is natural, not contrived. The author might say, "Looking at the results, we could conclude," or "The conversation may have gone something like this." Such statements are often necessary to fill in the blanks of a mysterious entity, as Brodie confesses in her preface Joseph to be. There are allowable techniques. But to announce, "It happened this way" is a perilous course. It leads, minus documentation, to haphazard or even bogus history. Filling in blanks with conjecture can be a leap of faith even a religious devotee should not be asked to make.

A few years ago when writing *Hamblin: A Modern Look at the Frontier Life and Legend of Jacob Hamblin*, I did a resource search to locate all that had been written on my subject. Two lengthy biographies stood out, one carefully documented, the other using alleged conversations in the desert between Hamblin and Major John Wesley Powell. Because no one else was present when the words were spoken, and no entries exist of such a conversation in either Hamblin's or Powell's journals, not only a red flag but also a flashing red light went up. The author of these dissertations in the desert may be correct, but since we have no way to verify it, the entirety must be considered apocryphal. Much of what Brodie has conjectured could well be true, but which part? No matter how colorful the language, no matter how precious to the writer's heart, the dubious matter must be waived if her work is to be labeled history.

However sincerely Brodie may have ventured forth, according to her preface, it appears her driving zeal to expose Joseph Smith gradually eroded away much of the record keeper's stock-in-trade: a painstaking penchant for unembellished accuracy. Certainly, she did more than anyone before her to research the life of her pariah from Palmyra. But research alone, no matter how diligent, does not amount to honest history. Facts must be sifted to weigh meaning, assign significance, and determine external corroboration and internal consistency, and they must be interpreted. The true historian must also discard, no matter how enticing or complementary to the theme, that data repudiated by other data—or at least give equal weight to the contradictory items.

Brodie announces in her prefaces (she has two in her second edition) that she will do this. But more and more she succumbs to the heat of her own agenda. The latter is defined in journalism as putting the author's own predetermined bias ahead of open-mindedly seeking the truth.[24]

It works like this: If I draw a map of Illinois with Peoria shown in large red letters, I could then show other in-state cities, including Chicago, in small or obscure letters. The visitor to Illinois would then get the impression that the most important thing to see in the state of Illinois is Peoria.

Why would I want to do this? It may be because of something as innocuous as my being president of the Peoria Chamber of Commerce. The Chicago Chamber could do its own map with no real harm done by Peoria. But Brodie claims a complete exposé of Joseph Smith.

Another example: Given opinions of others that Fawn Brodie was a courageous woman to go against the wishes of her family in writing *No Man Knows My History*, and reasonable evidence of this does exist, I might promote my own agenda, perhaps falsely, by saying that she did it out of ego or conceit. I could point out that she must have felt herself superior to the family, for she likely enjoyed a higher IQ than the others and, feeling superior, would rather go against her parents in some intellectual way than meekly do as they say.

True or not, such an approach carries more weight than simply saying, "It is my unsubstantiated opinion."

Or we could take the case of Abraham Lincoln. The *World Book Encyclopedia* records that as war between the states neared, President Lincoln stated, "Without the assistance of that Divine Being who ever attended [George Washington], I cannot succeed. With that assistance, I cannot fail."[25]

A historian with a working agenda might editorialize, "Lincoln must have been naive indeed, for surely the South would also be praying to God for victory." Or, "The president of the United States certainly must be weak to rely on divine intervention to guide the Union in winning this war when he should be busy amassing more military strength. Instead, he is spending his time vainly hoping for a miracle." Or, "The Republicans elected the wrong man for such a difficult time in American history."

Later, the encyclopedia includes this statement: "Lincoln denied he had any intention of interfering with slavery in states where the Constitution protected it."[26]

This could be followed with, "He was a clever man, for Lincoln knew the Constitution did not protect it." Or simply, "Since slaves were later freed by the Emancipation Proclamation, Lincoln lied." Or we could say that since the Union generals did not perform well in the early stages of the war, Lincoln must not have been adept at choosing his military leaders." Or even, "It is whispered there is evidence he secretly sided with the South."

This is not to compare Abraham Lincoln with Joseph Smith, one way or the other. It is simply that Lincoln was a well-known American we can relate to. Nor is it to say Brodie always did as outlined above. It is to show what a writer with an agenda can do to guide or manipulate the reader. It is something to be aware of, as the facts are laid out, in exploring Brodie's, or any historian's, efforts to fairly and accurately assess known facts.

To be fair, all of us must be wary of selective objectivity. Both Latter-day Saint and non-Latter-day Saint chroniclers have shown bias in the past by selecting only that material which proves their point. A writer can also distort the truth without actually lying by presenting only one side of an argument. The reader needs a realistic database to draw conclusions among viable alternatives. Too often on key issues, such as whether Joseph was a truthful person, Brodie gives only the negative possibility. The reader is unaware any other viable viewpoint was given, as we shall see in the case of Smith's early trial at South Bainbridge, New York.

Brodie does give Smith a listening ear in the Missouri persecution period, 1831–39, but the Missouri bias is so clear from court records that little doubt exists the Mormons were denied due process. She eloquently describes the plight of the Mormons in Missouri and their plea to Andrew Jackson's brand of Old

Hickory democracy for redress. Little argument exists that in far-off Kirtland, Smith did not comprehend the impossible situation faced by W. W. Phelps and others in Zion (Jackson County). The dream of resettling Zion in the near future was strong in Joseph's mind, but as history tells us, it didn't happen.

Yet more often Brodie does not reason with the evidence; she renounces it. Despite her spirit of intellectual adventure, no thread of direction exists, even with Smith pictured as an impostor. Why would he continue to perpetrate a masquerade against such terrible persecution as was mounting in both Ohio and Missouri, even at the point of death? Was it for material gain?

Let's examine this theory. Couldn't Smith have found an easier path than languishing in Missouri jails while refusing to give up on openly stubborn ideas? What was the material gain in lying in the Liberty Jail for four months? The mobocrats in Missouri often offered to halt persecution if any captive would merely renounce the Book of Mormon. None did, or at least no record exists of the same.

If money was a motive, wouldn't Smith give it up after a while, seeing that his course would only lead to a life of poverty? If he wanted to capitalize on the Book of Mormon, why not just label it fiction, enjoy acclaim as a creative novelist, and dispense with all the hardships, including four long years of hiding, or pretending to hide, gold plates, as reported in great detail by his family? If a fraud, he lived his fraud night and day, not only with his family but also with his wife, Emma, and all others. It would seem he'd grow tired of the masquerade at times and confide his perfidy to a confidante.

At one point, Brodie asserts that he does. She refers to *History of the Church* wherein Joseph says to Cyrus Walker while addressing a friendly audience in Nauvoo, "They are the greatest dupes." This makes it appear that Joseph is making light of his followers and that they are being deceived.

But a careful reading of Joseph's speech, recorded by fellow Saints Willard Richards and Wilford Woodruff, indicates Brodie is taking things out of context. Several sentences before the dupe comment, Joseph says, "I thank God that I have the honor to lead so virtuous and honest a people." Naturally, Brodie omits this comment, totally contradicting her assertion that he was poking fun at his own people.

Cyrus is there to talk about the Nauvoo City Charter and how it gives Nauvoo citizens the right to try writs of habeas corpus (release from illegal detention). Angry at being detained at that time by Missouri lawmen sent to extradite him and with Missouri harassment in general, Joseph says, "These are the greatest dupes, as a body of people who ever lived. I told Mr. Warren that I would not discuss the subject of religion with you. I understand the gospel and you do not. You understand the quackery of law and I do not."

Smith often fumed at lawyers and the lack of justice in both state and federal courts, particularly those in Missouri. In the speech mentioned, he seemed particularly angry at the Missouri mind-set. Joseph is speaking of those who follow the quackery of Missouri law, not his fellow Saints.

Brodie's Joseph is a mystic, magician, hypnotist, wizard, clairvoyant, and conjuror of spirits all tied together—in short, a frontier superman. To become so good, and at the rather tender age of seventeen or eighteen, he surely must have received professional training or practiced cryptic arts or at least shown some propensity for it over a period of time. The old records can be searched over and over, and no such thing will be found. His mother, Lucy Mack, says that Joseph was, of all her brood, least inclined to spend any time studying books or studying anything. Mrs. Smith says in her *History of Joseph Smith*[27] that she didn't even know him to spend much time studying the Bible in his youth.[29] (This will be examined more fully later.) She said the boy did much pondering and thinking, but where are all the books on magic and necromancy? If he was that good, why write the Book of Mormon at all? Why not just go on a magic tour and perform deception for quick money and open applause? But of course, it is possible we don't know the mind-set of the 1820–30s. Still, was Joseph just lucky to be born a master magician? No study required? It isn't that Brodie can't be right here. She just doesn't explain it in a way a rational mind can accept.

Brodie does not rely on the old rumors of Joseph being an epileptic. If that explained his visions, it did not explain how he carried them to fruition and influenced so many. If he was an epileptic, no one who knew him ever introduced that malady as a source for his magnetism. The early rumors of having fits or seizures seem to have all dissipated over the years. Wisely, Brodie does not try to resurrect them.

3
He Cast a Spell

Brodie confesses in one sentence in the preface to her second edition that her earlier (1945) book was one of speculations. The problem is this: Her thoughts weren't presented originally to the world as speculations. They were given as history in both first and second editions.

Let us reason together. We cannot use faith, which is difficult to measure and scorned by the secular world, in a work based on research and logic. But let us first remove bias from the mind. Forget for the moment that there might be such a thing as divine guidance. On the other hand, put it out of the mind that there assuredly is not. Focus instead, as in an impartial courtroom jury, on the evidence presented. Be as an umpire or referee, and maintain neutrality until fully examining the evidence before you.

Let us begin by scrutinizing one of Brodie's main themes: how Smith gained such influence over his thousands of followers. She says it was an evolutionary stepladder type of procedure due to the passing of time, plus Joseph's personal charisma. Many things can be explained if given enough time. The earth is said to be millions of years old, but Smith had a total of fifteen years, from 1829 to 1844, to do all he did. Is that enough time to accomplish all that even Brodie attributes to Smith in her *No Man Knows My History*?

According to Brodie, he accomplished it all by himself. On the other hand, if Joseph accomplished it all with divine guidance before being martyred in Carthage at age thirty-eight, he needn't be a genius. All he need be is obedient to a higher power.

One of Smith's greatest achievements was to attract thousands of loyal followers willing to face daily persecution. Did Smith do this by aspiring to be a king and dictator, as Brodie declares, or was it because he presented something of value to his followers? Consider the remarks of Brigham Young: "I feel like shouting hallelujah, all the time, when I think that I ever knew Joseph Smith, the Prophet."[1] Then there is Edward Partridge. He could have avoided a vicious tarring and feathering at the hands of an angry mob by rebuking the Book of Mormon. He chose not to.[2] Lyman Wight was told in Missouri he could save his life merely by rebuking Smith—otherwise, he would be shot. "Shoot, and be damned," Wight responded.[3] The cause he and Joseph espoused together was more important than either of their lives.

Let us explore the premise that Joseph's charisma was in presenting followers a meaningful cause to follow. Dale Morgan opined this when he advised Brodie to explain how Smith elicited so much magnetism over his followers: "Smith gave them something they never got from anyone else and in turn received a love they had never given anyone else."[4] Indeed, the loyalty of many people over such a long period of time indicated Smith to be more than a hollow voice. It doesn't prove prophethood but simply that Morgan was right. Joseph gave them something of value.

How could he gain loyal constituents, willing to spend years proselyting in England, for example, if not giving something of lasting value to them? Brodie never fully explored this issue.

Brodie's statement that Smith gradually gained power over his adherents in an evolutionary process, meaning that Joseph got better all the time, bears no logic.[5] Smith was highly influential in the early days of his prophethood when bringing forth the Book of Mormon. By 1838, during the firestorm of Missouri persecutions, some suggested Joseph could not have brought them there by divine revelation. Indeed, things seemed more precarious in Missouri eight years after the Church was organized. A few early key followers such as David Whitmer thought Smith "grew more worldly"[6] in the Nauvoo period. This does not lend itself to a snowballing, or evolutionary, effect on Joseph's part. Brodie does not address this aspect because it could derail her assertion that time made Joseph more convincing.

Brodie makes a colossal mistake early by declaring, "The source of his [Joseph's] power lay not in his doctrine but in his person."[7] Tens of thousands of converts in England and throughout Europe never met the Mormon prophet. Tens of thousands more in the United States didn't lay eyes on the man. Millions more today in South and Central America and Mexico also never met Joseph Smith. Perhaps less than one-tenth of 1 percent of all Church members immigrating to Nauvoo and later to Great Salt Lake Valley during the middle 1800s ever knew Smith personally.

The LDS movement seemed to take on a roller coaster effect after the Saints departed Nauvoo for the West in 1846. If their charismatic leader died in 1844, why would this be so? Brodie asserts that it is because the martyrdom of Joseph in Carthage brought greater strength to the Mormon cause.[8] But why? Why forego material possessions to trek a thousand miles through a danger-filled wilderness after the death of Joseph if he was the sole cause of their devotion?

And if converts responded to his mesmerizing presence so much more intensely than to his doctrine, why would so many apostles and Church leaders leave Nauvoo—and Joseph—to take the message of the gospel to foreign lands? Many were so sick they could scarcely walk as they set out for England, but history records they went.[9] The hard facts show that millions of converts today know Joseph only by the religion he founded.

Brodie receives accolades from many "reputable" sources for a basic theme that is flawed from the initial pages. She would like to convince us that Smith cast some sort of spell over investigators with his blue eyes, firm handshake, and personal charm. He probably did meet people warmly. Several LDS historians admittedly dwell heavily on Joseph's persona. But Brodie struggles to make him out as a man who could mesmerize people, thousands of people he didn't even know, via personality alone.[10] Was it magnetism that attracted these converts or a sincere appeal to those seeking to live God's word in the latter days? Right or wrong, the evidence points more toward these individuals seeking a faith to anchor their purpose and meaning in life. This doesn't prove Joseph inspired; however, Brodie does give an astronomical amount of credit to Joseph's personality, rather than to his doctrine, in attracting converts. She must do so, of course, if she is to achieve her agenda.

Of course, sheer number of followers proves nothing. If they did, conflicting Catholic, Jewish, Oriental, or Middle East religions would all be true. Some Mormons claim theirs is the fastest growing church of the twenty-first century. While that is a favorable indication that the Church has something of substance for many, it does not alone prove divine guidance. Russia's Lenin attracted many followers, and he was an atheist.

But if Brodie is wrong about Joseph's magnetism being in his person rather than in his teachings, she becomes a serious candidate for suspicion. For all her research, how much does she really know about the church established under Joseph's leadership? If she misses the mark here on such an important point, it could color other decisions throughout her lengthy treatise.

By the second chapter, an open-minded student is certain that her book would synchronize much more favorably with actual history had she presented both sides of the batting order: Smith had this in favor of his being a prophet and this against him. Instead, she seems to adopt a posture that strikes out.

Within The Church of Jesus Christ of Latter-day Saints, some feel that Dr. Hugh Nibley, a venerable exponent of LDS history, answered Brodie's book with the pamphlet *No, Ma'am, That's Not History*. One of those was historian Lavina Fielding Anderson, who has at times been seen as a critic of the Mormon Church yet embraces Joseph's claim to a prophetic calling.[11] She seems to consider Nibley as one ably answering Brodie's charges.

Nibley's pamphlet follows closely his law of parsimony, or that argument is best which is freest of contradiction, by which law he says Brodie takes an awful beating. He did not attempt to refute Brodie on technical points so much as disagreeing philosophically with the whole of her work. He specifically rejects her speculations in detail with his book *Tinkling Cymbals and Sounding Brass.*[12]

Nibley points out that on page 18 of *No Man,* when she is confronted with testimony she doesn't like, Brodie simply selects out what she wants. This is a strange illustration, however, for Brodie is apparently attempting to be generous by stating that fifty-one affidavits saying Smith was addicted to vicious habits can't be true. Joseph was actually gregarious, cheerful, and imaginative, asserts Brodie. But later, she tries to use these affidavits, gathered by Philastus Hurlbut, an avowed enemy of Smith, to discredit Smith's character. This is dangerous historicity, for if the fifty-one people who said he is vicious can't be trusted in this matter, how do we know they can be trusted in anything else they say? Brodie doesn't tell us.

To put it succinctly, Nibley does not think Brodie intellectually honest. Too often she says, "he might have," "if he went there," "if he did that," "quite possibly, perhaps," "one might guess," or, "it was whispered." Nibley points out many places where Brodie appears at a complete loss to explain the Book of Mormon, the witnesses, or devoted followers. For example, he says, if Smith dashed off the 275,000-word Book of Mormon at his young age all by himself with so little formal education, "What a hilarious document it will turn out to be . . . even if fiction."[13]

Many who have read the Book of Mormon from cover to cover have marveled for 175 years that it is such a compendium of disciplined teachings and stories for the moral betterment of mankind.[14] None of the above, of course, proves spiritual veracity. But common sense tells us that the author of such a book must be extraordinarily learned and wise, hardly an unlettered lad of twenty-three. Could the much-learned Fawn Brodie have written the Book of Mormon at age twenty-three? She has not attempted to answer this question.

Non-Mormon scholars pan Nibley and his sixty-two-page

pamphlet as being flippant, shallow, brief, and even asinine.[15] But Brodie makes some of her own asinine statements, including, "almost never these days did Joseph look with surprise and humility at what he had become."[16]

History? My own reaction is to recall the statement by *Time* magazine about detached objectivity. Here *Time* loses as much credibility to honest history as does Brodie. All that *Time* seems to be saying is that Brodie agrees with the magazine, which, since its review of the Mormon Centennial in 1947, has shown some bias against anything LDS, save monetary achievement.

Many LDS historians are galled by the idea, even displaying an annoyance at times, that almost anyone removing the supernatural from Mormon history, an absolute must for historian and novelist Bernard DeVoto, is eligible to receive an award for objective scholarship. We get the feeling that the Eastern press did so with enthusiasm. All that is needed is a debunking of all religion.

Did any of these publications, or forebears, castigate George Washington for his belief in a higher power? Can we say he was deluded when he prayed at Valley Forge? That he couldn't have been divinely inspired in leading the nation to victory in the Revolutionary War? That founders of our country were not inspired in drawing up those remarkable documents known as the Declaration of Independence and the Constitution? The hand of God is acknowledged by many in the birth of our country, but it couldn't possibly be extant in the birth of a new religion within that country?

Brodie has other such speculations. "He [Joseph Smith] stood proudly before his men, betraying nothing of the tumult and anxiety raging within him."[17] If he betrayed nothing of his feelings, how does she know he actually had those feelings? Or, while the story that Smith attempted to walk on water was unfounded, it was, claims Brodie, symbolic.[18] We could make up something similar to proclaim that Brodie admitted to always wanting to write a novel as her first book. Then we could add that while she didn't really say that, it was typical of what we know about her.

In Brodie's resolve to prove that Smith lied, she must do so but once to engender our distrust of him. On the other hand, to lose our trust, Brodie need only but once resort to obvious fabrication. So far, Smith is ahead.

However, Brodie has many more (499 in all) pages for us to critique. We must diligently search for every nuance in which she demonstrates that her love for the truth exceeds her prejudice.

Brodie insists throughout her work that anyone believing in God is in the throes of aberration. But surveys of the past few years and especially since the terrorist attacks of September 11, 2001, indicate that most of the population of the United States believes in deity.[19] While this neither proves nor disproves anything, it is a signal for critics to ask why. Why do people facing a crisis turn to a higher power? And why not Joseph Smith in his crisis to know which church would lead to his salvation?

Must a person claiming divine revelation necessarily be dismissed by academia without even an unbiased analysis? Certainly there have been strangers emerging from the hot desert sun with cryptic claims. But how many provided a 275,000-word book corroborating the Bible, with three eyewitnesses testifying it to be of divine origin and eight more providing supporting testimony?

Brodie pays scant attention to all this because she admits in her preface that she had an agenda before she ever started writing. Joseph Smith couldn't possibly be who he said he was; therefore, any explanation ruling out deity is better than none. And for those who passionately agree with her naturalistic premise from the beginning, she is their hero.

But our appeal here, again, is to logic. The author of *Gainsayers* wrote of turning his back on all teachings attributed to Joseph Smith and then returning to a deep belief in his prophethood; but it was because of experience, prayer, and comparison of his life before and after his return to the LDS fold, not a comparison of doctrines.[20] In other words, he liked himself better as a Latter-day Saint.

This won't sit with academia. Academia distrusts such a non-intellectual approach. Feelings of trust, love, and power to meet challenge—all exist, as most would affirm. Yet in an academic discussion, the above must be banned because it is too difficult to measure objectively. The call is to empirical evidence.

So where is Brodie's empirical evidence dislodging Smith as a prophet? She admits she had an iron-clad opinion that Smith wasn't a prophet before even starting her research. Doesn't a responsible historian start with an open mind and go wherever the facts go? With her agenda, Brodie must selectively amass only that which fits her preconceived notion, necessarily slanting all in that direction in order to make her point. In fact, several non-Mormon advisers warned her she was doing just that.[21] Did she desist? If so, there is no indication of it. She absolutely ignores all advice to show Joseph as a sincere man receiving direction from a higher power.

The lauded historian from Huntsville declares that Joseph's first vision was made up because there was never a revival, or unrest, in the 1820s as to which church was true, as Smith claimed.[22] But in her history, Lucy Mack Smith, Joseph's mother, tells of a family that was much divided trying to decide between the Methodists and Presbyterians, among other churches. It was confusing to the family, and it was confusing to a young boy.[23]

The whole idea that Joseph could not have been telling the truth because there was no hint of revival in Palmyra during the 1820s has been greatly blown out of proportion. It was a tenet of the Presbyterian minister Rev. Wesley Walters that Joseph Smith's reference to a revival shortly before claiming the first vision had to be the one in 1824–25. No one is arguing there was a general revival in the Palmyra area at that time. But a review of Walters's *Inventing Mormonism* by LDS historian Larry C. Porter (FARMS) says:

"In July 1819, Rev. Lane [Methodist minister] was just fifteen miles away from the Smith home for a period of eight days attending the annual Genesee Conference at Old Vienna (later Phelps, New York). . . .

"We know that many . . . preachments were given . . . to the congregation assembled for this auspicious occasion. This was an ideal time for the Prophet to have come under Lane's instruction. . . . Such conferences . . . were highlighted with stirring sermons . . . characterized by an impressive religious spirit."[24]

Porter concludes that Walters has substituted Joseph's claim to a revival in 1819–20 for one in 1824–25.

Historian Marvin S. Hill also states that Milton Backman, a Mormon trained at the University of Pennsylvania, found in his research that "a number of revivals occurred within a twenty-mile radius of Palmyra in 1819 or 1820."[25] In fact, in his book *Joseph Smith, The First Vision*, Backman includes a chart of revivals in those two years centered and advertised in Palmyra at that time.[26] Joseph said in the Pearl of Great Price that revivals "became general among all the sects in that region of country" prior to the first vision (see Joseph Smith–History 1:5).[27]

Revival or not, it doesn't prove Smith right or wrong in his claim to a heavenly vision. But why would the lad need an excuse to pray for guidance? Why can't he just pray if he feels like it?

Brodie claims that Smith's family remained in the Presbyterian Church long after his "supposed" vision.[28] Is it possible their names remained on the rolls after no longer attending? That Lucy believed her son was telling the truth in the early 1820s about a first vision and several visits by Moroni is obvious from reading her history. Based on what Joseph told the family, Lucy says, "We were now confirmed in the opinion that God was about to bring to light something upon which . . . would give us a more perfect knowledge of the plan of salvation and the redemption of the human family. This caused us greatly to rejoice."[29] Does that sound as if she wants to actively participate in a different religion?

What difference would it make if the Smith family left its names on the rolls of the Presbyterian Church as long as they believed what Joseph was telling them? Presbyterian minister Wesley Walters says the Smiths kept their names on that church's rolls beyond 1825. However, Larry C. Porter cast serious doubt on that.[30] You can accept Walters if you want, but it makes no sense if we believe what Lucy told us in her own history of Joseph.

Actually, this is a hollow argument about the Smith family's beliefs anyway, at least from Brodie's standpoint, for she admits that Joseph's family was with him: "Since his own family believed him (with the possible exception of his cynical younger brother William), why should not the world?"[31] As we shall see later, William may have been abrasive at times, but in his old age, he stated firmly that he believed his brother always told the truth about the Book of Mormon. Brodie commits a serious error in trying to cast doubt on Joseph through his younger brother, for as she knows full well, William bore strong testimony of Joseph's prophethood, even if arguing with Joseph when pushed to be an active Church member.

Critics have claimed that Joseph tried to join the Methodist Church in 1828. Pomeroy Tucker makes one such claim, but J. B. Gilbert who worked with Tucker at the *Wayne Sentinel* when the Book of Mormon was published said, "Nobody could believe the stories Tucker made up."[32]

Another reference to Joseph joining the Methodists in 1828 is made in the *Amboy Journal*.[33] If we believe Joseph Lewis in this statement, we must also accept the statement by Lewis that Smith got the plates from a bearded Spaniard who knocked Smith down three times. The Spaniard, claims Lewis, was bleeding from ear to ear with a slit throat, and Smith couldn't get the plates until Emma went with him. Or we could believe Orasmus Turner, who said Joseph tried to join the Methodist Church in 1828.[34] But this carries additional baggage: Turner said Joseph's brother "Alvah" [actually, Alvin], was really supposed to be the prophet of the Smith family, but he died of eating green turnips. And, notes Turner, Joseph was of feeble intellect. So how did he write the Book of Mormon? Even Fawn Brodie sees the lack of logic in that statement. How can anyone take these claims seriously?

Or we can believe Joseph Smith's own account that he was told to join none of the other churches in 1820?

Why did Joseph not inform the world more immediately about his first vision? Here, Brodie betrays her lack of knowledge about spiritual tradition. True, she was by all accounts an atheist;

but if she is going to launch a spiritual argument, she ought to be more versed in ecclesiastical scholarship. By that is not meant belief in a divine being (or in anything akin to it) but simply that she ought to have done some research on religious precedent. For example, she wants young Joseph to proclaim *now* to all what he has seen and heard from heaven. Here are four possible reasons, among many, that he did not do so.

1. In the early part of his mission, even as he began faith healing, Jesus told many whom he had healed not to yet share the event. As recorded in the New Testament, Christ also took Peter, James, and John to the Mount of Transfiguration where they had a special spiritual experience. Prophets long dead brought messages to them, according to the record. When the experience was finished, Christ told them to "tell . . . no man" (see Matthew 17:9). The time was apparently not yet right.

Even Christ's resurrection was not transmitted to the world at large for a time. Christ did not return to Pontius Pilate and say, "See, I told you so."

The time might never be right for the local *Roman Gazette* newspaper. Nor probably the *Wayne Sentinel,* as was later proven when Joseph was treated with contempt when the newspaper learned of his claim.

2. According to religious history, some things are sacred. You do not cast pearls before swine. You give people what they are capable of appreciating and respecting, living, and acting upon. They must be in tune. Even Jesus' parables seemed calculated to reach the spiritual level of the hearer (see Luke 8:10).

3. Joseph had not in his first vision been given any specific instructions to organize a church. He was simply told to join no existing church (Joseph Smith–History 1:19). It was not until 1823, with events leading to publication of the Book of Mormon, that he was given instructions to do anything other than prove himself faithful. He would also have, in the Book of Mormon, something tangible to show others. Following publication, no one need take his word alone for what he had claimed. If he was tired of ridicule, he now had eleven witnesses to help bear his burden.

4. Even the Apostle Paul waited twenty-five years to put pen to paper about his remarkable vision on the road to Damascus (Acts 7:58–8:3; 9:3–9). Perhaps it is difficult to place such a life-altering experience in proper perspective. Paul may have confided his vision to a few close associates, and he gave his testimony to King Agrippa well before writing it down. But he waited until later to declare it publicly in writing.

Joseph waited eleven years (1831) to officially begin writing down his first vision; but as we shall see, he was talking about it long before then. Chapter 6 explores Joseph's first vision more thoroughly.

4
Joseph, the "Hypnotist"

One LDS historian calls it laughable when Brodie passes off the eleven testimonies of the Book of Mormon witnesses with this statement: "At an early age he [Joseph Smith] had what only the most gifted revivalist preachers could boast of—the talent for making men see visions."[1] How easily and simply Brodie dismisses the sober testimony of eleven men. All risked ridicule, their reputations as honest citizens, even death, for the remainder of their lives rather than deny the witness of what they had seen. But Brodie must come up with something here if assuming that Smith could not be telling the truth.

Joseph put it this way: "For I had seen a vision; I knew it, and I knew that God knew it, and I could not deny it, neither dared I do it" (Joseph Smith–History 1:25). Is it possible that the eleven witnesses dared not deny it either, lest they come under condemnation? In such a matter, they would surely know the need for absolute integrity, not only in this life but also in the one they believed would follow.

Historian Roger Launius, who has much overall praise for Brodie's energetic effort, cannot let this one drop without adding: "The three key figures—Martin Harris, Oliver Cowdery, and David Whitmer—all were excommunicated from the Church in 1838, but none ever denied their testimony to the divinity of the scripture. This is remarkable."[2]

Remarkable, indeed. Most of them were disgruntled at Joseph

Smith and left his church but agree that it was founded just as Smith claimed—by gold plates and angels. They had to be well aware they would be ridiculed for such testimony, yet it made no difference to them.

Launius adds that Brodie credits the testimonies to their being "hypnotized" by Joseph.[3] Mormons ask, "Does psychiatry claim you can make someone believe something, like seeing gold plates, that you wouldn't otherwise believe?" But this premise is necessary for Brodie's thesis to bear up. Brodie insists there never were any gold plates or anything resembling them. The witnesses, eight at one time, gazed at nothing more than an empty box.[4]

Launius asserts that Brodie led historians down a blind alley with this one. The thing that really matters, Launius reminds us, is "what role the dissent of the Three Witnesses from the Church played. . . . These are important questions Brodie did not raise and that have gone begging."[5]

Reference has been made by many Mormon detractors that Martin Harris said he saw the angel with his spiritual eyes. A Stephen Burnett, who was angry at the Church for some reason, made that claim. He said that Harris told him he had seen the angel and plates with spiritual eyes, but Harris himself later said he had been misrepresented. Believer and nonbeliever alike should read a long litany of public statements made by Martin, including, "Do you know the sun is shining on us?" Or, "Do you see that pencil?" Once asked if he believed the Book of Mormon was true, Harris answered, "No. I know it is true." He then described the plates in detail.[6]

How many times did Martin affirm that he had seen the gold plates in presence of an angel? How many times did he correct people who said he had not? Harris repeatedly attested until his death that he was shown golden plates by a heavenly being.[7]

At first, Martin did not succeed in receiving a witness, as explained in Joseph Smith's history. There is parallel precedent. As he neared the burning bush, Moses was told to prepare himself spiritually for holy instruction with these words: "Put off thy shoes from off thy feet, for the place whereon thou standest is holy ground" (Exodus 3:5). Is it consistent with Old Testament revelation that some preparation must be made to be ready for the things of God? If we do not accept that, let's look at the bottom line: the profound difference the witness experience made in the later lives of these men. If anyone at any time attempted to suggest that they did not actually see the angel or the plates, they were immediately corrected.[8]

Harris once said that he saw the plates through a veil, which was confused with his testimony as one of the Three Witnesses. But Martin was then explaining the process of helping Joseph in translating the plates. Harris never said there was a veil across the plates when fulfilling his role as one of the Three Witnesses.

Ask yourself this question: If Joseph is an impostor and wrote the Book of Mormon himself, why in the world would he bother to include 2 Nephi 27:12 wherein the plates must be shown to three witnesses? Even if he is a hypnotist of the highest order, isn't this risky business? In all, eleven witnesses must be hypnotized, eight of them at the same time?

Not only that, but Smith must hypnotize Oliver Cowdery, who was with Joseph when the two said they had visits from John the Baptist and Peter, James, and John. He also must include Sidney Rigdon in his vision at the Kirtland Temple (see Doctrine and Covenants 76). Many other visitations from heavenly messengers were recorded by Church members at the dedication of the Kirtland Temple, and not all were in Smith's presence.[9]

Throughout history, of course, many people have claimed to see visions, some in contradiction to others. Catholics claim to have seen the Virgin Mary, but Protestants have pooh-poohed the idea that revelations should come from the mother of Jesus. They ask why they don't come directly from Jesus himself? Religionists say some "revelations" are of the devil, while all academia shudders at such a thought.

Even if God-fearing, you can't accept them all. But at the same time, can you reject them all? Science might suggest you try, as did the associates of Dr. Raymond Moody who heard so many patients report life-after-death experiences following recovery on the operating table that he kept a record of their statements.[10] "Superstition!" cried his colleagues, as if he was a throwback to the Stone Age. Yet why was it more scientific to ignore the statements than to record them?

The December 2001 issue of *Reader's Digest* contains an article titled "Searching for the Divine" about physicians measuring human brain waves of people who are praying. These scientists tell us changes take place in the brain at such times; a diagram accompanying the article shows in what ways. So, changes do take place in the human mind when individuals pray. Are those changes linked to heaven? No one has yet measured that with irrefutable evidence, but science has come a long way in just being open-minded enough to begin such experiments.

Let's get back to prayers during Joseph's time. He is surrounded by many people such as Cowdery who say they prayed on their own and received revelation that they should assist Joseph in his latter-day work. Smith is not present to hypnotize Cowdery. Oliver adds that after his religious experience he was told to tell no man (D&C 6:12, 20-25); there is that admonition again. Cowdery's experience is referenced in Carter E. Grant's *Kingdom of God Restored*, where Grant emphasizes that what Joseph accomplished would "seem far beyond his natural ability at age twenty-three."[11]

This isn't to say things happened the way Smith said they did, but how can they happen the way Brodie said they did: hypnotizing people without being present? One example: the Kirtland Temple experiences previously mentioned.

The assertion of hypnotizing is, at best, a fragile one, for what if it backfires? What if Joseph tries to hypnotize someone, or even better, a group of eight men, and fails? What if everyone can't be hypnotized? Why is it that no one Joseph practiced his black magic on ever complained of him trying—and failing? What if someone in the group, say one of the Eight Witnesses, isn't cast under the spell and complains that "Joseph tried, but he couldn't put me under"? Not a single word exists, other than those from Brodie, in all that has ever been written about Smith, including by his enemies, of anyone who has ever put forth such an allegation. And what if there are unpleasant aftereffects, as the *World Book Encyclopedia* says often happens?[12] There is no record of such a claim. Not one word from any of the witnesses, or anyone else for that matter.

But we have Brodie's word for it: Smith was one of the best at his black magic—seemingly, the best ever.[13]

With such logic, could we not dismiss Jesus Christ himself as one who hypnotized his followers? But this is not a good analogy, for Brodie did not profess to believe that Christ was divinely inspired. Suffice it to say that anything can be explained, including the greatest of miracles, by inserting the phrase "with the talent to make men see visions." We could say that Washington won the Revolutionary War because he hypnotized enemy leaders to no longer fight. Or he hypnotized his own men into thinking God was with them, and thus, they could not fail. Surely a better explanation exists for Smith's success than hypnotism.

At one point, Brodie says, "Exactly how Joseph Smith persuaded so many of the reality of the gold plates is neither so important nor so baffling as the effect of this success on Joseph himself."[14] Here, Brodie cops out big time. She tries to persuade the reader to ignore evidence against something she doesn't want to believe. In journalism, such lack of objectivity is called an *agenda*. It is totally shunned by investigative reporters attempting to arrive at truth and utterly banned in any text teaching objective writing. Students who employ it receive a failing grade. Professionals, as Brodie claims to be, would likely find themselves terminated.[15]

Yet Brodie tells us in her preface to the first edition that she has not included any fallacious data so as to avoid treading into yellow journalism. *The American Heritage Dictionary* explains the phrase this way: "Journalism that exploits, distorts, or exaggerates the news to create sensations and attract readers." Brodie sets up the standard and then ignores it.

For example, Brodie makes much of the fact that Dr. Charles Anthon of Columbia College wrote two letters in which he called the translation of gold plates brought to him by Martin Harris ("a plain looking countryman") a hoax. Anthon complained that the translation included a crude collection of alphabetical characters from different languages, and he labeled those who believed in them "wretched fanatics."[16] But Anthon's two letters contradict one another in a significant way.[17] In the one to E. D. Howe (1834), Anthon said he refused to give his opinion in writing. In the one to Dr. T. W. Coit (1841), Anthon said he gave, without hesitation, a written opinion to Harris. It could simply be that when writing the letters seven years apart, the latter twelve years after Harris's visit, that Anthon didn't remember what he did say. Or Anthon simply stretched the truth in one letter or the other to separate himself as a scientist from any connection with an unpopular religion.[18]

When Martin gave his report to Joseph Smith, he told the Prophet that Anthon not only gave him a written opinion but also that it included a statement that the translation was the most correct he had ever seen. As is well known in LDS history, when Harris told Anthon the gold plates from which the translation was made had been delivered by an angel, Anthon tore up the note.[19] So, do we believe Anthon with his contradictory statements, or do we believe Harris?

The evidence would seem to weigh on Harris's side for a very good reason. Harris was a skeptic who certainly didn't want to give any money to a fraud. Thus, if Anthon didn't make such a statement, why would Harris return to Palmyra prepared to finance publication of the Book of Mormon? Then too, as LDS historian B. H. Roberts points out, Anthon contradicts himself a second time.[20] He tells Rev. Coit that no one previously had asked him for his version of the Martin Harris visit, yet E. D. Howe had made just such a request and received an answer in 1834. Maybe the learned professor had a bad memory; but if so, how much can the student of history believe in Anthon as a reliable source?

In addition, recent scholarship strongly indicates that so little was known in 1829 about Egyptian languages that Anthon may well have been less than advertised in that field. Being known as a language expert at Columbia College in New York in 1829 doesn't prove Anthon was proficient in any particular ancient language. LDS historians Leonard Arrington and Davis Bitton, two veteran researchers, say that in 1829 "Prof. Anthon could have had no knowledge of Egyptian script."[21] There wasn't that much known about it then, say these historians, especially about reformed, or shorthand, Egyptian.

Where does that leave Brodie? She supposes Egyptian, let alone reformed Egyptian, to be an open book to the world, an exact science in the year 1829, and she relies on Anthon totally. Yet with her supposedly meticulous research, she must have known about the two discrepancies in the letters, even if not the statement pointed out by Arrington and Bitton. Why is it she doesn't mention them?

Brodie also makes hay with regards to the 116 missing pages episode. Briefly, Harris lost those pages after dogging Smith to borrow them, and when Harris couldn't return them later, Joseph is greatly despaired. For if Smith were to do the translation again, those who had the 116 pages could alter them, and when the new translation differed, they could declare Joseph a false prophet. This is an admittedly awkward public relations matter for Smith, even if he is telling the truth. In translating the missing pages from a different set of plates provided him, enemies could say that it was just too convenient. Maybe so. But there were different accounts made during the Old Testament period, as the Dead Sea Scrolls attest.

Brodie takes a strange stance in regard to Smith's faith-healing activities, which are extensive and well documented. This is especially true during the Nauvoo period when the Saints were transforming a malarial swamp into a robust community, the largest at that time in Illinois. Smith's contemporaries, including Wilford Woodruff and Heber C. Kimball, mention such healings with great respect.[22]

Brodie shrugs them off. Doesn't Smith know that such healings are commonplace? If they are, did Smith say they weren't?

That other faith healers preceded Joseph is correct, but some of Smith's multiple healings parallel those of Jesus' disciples in the New Testament—all of which proves nothing to the non-believer. But it is one more factor Brodie can't explain, other than that faith healings are routine. Thus, she dispenses with it.

Brodie is candid in her preface to the second edition: "New discoveries do not necessitate important revisions in this biography. On the contrary, I believe that the new data [since the 1945 edition] tend on the whole to support my original speculations about Joseph Smith's character."

What new discoveries? How do they authenticate her speculations? What are speculations doing, anyway, in a supposedly documented history?

As for new discoveries, a good many seem to lean toward authenticating the theme of the Book of Mormon. For example, the American Indians are not as primitive as once believed in the 1800s, and they followed a religious course much like the Jews of the Old Testament. Archaeological findings indicating that the Mayans and Incas developed a sophisticated civilization in South and Central America continue to come forth almost annually. They were obviously far more than mound builders. Then there is Quetzalcoatl. Brodie affirms that modern paleographers have fixed the date of this Christ simile "at A.D. 1208," well after close of the Book of Mormon in 400 A.D. But Bruce Warren and Thomas Ferguson spent years researching *The Messiah in Ancient America* and fix the date of Quetzalcoatl's death at A.D. 30.

Brodie also doesn't mention further linguistic studies indicating that the Book of Mormon was written by many authors, as claimed, rather than by one person.[23] Another new "discovery" deals with news reports of boats drifting or being rowed across the ocean from Europe to South America, as claimed in 1 Nephi. And how could Brodie overlook the fact that she said Smith did not relate his first vision until 1838 when further scholarship, well before her second edition in 1971, agrees he wrote of the first vision in 1831–32? Is this an oversight, or is Brodie, in her zeal to prove a point, manipulating the reader, who is supposed to take her word for it?

She also makes light of the book of Ether, which she says Joseph added as an afterthought. It discusses people migrating to America at the confounding of tongues at the Tower of Babel when the people were scattered abroad upon the face of the earth (see Genesis 11:4–9).

If the people were so scattered, they would be in America as well as Europe. So why isn't it consistent for those in the New Country to receive divine guidance as did the Hebrews in the Old Country? In John 10:16, Christ says, "Other sheep I have, which are not of this fold: them also must I bring, and they shall hear my voice; and there shall be one fold, and one shepherd." In this, Smith is only being consistent in linking the Bible with the Book of Mormon as God's word to people in two parts of the world. It is an easy matter if he's inspired; but if he depends only on his own education, it would obviously be most difficult for Joseph to produce without contradicting known and already-accepted scripture.

To be completely fair here, it must be added that no one knows for sure just how much time Joseph spent in his boyhood studying the Bible. We know he was reading James 1:5 at about age fourteen, but this verse could be heard at any camp revival meeting of the period.

I believe Joseph did know more than a little about the Bible even though his mother says he read little of anything. There is some sophistication in Smith's report of what the Angel Moroni quoted to him from the third and fourth chapters of Malachi, "though with a little variation from the way it reads in our Bible," and from Isaiah 11, Acts 3:22–23, and Joel 2:28–3:32 (Joseph Smith–History 1:36, 40–41).[24]

Even with three visits in one night by Moroni impressed on his memory, it would appear that Joseph had more than a passing knowledge of the Old Testament. Perhaps Joseph immediately wrote down all Moroni had told him, but even then one might pose an argument that Joseph was more than a dunce on Bible scripture as early as age seventeen. But Joseph seems fairly well at home with both Old and New Testament early in his prophetic career.

Still, with all the possible places to mess up, Joseph (or someone) does a remarkable job of seemingly to never miss a chance in linking the Bible and the Book of Mormon as scripture. Many connections exist between the two works, more than Brodie seems willing to admit. She may not, of course, have perused the work of Dr. Sidney Sperry, Dr. Hugh Nibley, Dr. Richard L. Anderson, and B. H. Roberts, who spent their entire professional lives studying the Book of Mormon.

If some nonmembers don't want to accept these LDS researchers, fine. But if not, it remains for other historians to make such an exhaustive study. Most won't, Nibley hints, because they don't approach it with an open mind, for they dismiss the book without examination.

Some LDS historians have opined that the Book of Mormon does not approach the Bible—books such as Ruth, Psalms, and Isaiah—in literary eloquence. Brodie does not bring this up, probably because she sees no reason to read the Bible at all. It is not within the scope of this treatise to compare the works as literature other than to say that writings which are heavily edited, as is claimed in the Book Mormon, dwell on conclusions rather than on flowery description. Someone editing hundreds of years later is apt to ask, "What is the point?" and exclude extraneous material. If the purpose of the Book of Mormon is to present a companion message to the Bible of salvation in following Christ, it would appear to do so.

Adviser Dale Morgan complained throughout Brodie's work, while somehow praising the final product, that she too often claimed to get inside the mind and heart of Joseph Smith, whereas she can only be speculating.[25] Anti-Mormon novelist Vardis Fisher says she "used the tools of fiction" rather than documented research and relied "too heavily on bitterly apostate Mormons."[26] He suggested Brodie had written a novel and was good enough at it that she ought to try her hand at doing a few more.

Growing up in eastern Idaho Mormon country, atheist Fisher was one of Mormondom's severest critics. In all his thirty-six novels, Fisher never once allowed that Joseph Smith could be divinely inspired. Thus, it is interesting that he should find fault with someone (anyone) lifting a cudgel against the church in which he also found so much fault. Yet Fisher seems genuinely disappointed in Brodie pretending to be writing an honest biographical history. According to Newell Bringhurst in his *Fawn McKay Brodie: A Biographer's Life*, this criticism by fellow atheist Fisher stung Brodie more deeply than any other. Afterward, she is quoted as saying, "Why should I bother when historians are bound to find errors?"[27] DeVoto is also quoted as follows: "Brodie offers no satisfactory alternative [to Smith not being a prophet]."[28] Yet this did not prevent DeVoto from praising her work.

Brodie elaborates on Smith's many political intrigues, of which little fault can be found by this author. But when it comes to spiritual matters, she uses a subtle ploy to make us think she is providing a scholarly and balanced view. She links objective statements with totally subjective, and oftentimes absurd, conclusions. An example is when she implies Mormons use phallic symbols in their temple ceremonies. Then, her damage done, she abandons the subject.[29] We can readily venture that if you were to interview a thousand LDS temple goers, they would not have the slightest idea what Brodie is talking about.

In another instance, Brodie presents a totally unfounded statement with no explanation of any kind: "But Joseph laid no great emphasis on temple work."[30] All the work done on the Nauvoo Temple at an estimated cost of one million dollars for a people already struggling in near-poverty while trying to elude enemies wasn't important? He went to all this trouble for the pomp and ceremony?

Even a casual glance at the headings of the Doctrine and Covenants indicate the importance of temple work to Smith. It was vital, the heart of the new religion he taught. It is one more example that if Brodie is not a rebel without a cause, she is a crusader without a reason.

If determined to expose Smith as a man "so deified [by Mormons] as to rob him of his healthy, earthly qualities,"[31] Brodie has a valid starting point. Smith did a number of things that can be easily analyzed as tactical mistakes, prophet or otherwise, including ordering, as mayor of Nauvoo, destruction of the *Nauvoo Expositor*. This decision, even if the newspaper was deemed a public nuisance under the generous Nauvoo Charter, clearly hastened Smith's death. Maybe, but as Joseph told Brigham Young several times, he was going to die before age forty anyway[32] and didn't care about consequences.

But government and non-Mormon bystanders considered the act an unforgivable outrage. Journalistic research shows there is no faster way to bring down wrath than to violate the First Amendment. Or, in other words, to destroy an opposition printing press. Joseph wrote to Illinois governor Thomas Ford that he would make himself available if the governor should demand an investigation.[33] But it was more than that; the act violated a constitutional right, even if the *Expositor* was printing pure libel to destroy the Church, as claimed by Nauvoo city leaders.

Mormons might recall their unmitigated anger when Missouri mobs destroyed the press used by W. W. Phelps to print the first Book of Commandments, forerunner to the Doctrine and Covenants. While the *Expositor* might have been printing lies, such a matter finds relief in America under the First Amendment via lawsuit, not violence. True, the courts had not been kind to Mormons. Joseph may have had no trust in the courts, even in Nauvoo, "his" town. But it was the only legal and ethical avenue available for relief. By not following this course, the Mormon leaders only added fuel to the conflagration beginning to erupt in the capital at Springfield and strengthened a growing animosity among Nauvoo's neighboring villages, including Carthage. Destruction of the *Expositor* confirmed in the mind of many that lies being told about the Mormons were true.

So, Brodie has another point. Joseph could cause trouble for himself when it came to public relations. But the woman didn't know when to stop. And when is that? When the documentary trail runs out and speculation starts to take over.

For example, Brodie says she had fun in declaring that there was nothing in the Book of Mormon not found in the Smith neighborhood in Ontario County, New York.[34] In the process, she contradicts herself. She asserts that Smith had a vivid imagination; so why must he rely on what is observable around him to write a book? But that is not the point. The point is that seeing Indian mounds and writing the Book of Mormon with its multiple plots and characterizations, with evidence of many authors, are two different things.

Brodie did the Mormons a favor by helping to dispel the notion that Smith purloined the book from Solomon Spaulding. Since that does not answer the broader question of who did write the Mormon book, however, Brodie is among many detractors who point to Rev. Ethan Smith's *View of the Hebrews* as an answer. If Smith's vivid imagination was not the root source, and apparently Brodie does not rely entirely on this explanation, she holds *View of the Hebrews* as a trump card.

View of the Hebrews, written in 1823, is such an important issue that a future chapter is devoted to it. But the Rev. Smith did not attempt to write a narrative of the American aborigines being descendants of the ten tribes of Israel and coming to the new land across the Bering land bridge; he simply presented the theory they somehow did (see chapter 9).

The value of the Book of Mormon is more than describing an ocean voyage, or even three of them. It contains considerable doctrine answering the religionist's many vexing questions through the ages—so many, in fact, there is not enough room here to enumerate them all. One is whether salvation is gained by grace alone or by grace and works. Smith (or God) answers the question this way: "For we know that it is by grace that we are saved, after all we can do" (2 Nephi 25:23). This principle has been a guideline in LDS philosophy since 1830. With it, missionaries have taught many converts the Mormon message. The idea seems simple enough. So why was it left to an obscure farm boy to promulgate?

We also have these verses from Mormon 6:16–20, and we must ask if something so almost poetic could actually be written by a young man whom Emma Smith says couldn't even write a literate note to a friend[35]:

> And my soul was rent with anguish, because of the slain of my people, and I cried:
>
> O ye fair ones, how could ye have departed from the ways of the Lord! O ye fair ones, how could ye have rejected that Jesus, who stood with open arms to receive you!
>
> Behold, if ye had not done this, ye would not have fallen. But behold, ye are fallen, and I mourn your loss.
>
> O ye fair sons and daughters, ye fathers and mothers, ye husbands and wives, ye fair ones, how is it that ye could have fallen!
>
> But behold, ye are gone, and my sorrows cannot bring your return.

This is not showcase poetry, even for an eighteen-year-old, but it makes a point: if the book evolved as Joseph said, it reflects a lamentation on the part of one of the writers who felt a deep sense of loss. It is possible that other prophets of the Book of Mormon or Bible might also reach out to a Supreme Being in such words? That is, the thought process in scripture can move from the bottom up, as well as from the top down. If the former, it is apt to be less eloquent, depending on the skill and experience of the writer, than if rendered by God.

Even if it is all Smith's doing, however, his would seem to be a mind keenly sensitive to the things of God.

One of Brodie's greatest missiles thrown at the Book of Mormon is the theme that Joseph borrowed so heavily from the Bible. Common sense tells us that if a people came to America from the Old World that they would bring their moral teachings, customs, revered history, and nomenclature with them. Thus, it is not strange that the Book of Mormon should reflect the same, with Isaiah being the favored icon. As Nibley points out, twenty-one chapters of Isaiah show up in the book.[36] However, Isaiah's wisdom and prophecies as written on the brass plates of Laban, do not appear exactly as in the King James version. Nibley says, "So far as Nephi's translation being a slavish repetition of our Bible . . . there is hardly a single verse that is identical in the two translations."[37] Most of the differences are in a word or two such as a preposition; but the meaning is much different in several places.

To the skeptic, it might mean Smith took the trouble to make these changes so that his product would appear more credible. To others, it likely means that translators everywhere come up with varied renderings. In any event, it does not appear to be lazy action on Joseph's part, as Brodie alleges, for it would require almost as much effort by Smith to alter so many words as to simply fill the space with his own thoughts.

Some may marvel at the many new names in the Book of Mormon, but as one who has had thirteen books published, fiction and nonfiction, I don't see conjuring up place names nearly as difficult as thinking up intricate plots and defining characters to interact logically with them. Many of these exist in the Book of Mormon.

The authors of the *Wizard of Oz* and *Gone with the Wind* came up with many new names. The hard part is coming up with characterizations and plots. Creating these can take considerable time, and not only that, all statements, prophecies, moral teachings, and references to names and places in such a historical work as the Book of Mormon must link together with the Old and New Testament. Any fiction writer will readily admit that coming up with something original is difficult enough without the handicap of making it all tie in with past events. For example, one veteran author who did so in his story of a family wending westward in pioneer times took five years to write a book, and he had been at his profession for decades.

Even the great Shakespeare, one of the keenest intellects of all time, made mistakes in writing of historical events. For instance, he has a clock strike three in one line of Julius Caesar, but in Caesar's day clocks did not strike anything.[38]

In the Book of Mormon, 1 Nephi 18:24 speaks of horses, but

in 1830 it was a consensus of historians that there were no horses in America before the Spaniards. However, the LeBrea Tar Pits in southern California have yielded horse remains from an earlier period.[39]

Brodie does claim to have a major point of geographical contradiction. The Bible says Jesus was born in Bethlehem (see Matthew 2:5–6), and the Book of Mormon, claims Brodie, says in Jerusalem. Actually, Brodie commits a serious breach of research here. Alma 7:10 prophecies that Christ will be born "at Jerusalem which is the land of our forefathers." It is the land of Jerusalem, not the city, which is being cited. Nothing here suggests that either Joseph Smith or Alma did not know that Jesus was born in Bethlehem. It is straining at a gnat.

But nowhere does Brodie tip her hand about a shallow comprehension of the Book of Mormon's appeal more than when she says, "If his book is monotonous today, it is because . . . the burning questions that the book answered are ashes. This is particularly true of the religious matter."[40]

Perhaps Brodie could have more ably critiqued the Book of Mormon if she'd done any serious research on the matter. She can't get out of her agenda long enough to ask: How many books have been sold? In how many languages? What is the appeal of this book to so many people? By the time she had published her second edition in 1971, many million copies of the Book of Mormon had been sold; it appeared by that time in nearly a hundred languages. And today, readership is growing even faster, according to LDS accounting.[41]

Certainly if we were writing a book about a best-selling Koran, New Testament, Torah, Tripitaka, or revered writings from any other religion, and pretending to be objective, we would not dismiss a best seller with, "It has turned to ashes." We might say, "We can't in all the world understand its appeal," but we would definitely try to determine what it was that attracted so many to its pages. In this particular instance, we would surely attempt to answer the question that Brodie herself raises: If the Book of Mormon was only a reflection of the Palmyra frontier of

1830,[42] what makes it so popular so many years later?

Closer to the truth is the statement by Sidney Sperry that the Book of Mormon "has had great impact on the world."[43] This is hardly a speculation, for sales of the book are documented, as are miles traveled to disseminate it.

Nibley gives this opinion: "In view of the newly discovered insights into the nature of the ancient scriptures, it is getting harder and harder to find any real objections to the Book of Mormon."[44]

Of course, many critics have not really examined the book any more fully than Brodie. Her ashes statement isn't much of an indictment against the book or even a meaningful critique because she has so limited its parameters.[45] Her famous exegesis would appear to be mostly cathartic. We must ask if she is writing the book for an at-world audience, or simply for herself.

In so doing, Brodie may simply be purging out years of animosity growing up in ecclesiastical surroundings with which she didn't agree. Undoubtedly, the Book of Mormon was a subject of frequent discussion in the McKay home.

Even though Dale Morgan lauded her overall effort, he made this comment in a letter to his protégé after seeing her first draft: "You are positive beyond what the facts will support."[46]

Is Brodie purporting to write a polemic about herself or one about Joseph Smith? She only succeeded if she was attempting the former.

5
And It Came to Pass

Mark Twain said if the phrase "it came to pass" were deleted from the Book of Mormon, the book would be only a pamphlet. While somewhat exaggerated, much like reports of Twain's death, new studies by statistics professors Wayne Larsen and Alvin Rencher indicate that the phrase was probably one word in the reformed Egyptian lexicon.[1] Hugh Nibley calls it a very Egyptian way to begin a sentence.[2] Fawn Brodie disagrees, but since she is no Egyptian scholar, Nibley's word means far more.[3]

As for so many sentences starting with "And," Brodie has this to say: "The typesetters broke up the clauses as they saw fit, with the result that of the first 200 sentences, 140 began with the word 'And.'"[4] Her implication, of course, is that much of the Book of Mormon was the work of those who happened to be employed at the Grandin printing press who did a rather clumsy job of it.

But it may be that prophets like to begin sentences with the word "And." The first five verses of Acts 28 begin with "And," as do sixteen of the chapter's twenty-five total verses. In Revelation 12, all seventeen verses, except for verse 12, begin with "And." The same goes for fourteen of eighteen verses in chapter 13. These are only random samples. "And" seems to be a connective word that works for writers of scripture, ancient and modern.

Many of the above Bible references are narrative. Since the Book of Mormon's opening chapters also tell a narrative story, the book seems in harmony, format wise, with the Bible. As stated earlier, Brodie apparently didn't read the Bible. That is understandable for an atheist, but if Brodie had done so, she might have panned the Bible as well, or skipped seemingly empty criticism on this point.

But let's first examine how the Book of Mormon made its way into print. When Joseph Smith sent Oliver Cowdery with the Book of Mormon manuscript to Egbert B. Grandin, publisher of the *Wayne Sentinel*, for typesetting, the manuscript was one long paragraph.[5] John Gilbert, Grandin's printer, was told by Cowdery to put in punctuation as necessary to make it more readable. Clearly, Oliver did not want Gilbert, or anyone else, to change any of the meaning from what he and Joseph considered holy writ. But this opened the door for punctuation placed at the printer's discretion or possibly even arbitrary spelling, for some words were not spelled the same way twice.[6] That errors could creep in by Gilbert's hand is not unthinkable.

One reason Joseph might proceed this way was that he was so unlettered he didn't trust his own grammatical judgment and relied on a professional with more experience on the proper mechanics of book printing.

But that of itself does not solve the problem. The original Book of Mormon in 1830 drew howls of protest from enemies because it was apparent the language was in the idiom of the day; in fact it was in Joseph Smith's western, New York, semiliterate lexicon. Brodie mocks it all as the work of a clumsy author with a rich imagination.

But some readers of today's Book of Mormon may have a mistaken idea about how Smith translated the book in the first place. It is supposed by even many LDS Church members that Joseph simply looked into his Urim and Thummim and then God placed the words there for him to read. Joseph relayed them to a scribe, usually Oliver Cowdery, who repeated the words as he wrote them down. If correct, the phrases would disappear and new words would replace them. This is the way Martin Harris seemed to describe the process.

But Sidney Sperry, Hugh Nibley, and B. H. Roberts, all students of the translation process, describe it this way: When Joseph looked at the "screen," he saw what the writers said in their day. Then, focusing prayerfully on the task at hand, he translated it into his own words for his own day.[7]

It had more meaning that way for the audience to follow, say these scholars. If you were, for example, trying to explain to an Eskimo the meaning of Psalm 23 talking about sheep in green pastures, they would have no idea what you were talking about. Thus, ideas, terms, and phrases that made perfect sense in the Egyptian shorthand some two thousand years earlier were translated into the English of Smith's day.

In many ways, Smith's limited use of the English language short circuits the idea that he wrote the book by himself. His not being literate, as Emma says ("Joseph didn't even know how to write a literate letter"[8]), lends credence to the idea that he couldn't write a complicated work such as the Book of Mormon. Because he was so impoverished in any formal education, Joseph rarely wrote anything in his early life, save a few letters to Emma, without relying on a scribe. Yet strangely, he is accused of somehow putting together a 539-plus-page book that has influenced millions of readers the world over. Even if he had been a literate and prolific writer, when did Smith vanish for months at a time to write what would certainly seem to require even a veteran author years to produce—and on his first try? Surely, someone would have noticed his absence in some phase of this lengthy process.

As for the one monster paragraph, it smacks of being so because Smith translated it without backing up to read before continuing on. As Emma said, her husband would leave for an hour or a day and return to pick it up right where he left off, never asking a single question about where he stopped.[9]

As for the Urim and Thummim, this is more nonsense for Brodie; she acknowledges that it was an instrument of translation used in the Old Testament yet still treats it as an invention of Joseph Smith.[10] But again, Joseph is being consistent, for the Urim and Thummim, meaning light and perfection in Hebrew, is mentioned in Exodus 28:30, Leviticus 8:8, Numbers 27:21,

Deuteronomy 33:8, 1 Samuel 28:6, and Ezra 2:63. If Joseph is really a prophet as he says, why not proceed, as did the Old Testament prophets?

Brodie says Smith offers "nothing not already found in frontier America."[11] Again, she couldn't have been more wrong. Smith's new religion challenged conventional ecclesiastical wisdom to the core. What about the concept of God and Christ as two physical entities in contradiction to the Nicene Creed, the traditional standard of deity for so many centuries?[12] What about the concept of the Restoration itself, that gospel truths which had been lost from the earth in an apostasy as prophesied in Acts 3:19–21 were now fully restored, including divine messengers bringing back what had been lost after the death of Christ's apostles? The gathering of Israel in the last days? The keys mentioned by Elijah related to the family history work the LDS Church is so busy with today? The concept of the Garden of Eden being in America? What about polygamy, baptism for the dead, and modern revelation—in the 1820s?[13] These were not new concepts for that period of time? Where was Brodie when all this was going on?

Ironically, while panning it, Brodie fails to ascertain the fact that Joseph's claiming modern revelation was an innovation in itself. Nothing new in Smith's religion? It would be difficult, indeed, to name any other church teaching daily communication from God in America of the 1820–30s as Smith taught.

Smith's claim to a restoration of all things was so innovative that in faraway Russia, Count Leo Tolstoy took note of the "American religion," telling Dr. Andrew D. White, United States Foreign Minister to Russia, of his admiration for the new faith in 1892. "The Mormon people teach not only of heaven and its attendant glories, but how to live . . . on a sound basis."[14] Tolstoy heaped other praise on the American church, but it is not pertinent here. What is significant is that around the world the teachings promulgated by Joseph Smith were perceived as very different from existing religions. The Mormons asserted boldly that they were not Catholic, Protestant, Jew, or any other conventional ecclesiastical category. The LDS Church should properly be classified as restored.[15]

Brodie says almost nothing about these bold new claims of Joseph's church; indeed, the word *restoration* does not even appear in her rather sophisticated index. She fails to comprehend the religious significance of the apostasy and restoration claim of the latter days. Either she is ignorant of how these claims relate to the Bible, or she chose to ignore them. Right or wrong, the doctrines introduced by Smith seem not only new but also revolutionary. That doesn't prove they are true, but they are certainly different.

They were so different from conventional wisdom of the day that it is not surprising the same would invite persecution. Obviously, the tenets of the early Mormons varied so greatly from their neighbors that ridicule and scorn were certain to follow. It is worth noting that the religion taught by Jesus also drew criticism because it differed from the law of Moses.

Was this strange religion not the reason given for the Mormon Manifesto issued by anti-Mormons in Jackson County, Missouri, in 1833? The manifesto proclaims: "The evil [Mormon religion] is one that could not have been foreseen and is therefore unprovided for by the laws." Missourians mocked the Mormons for "their pretended intercourse with God."[16] This people who called themselves Latter-day Saints were hardly treated as orthodox Christians then, and in some quarters, are not today.

For one who sets forth that she is singularly qualified to write about the Mormons because she spent twenty years among them, Brodie leaves herself open to criticism regarding how much she actually understood about the church Joseph founded. She has the outer rudiments of scholarly inquiry, but if we were going to expose someone as a charlatan, it would seem the first order of business would be to know what that person, in actuality, is setting forth to accomplish.

Of course, it is known today that Brodie did not have access to many LDS libraries, which could have provided more sympathetic insight into why Mormons believe as they do. Because Brodie spent most of her time at Chicago and New York public bookshelves, many featuring local hearsay and gossip, her understanding of Mormonism, even if only to criticize it, suffered a leanness of depth.[17]

If you or I set out to find the truth about say, flying saucers, we might carry some baggage of bias. I personally do not believe in flying saucers anymore than I do in the existence of Bigfoot. But if writing on it, I would still have to examine the evidence and report on it truthfully from my findings. Due to vivid reports of saucers in many parts of the world, including thousands of people claiming sightings in Belgium near the German border, I would have to honestly admit that things are going on there that I do not fully understand.

In fact, Brodie confided to mentor Dale Morgan that she "still didn't know what to do with him [Joseph Smith]. . . . Smith's career continues to astonish me . . . the more I work with the man the more of a challenge he becomes. . . . The success of his church is astonishing."[18] Yet we find no such admission in her book, for by the time she sends it off, she has expunged all such concerns.

Even some non-Mormon scholars differed with Brodie's "nothing not already found in frontier America" remark. Richard Bushman, of Boston University, stated emphatically that the Book of Mormon "did not consistently reflect American democratic values of that [Joseph in Palmyra] period."[19] He finds no common ground on that point at all.

It is also interesting that Alfred Knopf, who published Brodie's book on Joseph Smith in both 1945 and 1971, invited two LDS historians to provide a different, more positive, point of view about the subject. Using the same resource materials as Brodie, Leonard Arrington, official historian for the LDS Church for a number of years, along with Mormon historian Davis Bitton, reached many different conclusions than Brodie.[20] From this we might deduce that Knopf recognized the need for a more balanced presentation. The detailed work of Arrington and Bitton did not fetch any national awards for objective reporting, of course, any more than had the exhaustive research of Nibley, Sperry, and the introspective B. H. Roberts. Since all were LDS, that alone seems to exclude them from being labeled objective by a non-Mormon audience.

But the greatest weakness in Brodie's argument is that she leaves out the hard parts. She never does address how Joseph, according to wife Emma and scribe Oliver Cowdery, could finish dictation in the middle of one page and then several days later resume precisely where he had left off without so much as a glance of the manuscript to date. Emma makes a most damning statement to Brodie's agenda when she says: "I know Mormonism to be the truth and believe the Church has been established by divine direction. . . . Joseph Smith could neither write nor dictate a coherent and well-worded letter, let alone dictate a book like the Book of Mormon. . . . I am satisfied that no man could have dictated the writing of the manuscripts unless he was inspired; for when dictating to me hour after hour, and when returning after meals or interruptions, he would at once begin where he had left off, without either seeing the manuscript or having any portion of it read to him. . . . It would have been impossible that a learned man could do this and for one so ignorant and unlearned as he was, it was simply impossible."[21]

Brodie does not mention this. But who should know what happened better than Emma Smith, Joseph's wife for nearly twenty years. Brodie has no answer for this. She doesn't try. Nor does she challenge Emma's honesty.

Let us ponder the improbable once more. Could any writer produce a full-length book without ever checking notes or looking back? Could Brodie? Did Brodie? Could anyone? How often did she refer to former notes or pages while working on *No Man Knows My History?* Both books were, incidentally, about the same length: 539 for the Book of Mormon, including preface pages; and 534 for *No Man Knows My History,* including notes and index.

From the time Joseph was known to begin his work until finishing the Book of Mormon, less than three months elapsed. This is difficult to explain for an uneducated person of any age; Joseph was about twenty-three at the time. And why, if he wanted to foist off a fraud, let anyone else see what he was doing by dictating to someone, anyway? Why not go off in a corner and hide while committing such a colossal deception? And how does Brodie explain the obvious: why would someone committing a fraud wait seven years, from spring 1820 to 1827, before realizing a payoff? Doesn't it seem unlikely that if Joseph wanted to perpetuate a hoax for some sort of gain from golden plates that he would wait for such a long period before announcing the existence of the plates? Is that the way of frauds?

Brodie mentioned that others besides the Eight Witnesses felt or hefted the plates, but then she passes over the matter quickly.[22] If Smith had something remotely resembling metal plates, why not show them to the witnesses rather than an empty box as Brodie claims? The reason given by Smith is that he was under strict orders to show them to no person other than as directed, even members of his family. Brodie did not accept this. But if he was a fraud, wouldn't Joseph really rather show his witnesses something rather than nothing? Brodie's reasoning here seems to become totally illogical.

Brodie says that it was after he began rewriting the New Testament in 1831 that Joseph learned the "power of words."[23] So, he didn't have such power earlier when he wrote the Book of Mormon by himself? Brodie has, in such a manner, committed dozens of contradictions. She inserts conclusions whenever she feels a need to prove something for the ambiance of the moment.

Her research and conclusions can appear linked because she is clever in the use of false transitional conclusions, such as saying Joseph (1) "laid no importance on the temple ordinances," and (2) "the costuming, pageantry, and general abracadabra had attracted him to the Masonic ritual in the first place."[24]

But what if he was sincere in introducing the temple rite as God's word from a Masonic ritual that had also come down from religious tradition? How does she know it was the costuming and pageantry he was interested in? For instance, I can make a point by claiming that Abe Lincoln never was interested in winning the Civil War. To command a large number of soldiers with their colorful uniforms was what captured his fancy.

Jack H. West, in his *Trial of the Stick of Joseph*, explains how he presented the case of the Book of Mormon with its many witnesses to a mock trial in law school. The non-Mormon professor told West that he had presented "the most perfect case I've ever witnessed."[25] West explained why the stick of Judah (Bible) and the stick of Joseph (Book of Mormon) were compatible and logical, while backing the Book of Mormon with eleven eyewitnesses. Brodie does not mention the parallelism in the sticks of Judah and Joseph as mentioned in the Old Testament.[26]

While she sometimes brings in opposing opinions, Brodie frequently selects straw men who can be easily pushed over. An example is quoting Josiah Quincy, who visited Joseph in Nauvoo, as saying, "If the reader does not know what to make of Joseph Smith, I cannot help him out of the difficulty. I myself stand helpless before the puzzle."[27] This is too much in Joseph's favor, so she must add, "What had overpowered Josiah Quincy, as indeed it did most of the Prophet's visitors, was Joseph's magnificent self-assurance."[28] She inserts this declaration as if it were a sure sign of Joseph's artifice. But wouldn't he also possess magnificent self-assurance if he were what he claimed to be? Maybe even more so?

Sometimes Brodie creates silly conversations that do no one any harm, such as the one between Joseph and Martin Harris, after Harris loses the first 116 pages of the Book of Mormon manuscript. Brodie has Joseph saying, "'I must return to my wife with such a tale as this,' Joseph cried. 'I dare not do it, lest I should kill her at once.'"[29]

Why kill Emma? Brodie appears here to merely get caught up in her own imagination without adhering to any logic. Elsewhere, Emma is depicted as a trusting wife who just goes along with what Joseph tells her; but then it is apparently decided she should take a more active role in her husband's work. There is no footnote to the conversation; it simply seems a benign innovation that makes for a more interesting narrative provided by the author of *No Man*.

Brodie sidesteps the David Whitmer family as having

fantasies. All were deceived, nuts, crazy, weirdos, and whackos.[30] In this she is being consistent, for she treats with contempt any and all who claim to have heavenly insight. It is a good thing for America she did not write a history of George Washington or Abraham Lincoln, who often credited divine guidance in their successes in preserving their country. Or the founding fathers. Had she done so, there is no doubt she could have located a control group of leaders in some ancient country who worshipped trees and managed to do what Washington did, only better. The Druids perhaps.

The point is that the reader must be careful not to become mesmerized by the rhetoric. The Jewish historian Flavius Josephus had every reason, especially being under control of the Roman Empire, to write Jesus off as a fanatic and fraud. Instead, in his *Antiquities of the Jews*, Josephus manages to describe the importance of Christ from a believer's point of view,[31] "for he appeared alive to them again the third day." He then writes another 752 pages about the political intrigues of the Romans, but at least he has provided posterity with an insightful view of those who did not believe as the Romans.

Brodie names people during Smith's Palmyra period who claimed to see visions and have "spiritual dreams."[32] Many are listed in an article by Richard L. Bushman titled "The Visionary World of Joseph Smith." Bushman also tells of a Solomon Chamberlin, who prayed in 1816 to find the "true religion of Jesus Christ."[33] Chamberlin says he was told that such a church was not yet on the earth but would be later. In 1829, he was impressed to stop in Palmyra, making his way to Joseph Smith's residence. "Is there anyone here who believes in visions or revelations?" he asked. Chamberlin was later baptized into this new religion.

This account might have been embellished somewhat along the way. But wouldn't a mention of it by Brodie give some semblance of objectivity? She did not mention it. Perhaps she did not know of it with all of her lengthy research, for she wouldn't likely find it in the hostile libraries where she spent most of her time after she left Utah.

She lumps together all the visionaries of the Palmyra neighborhood as impostors because they committed the sin of claiming inspiration of one sort or another. Some were listed in *Mormonism Unvailed* [sic], which borrows heavily from anti-Mormon Philastus Hurlbut's controversial list of Smith's neighbors who, once he claimed prophethood, had little good to say about him.[34] Research has indicated that Hurlbut himself penned some of the castigations and then later got signatures from people who had never met Joseph Smith but had "heard rumors."[35] Centuries later, how do we know he didn't also make up a few of the names on his list?

As pointed out by Brodie, most of these visionaries later doubted they'd seen any vision at all. Smith stood out and frustrated his enemies by never recanting his own claim to prophecy. Brodie asserts as much with her *No Man Knows My History* title, but her interpretation of its meaning is clearly subjective. Did it mean he carried out a secret life as an impostor or, as he often stated, that he received precious inspiration beyond human invention? We may never know for sure from those mystical words. Only Brodie seems to have the answer.[36]

While she has much interest here in the alleged visions of people in western New York, she summarily throws Joseph out with the bath water. Read Bushman for a more balanced account of what happened and to whom. In some places, Brodie assesses the entire Smith family as being spiritually minded, but instead of saying they were complementary in this, they are described as being in rivalry with one another for attention from God.[37] The same doesn't do much for Brodie's appearance of fair play, for why must they be competing with one another? Were Christ's apostles competing with one another simply because all professed spiritual insight—from the same source?

Brodie states that Joseph's family must not have been much impressed with his vision, since most members remained in the Presbyterian fold for so long. But how does Brodie explain that within a few years Joseph had the unwavering devotion of his entire family—Joseph Sr., Lucy Mack, Hyrum, Samuel, and his sisters—to his dedicated missionary journey? And William? While hot and cold to Joseph's religious urgings, the younger brother did not oppose Joseph's announced prophethood. William clearly stated just before he died at age eighty-two that he believed implicitly in Joseph and the Book of Mormon. Asked about the book, William replied succinctly, "Joseph was a truthful man. . . . No sir, we never doubted his word for one minute."[38] To suggest that Joseph's family was not impressed with his claims is misleading in its entirety.

Brodie has a parallel somewhere for everything. Joseph's new church is blasé, for in her studies and travels, she has seen everything Smith did. If Joseph pens anything eloquent or gazes into a crystal stone, then the Masons or Shakers or ancient civilizations have done it before. The Gadianton robbers of the Book of Mormon were nothing more than a form of freemasonry found in New York. Brodie goes into great detail about anti-Mason violence in that state, which proves nothing about violence in the Book of Mormon.[39]

She is off on another tangent in saying Joseph looked "in his crystal" for gold in "every odd-shaped hill."[40] This does little to suggest an honest appraisal, for Brodie knows Smith never intimated such a thing. There was one source for the gold plates, the Hill Cumorah. But she is not the first critic distorting this account in Mormon annals. Historian Milton Backman, compiling a study of non-Mormon writers, found that among fifty writings studied, none related the first vision and Moroni accounts as Joseph told them in the official history he began in 1838. Hugh Nibley did isolate one, a government publication covering the year 1844, which carried the first vision as Smith wrote it.[41] That this should be so unusual is a sad commentary on the role of those who call themselves religious historians.

It would seem that serious biographers, Mormon or non-Mormon, could agree on some standards in order to attain more meaningful and less polarized historicity. A starting point might be to write down the claim of any religious figure, or one who pretends to be, and begin the dissection after first getting the facts down as presented by the subject. If the original premise is flawed, how can truth possibly be served?

On this, Brodie need not draw condemnation. She simply distorted Smith's account of his claims, as did other non-Mormon critics.

At times Brodie lapses into imaginative prose, which could be taken as offensive. For instance, she says that when Joseph was born on 23 December 1805, "he was accepted that cold winter night probably with more resignation than delight."[42] Why more resignation? Is this meant to suggest a portent of some ill-boding future event? If so, what?

Maybe the family actually thought it was wonderful to have a new baby in the family. True, the Smiths were as poor as anyone around, but with love and close-knit bonding, which their family history seems to indicate, why would they not welcome a new addition? The comment seems to carry no purpose, and with it Brodie comes off as assumptive, if not arrogant. Even if she did know what the family was thinking, why is she invading such a private family matter? In this, she gives a clue regarding what we can expect later.

Such a thing as creative nonfiction exists in the writing profession, but it carries rules: characters must interact within the framework of documented events. Characters should not act contrarily to known behavior. If new characters are introduced, as in Gerald Lund's *Work and the Glory* sagas, we should differentiate between fact and fiction, as Lund did. Truly, Smith presents a conundrum for those faced with drawing the line between tinkering and truth. As Marvin Hill puts it, Joseph's visions create an "awkward" situation for historians.[43]

Many who have written about early Mormon history can be quite generous in matters not involving deity. Novelist Vardis Fisher was particularly kind to Brigham Young in matters of organizing the westward trek and in colonizing it, but then Young didn't claim the visions that Joseph had claimed. Joseph's visions seemed to anger Fisher, as if they were an act of putting on airs and being "holier than thou." But this same mind-set would simply seem a reflection of human nature. Many in Joseph's Palmyra neighborhood seemed to share Fisher's idea that anyone claiming divine inspiration must be making things up. In his *Children of God*, Fisher's Joseph was kind to strangers and loved little children but was, nevertheless, deluded.[44] Claiming to see deity can't be allowed.

In an earlier era, western writer Zane Grey's modus operandi was to rescue Mormon damsels from the clutches of lecherous and polygamous priesthood bearers. Grey did not get this notion from any actual experience, for he personally knew only a few Mormon men, and those he did know he said he admired.[45] You don't see this in, say, *Riders of the Purple Sage*. It was written to pander to audiences willing to spend millions of dollars in confirming what they wanted to hear, which rescued Grey from his dreary life as a New York dentist.[46]

I do not think Brodie wrote primarily for money, as did Grey, although with sales of her book, Brodie must have become most comfortably fixed. It does not appear that she lied her way through the book merely for popularity's sake, as did Grey. But I believe Brodie held herself up as a scholar who couldn't fail and then succumbed to her agenda. As Fisher hinted, it appears what Brodie wanted to do in the first place was write her suppositions (a novel), but seeing herself as an academic superior, she could gain greater acclaim in scholarly circles by transforming her work into a documentary.

Like Fisher, Brodie is willing to praise Mormon leaders, provided that doing so does not link them with deity. She shows them as having considerable grit and courage to maintain religious convictions and devotions against fanatical mobs, even migrating a thousand miles into a wilderness to practice their beliefs. She heaps praise on the dynamics of the Mormon Church in surviving the murder of its prophet at Nauvoo in 1844 to colonize and build up the Great Basin under the leadership of Brigham Young. She avoids the temptation to claim that Joseph could not have taken the Saints west, as did Young. She avows that thousands followed Joseph from New York, to Ohio, to Missouri, and to

Illinois, and would have followed him wherever he went. She also dispelled the myth that Emma refused to go west because she did not believe in the church founded by her husband. "Emma did not believe in Brigham Young," asserts Brodie.[47] In this, she would seem to be correct.

Brodie appears to strike a fierce blow to Mormondom when she says Joseph never took his message (his first vision) to the newspapers. He did eventually publicly share what to him was a sacred experience, or at least Oiver Cowdery attempted to do it for him. But when Ontario County-area editors heard of it in 1831–32, they did what you might expect—they pooh-poohed the entire account. When they heard it again in 1838, they pooh-poohed it all over again and then ignored it.[48]

After studying newspapers for a master's thesis, visiting *The New York Times,* and working among news gatherers for half a century, I concluded that newspapers refuse to print all they hear. Skepticism is the byword. Thus, a newsman worth his salt would not necessarily set to flogging Joseph. He would simply say, "Bring in the proof." In other words, have your vision here in our newsroom.

It does not seem to have crossed Brodie's mind that Joseph might have considered the matter deeply personal for a time and did not want to share it with a world of nonbelievers right away. Joseph did announce guidelines for organizing the church he founded—in the early sections of the Doctrine and Covenants and intended to reach believers—and he sent out missionaries for nonbelievers. He tried to disseminate his message to believers but was not energetic in casting pearls before swine. Did not Christ do the same?

6
First Vision Under Attack

Joseph Smith might have been spared a lion's share of persecution had he been content to simply claim inspiration rather than revelation. Using the dramatic words "I saw" ensured that Joseph's life would never again be the same.

Attacking Joseph Smith's first vision (the term is capitalized by LDS believers, but herein it is accorded a neutral label) has been a favorite sport for one hundred seventy-two years. According to LDS historical researcher David Whittaker, more than two hundred anti-Mormon books have been published since Brodie's "exposé" in 1945.[1] The first vision draws the major attack.

This fact tosses some cold water on the idea that Brodie (or anyone) wrote a definitive history of Joseph Smith. If so, why are so many still trying? Almost certainly many critics would like to totally dispose of that first vision.

Despite repeated virulent attacks, as Whittaker labels them, on the beginning of Joseph's spiritual career, response from the LDS Church has been almost nonexistent. Is the Church's reason "Why repeat the abuse?" Perhaps, but enemies might label it apathy, or even neglect.

One LDS historian who has responded is Hugh Nibley, with a humorous treatise titled *How to Write an Anti-Mormon Book, a Handbook for Beginners.* His first rule is "don't be modest," or, in other words, "boldly state your credentials and irrefutable objectivity, then fire away with both barrels."[2] E. D. Howe began firing both barrels, assuring us he had received his information on the best authority.[3] But the shots he fired proved to be blanks. No one takes Howe seriously anymore because he didn't set out to present honest research. As for Abner Coles, who wrote *Pukei*, he didn't do a satire on Joseph Smith so much as he simply invented a Joseph Smith no one knew. Not even non-Mormons take the book seriously as a history of Joseph Smith.

But a few detractors such as Brodie have actually seriously studied the first vision and raises doubts among some LDS members, including several known to the author. Thus, it seems proper to address Brodie's most damning allegation: Joseph gave three different versions of his first vision.[4]

Four, actually, says LDS historian Richard L. Anderson.[5] They came in the years 1831–32, in the handwriting of Frederick G. Williams, Joseph's scribe; in 1835, in the hand of Warren A. Cowdery, Oliver's brother; in 1838, in the official history of the Church, started by Joseph and written by various scribes but not completed until 1842; and in 1842, in the Wentworth letter from Smith's hand. The latter included what later became the thirteen Articles of Faith, including the first article of faith: "We believe in God, the Eternal Father, and in his Son, Jesus Christ, and in the Holy Ghost."

But the first article of faith provides no details on the nature of the first vision, so focus settles on the others. Another reference listed by LDS historian Dean Jesse, who extensively researched Joseph Smith's vision,[6] includes one in 1835, shortly after number three. But it appears there are no significant differences, so we will settle on four. Why two first vision statements within a relatively short time? Because two different men whom Joseph accepted as honest seekers of truth requested them, says Jesse.

The main complaint of Brodie and cohorts is that Smith referred only to Christ in the first account, in which he says he was in "the sixteenth year of my age," and to both Christ and God in the other accounts.[7] Later, Joseph also changed his age, a matter for later discussion.

We refer to Jesse's listings chronologically.[8] It is clear in the first account (1831) that Joseph is speaking of Christ, for he says, "A piller [sic] of light above the brightness of the sun at noon day came down from above and rested upon me and I was filld [sic] with the spirit of God and the Lord opened the heavens upon me and I saw the Lord and he spake unto me saying '. . . I was crucifyed [sic] for the world that all those who believe on my name may have eternal life behold the world lieth in sin. . . . They have turned aside from the Gospel and keep not my commandments . . . they draw near to me with their lips but their hearts are far from me.'" The reference "I was crucifyed" [sic] makes clear that this is Christ, not God, speaking—the later deity not being mentioned in the initial account.

Some Church critics have complained that Joseph received nothing in the 1831 version, save a forgiveness of sins. But Joseph learned that man could, beyond the Bible era, receive a direct answer to prayer. Man might communicate with heaven. Joseph was also told to "go thy way and walk in my statutes and keep my commandments."[9] For what reason? To be a future tool in restoring the true church? There is no direct mention that this would be the case, but could Joseph be that instrument if he was to prove himself worthy and "keep my commandments"?

That there was to be a restoration would seem a logical conclusion, for Joseph was told, "Mine anger is kindling against the inhabitants of the earth to visit them according to this ungodliness and to bring to pass that which hath been spoken by the mouth of the prophets and Apostles."[10] Could Joseph, if he gained experience in what God had in mind, qualify to be part of such a glorious restoration?

In the 1835 version, Joseph mentions two personages: "The second testified unto me that Jesus Christ is the Son of God." He also mentions the presence of angels. "I was about fourteen years old when I received this first communication."[11] Joseph said he felt a darkness overcome him, consistent with all four accounts. "I made a fruitless attempt to pray." At first he could not utter a word. His tongue was finally loosed as he "called upon the Lord in mighty prayer."[12]

In the third account, Joseph explains the first vision for the first time more fully in his own words. (Frederick G. Williams and Warren A. Cowdery had penned the other accounts.) In the 1838 version, Joseph is more inclusive. He explains that God introduced Christ and said, "Hear him." The particulars can be found in the Pearl of Great Price. In this account, Joseph emphasizes that he was told that he must join no church. "I was answered that I must join none of them. . . . And many other things did he say unto me, which I cannot write at this time." Joseph includes the following words that were not mentioned in the earlier accounts: "for at this time it had never entered my heart that all were wrong" (Joseph Smith–History 1:18–20).

In the Wentworth letter, written at the request of John Wentworth, editor of the *Chicago Democrat*, Joseph summarizes the first vision for an audience of mostly nonbelievers. He mentions two glorious personages who told him that all religious denominations were believing in incorrect doctrines and that none of them was acknowledged by God as his church and kingdom. "And I was expressly commanded to 'not go after them,' at the same time receiving a promise that the fullness of the Gospel should at some future time be known unto me."[13]

This accounting is more conscious of public relations in that Joseph doesn't allude to no man being righteous as in previous versions. He emphasizes in this one that it was denominations, not people, that were incorrect. This is also the first account that he wrote in his own hand, the others taken down by scribes via notes or dictation. It is noteworthy that in this account Joseph refers specifically to "a fullness of the gospel which should at some time be known to me."

Differences of opinion obviously exist about whether he simply supplies more information in some, or whether he contradicts himself. Historian B. H. Roberts sees no contradiction.[14]

Still, I see three possible points of contradiction in the four representations: one, age; two, angels are mentioned only in the second version; three, only Christ is mentioned in the first accounting, while both Christ and God are referred to in the next three.

It is possible Joseph focused in the initial version on the one person who talked to him, Christ, since it was he who told Joseph to "walk in my statutes" and "keep my commandments." Joseph did not say that God didn't appear to him. He just focuses on the message that Christ had for him.

Mixing up numbers of divine beings in scripture has happened before. In the New Testament narrative of Mary Magdalene and others visiting Christ's tomb three days after the crucifixion, one account says she saw two angels; another account of the same incident mentions only one angel.[15] No one worried too much about it in the Bible. In Smith's history, they do.

As for age differences, Brodie makes much of Joseph giving his age in the first version as "in my sixteenth year." Later, in all versions, he says fourteen, or in "my fifteenth year." Brodie says he is two years off. But actually, Joseph says he going on fifteen or he is fourteen. Well, my mother is ninety-four but is going on ninety-five. So, Brodie is off by a year, just as Joseph Smith is. Perhaps Joseph didn't worry about it in 1838 because he deemed the *what* more important than the *when*.

Believers would say that answers are given much as a parent responds to the question: Where do babies come from? The responder must decide what amount of detail answers the question adequately. That might account for a mention of angels in one account, none in the others.

I do not see Brodie's claim of a "remarkable evolution"[16] in any accounts of the above. There are questions, but there are questions about Paul's vision as well. In one account, he "saw a light and heard a voice" (Acts 9:7), but in another place, he "heard not the voice" (Acts 22:9). It does not merit throwing out the whole of it and, consequently, the entire Christian church.

Interestingly, Joseph says in the "official" version that when he returned home he told his mother, "I have learned for myself that Presbyterianism is not true."[17]

Unfortunately, nothing exists in Lucy Mack Smith's *History of Joseph Smith* to tell us of a detailed response. But Lucy does tell us something of great importance. After giving Joseph's account of the first vision, she says, "From this time [time of the first vision] until the twenty-first of September, 1823 [Moroni's first visit] Joseph . . . suffered every kind of opposition and persecution from the different order of religionists."[18] Her statement tells us clearly that Joseph was experiencing persecution before the coming of Moroni. Why? Why is this obscure teenage boy being persecuted by religious leaders if not for speaking about the first vision?

Brodie lists many reason that Joseph might be persecuted.[19] But if Lucy Mack's statement is accurate, doesn't it seem unlikely this would be so if Joseph wasn't making a claim of some kind? And what kind of claim would he be making between 1820 and 1823 if not about the first vision?

Brodie asserts in her first edition (1945) that Smith didn't even think of coming up with a first vision until 1838–42 in his official history. She then backs up in 1971 and says that based on more information from the LDS Church, it was actually 1831. Yet incredibly, in her second edition in 1971, she declares that there is nothing new since her 1945 version. Surely, she must have known about the 1831 account. Did she miss it (poor scholarship) or choose to ignore it (poor history)?

She asserts in both editions that Joseph looked back and remembered a half-forgotten dream, or perhaps it was "sheer invention."[20] Unlike many hostile writers, however, Brodie is honest enough in this particular instance to acknowledge that LDS historians don't agree with her. She is correct.

Mormon historians say the alterations could be attributed to gaining new perspective as one gets older. The attack on Pearl Harbor, for example, is a well-known event told over and over by historians and filmmakers since 1941. It becomes more detailed and sophisticated in the telling. Essential facts are not necessarily altered, but previously unimportant details may be considered more important and, upon reflection, receive new emphasis. This is especially true as time goes on and one determines what questions are being asked that need to be answered more fully.

Smith is, it should be remembered, a very young man trying to put what can only be described as an awesome experience into proper perspective. Should God have intervened to help him tell of his experience sooner than 1831? Or at least prior to the Church being organized 6 April 1830?

Actually, Joseph did mention information linked to the first vision (God is with the new church to be organized) in D&C 20, received in April 1830. Verse 1 of the revelation says the Church is being organized and established according to the will and commandments of God. Verse 2: "which commandments were given to Joseph Smith, Jun., who was called of God, and ordained an apostle of Jesus Christ"; verse 6: "God ministered unto him"; 8: "and gave him power from on high"; verse 16: "for the Lord God has spoken it; and we, the elders of the Church, have heard and bear witness"; verse 17: "by these things we know that there is a God in Heaven"; verse 21: "wherefore, the Almighty God gave his Only Begotten Son"; verse 23: "He was crucified, died, and rose again the third day"; verse 24: "and ascended into Heaven, to sit down on the right hand of the Father, to reign with almighty power according to the will of the Father."

This makes it plain that even though there was no known published account of the first vision until 1831, the six members who organized the Church in 1830 were not left ignorant of Joseph's claim that those then joining, or those to come later, were acting under the direction of God and his Son, Jesus Christ.

Some critics issue this challenge: How could Joseph be telling his family he had received a vision that he and his family should join no church, and yet family members remained in the Presbyterian Church? As mentioned, Presbyterian minister Wesley P. Walters claimed that Lucy remained in the latter church in 1825, five years after Joseph said he had received the first vision. This does, indeed, appear to be incongruous.

But historian Marvin S. Hill says that by 1823, when Joseph began to translate the gold plates, Lucy believed him and had "separated from Presbyterianism. There would be little reason to do so if she doubted Joseph's vision."[21] The bottom line, as Hill concludes, is that the Smith family believed Joseph, a point affirmed by brother William many times over, including in a statement to that effect in the *Deseret News* of 20 January 1894. William never vacillated on this point.

Then there is this: Historian Richard L. Anderson says that a committee headed by Deacon Beckwith visited Lucy from the local Presbyterian Church. He charged Lucy, "Upon the possibility of losing you," that she not say anything further on the subject of the new revelation. It is not known if the deacon's reference was to the first vision or the coming of Moroni. To this Lucy made a defiant reply. The group then "sought a recantation concerning the Book of Mormon from Hyrum, who stood firm in his convictions."[22] The family was subsequently cut off from the Presbyterian Church. Anderson footnotes this incident with Records of the Sessions of the Presbyterian Church in Palmyra 2:11–12.

Whatever the Presbyterian membership records show prior to 1830, it is clear that Lucy Mack Smith allied herself with son Joseph and no longer wished to be associated with the Presbyterian faith. As for not being excommunicated until 1830, it really makes little difference how long the Presbyterians tried to woo her back to their fold. Lucy might have even associated with them for a time out of friendship. But she makes it clear she feels her future belongs with the church linked to Joseph's revelation and the Book of Mormon. Ditto for Hyrum.

As for the comment by Brodie that Joseph never even verbalized the first vision until 1831, she is dead wrong, as we have seen from his mother's statement. Joseph also says in his church history that a Methodist minister told him that his vision was "of the devil, that there were no such things as visions or revelations in these days" (Joseph Smith–History 1:21). We have in Lucy Mack's history between 1820 and 1823 a corroboration of her son's statement about the first vision.

Why did Joseph not write about the experience until 1831, even though talking about it earlier? Joseph explained in his *History of the Church* 4:89 that he was commanded to keep a record in 1830, when the Church was organized. He says he started one several times but lawsuits, persecution, vexatious enemies, and death of scribes delayed his work.[23] Scribes James Mullholland and Robert Thompson died, and Joseph said a Dr. Foster had failed him. It was not until Willard Richards took over in the Nauvoo period that faithful records were kept. How could the Lord allow such inefficiency? The only answer faithful Church members would give is that man has his agency to obey or otherwise. If he doesn't get the job done, another will be called.

Still, it could be argued by non-Mormons that Smith should have found a way to get the history begun in 1830, since it was commanded in 1830. Even Mormons might well agree with this conclusion, for it seems to be a commandment late in being fulfilled for whatever reason.

Mormons would also say that not writing down every detail of his history could work as a vote against chicanery on Joseph's part. If he was out to defraud, why wouldn't he work out an iron-tight alibi in every step he took? And write it down? On this basis, it does not appear that Smith set out to purposely defraud. If he did, he was not skillful at it.

Smith consistently focuses on his role as an instrument in bringing forth a restoration of all things known to Christ's early church that were lost in an apostasy after the death of the Lord's apostles. Examples of the restoration process include a return of the Aaronic and Melchizedek Priesthoods and the coming of Elijah, as mentioned in the Doctrine and Covenants.

Mormons would argue that if a restoration was needed, it didn't especially matter whether Smith was the tool to get it done. If Joseph failed, they argue, and God needed a restoration, which could only come at a time and place when freedom of religious speech was allowed, someone else could be found to meet the challenge. Smith wasn't the only one who could do it. But, of course, in pointing out Smith's accomplishments, Mormons would argue that he completed the restoration as he was expected to do, and with considerable success.

None of the above, of course, proves revelation—only that a revelation was needed if all that was lost in the days of the primitive church was to be restored.

Visiting what the LDS Church labels the Sacred Grove, the site of the first vision received by Joseph Smith, near Palmyra, New York, I did have a special feeling about the place. It was not necessarily born of deity; it could just be what I'd learned about the history of the site. And walking it posed a question: Wouldn't it be interesting for a moment to speculate what we would do if asked to do what Joseph Smith said was asked of him?

I have never received a vision or even had a dream that could be construed as such. I don't think I want one. If a heavenly messenger should appear, I would be asked to do something difficult. It would take me out of my comfort zone. I would be reticent to share it with anyone, save for a few trusted confidantes, and then I would extract a promise that something so sacred and personal not be blabbed about all over the neighborhood, let alone expose me to ridicule in the newspapers. Yet it is true I would have to find a way to disseminate it to the world, as did the Apostle Paul—if it was meant as a message for mankind. Paul did so but not in writing, for a quarter century. (See chapter 11.)

Clearly, being a bearer of such a message would not be an easy thing, especially if I was expected to organize a church and send missionaries around the world to render testimony based upon my experience. Many of those who heard it would accuse these emissaries of being haughty and holier than thou, when in truth we would all be obligated with the great burden placed upon us to do so. We would have to forgive and forget detractors, even though they dragged us into the night to tar and feather us. We would focus on the only thing that really matters: living up to the instructions received. If we received such a mandate, or revelation, we would do our best not to fail such a monumental responsibility, for our personal salvation and that of others would depend upon the same.

No thanks; why would anyone want it?

Of course, the atheist would not see it this way. But it is something to ponder when supposing, as some have, that Joseph did all the foregoing for some sort of pecuniary or other gain. For what other cause would he do it? The argument has been advanced that he might have reaped any profits from the Book of Mormon since under the laws of the state of New York Joseph was listed as the author. But since there were no profits from the Book of Mormon in Joseph's time, all we have is conjecture.

Joseph would forego any profits from sales of the Book of Mormon in authorizing Oliver Cowdery by revelation to sell copyrights to the book in Canada. Why sell the copyright anywhere? Was the Church in desperate need of money? In any event, Cowdery was unsuccessful in the attempt, as recorded by David Whitmer's pamphlet, *To All Believers in Christ*, written fifty-seven years after the alleged revelation. It is interesting that anti-Mormon elements say Whitmer recalled correctly this event in his old age but must not have remembered correctly when testifying of his Book of Mormon witness.

Did Joseph act out a charade of prophethood because of a super ego? If so, Church members would say, bring on the evidence. Those who followed him, such as Parley P. Pratt and Edward Partridge, say Joseph was a humble man; Pomeroy Tucker and E. D. Howe say he was not. Yet it would seem the burden rests on those who challenge Joseph's claim that he followed divine instruction. Perhaps the possibility of ego, or other failings, getting in the way of Christ's church was a reason that Joseph had to wait ten years from his announced first vision before organizing the new church. It is clear that from Smith's history he was not ready to govern Christ's new church in 1820, nor in 1823. He was required to wait, apparently, to prove he was worthy.

Yet let us look at broader parameters—the entire concept of visions. In *No Man Knows My History,* Brodie has William Marks listening to Smith saying, "We are a ruined people." How so? asks Marks. "The doctrine of polygamy. . . . I have been deceived."[24] Brodie strikes a hard blow here, for if Smith isn't certain of his own revelations, or if he made them up, he is not only a deceiver of others but also of himself and his own announced divine mission. She depicts Smith as striking blindly for a way out of his dilemma; he is embarrassed and discards his decision by sundown. A footnote says Marks's account may be colored somewhat by his profound antipathy to polygamy. So, how much can we believe of what is attributed by Brodie to Marks?

Brodie could make anything out of this she wanted. She could have written about Moses being embarrassed and blindly striking out to find a way out of his dilemma after telling the children of Israel he had a vision that they should refrain from worshipping idols. So, if Brodie doesn't believe Moses was following God's will, she could have Moses change his mind by sundown. Her conclusion doesn't change what really happened.

Brodie commits a monumental miscarriage of historical justice when she quotes extensively from the bitter apostate Ezra Booth. Booth was quite possibly one of those Fisher had in mind when complaining that Brodie quoted from unreliable sources. Booth passed himself off as an authority on Mormon doings from a several-week visit with Mormon leaders in Missouri. It is asserted in a series of letters Booth wrote after this visit, which appeared in the Ravenna, Ohio, *Star*, that Bishop Edward Partridge rebuked Joseph for unwisely choosing Jackson County, Missouri, as Zion. Brodie quotes Booth as saying Partridge complained it was a "poor" land. Then, after being corrected by the Prophet, the bishop says, "I wish you to not tell us any more that you know these things by the Spirit when you do not."[25]

Let us analyze this statement by Booth about Partridge more fully. Brodie is quoting Booth's twenty pages of unnumbered, single-spaced epistle (in present form) written to Ira Eddy, former Methodist minister. Booth had left Eddy's congregation after being converted to Mormonism when witnessing Joseph Smith perform a healing on behalf of an elderly Mrs. Johnson.

The conversion obviously didn't hold up. Booth addresses a letter to Partridge thusly: "Have you not often proven to your satisfaction that he [Joseph Smith] says he knows things by the spirit when they are not so? You know you have." It appears that Booth is not quoting Edward but putting words in his mouth. They are the precise words Brodie wants to hear, and she doesn't hesitate to use them as an indictment against Joseph's prophethood, never mentioning the praise Partridge gives to both Joseph and Zion the remainder of his life. (No indication exists that Edward ever received this letter, if indeed it was ever sent.)

Brodie also quotes Booth as saying Edward's faith was shaken and that he was insolent toward the Prophet. He would surely be removed from his office as bishop "and the office bestowed on a more trusty . . . person like Joseph's father." But when Joseph wrote his history in 1838, he said of Partridge that he was "a pattern of piety, one of the Lord's great men."[26] Even Brodie refers to Partridge as sweet-tempered. There was simply never any known animosity between Smith and Partridge other than Booth's allegations.

Brodie was not present when Smith, Partridge, and Booth conferred. So she must rely on someone who was. Since there is no mention of it in Edward's or Joseph's writings, she has only Booth to say what she wants Edward to say. If she had researched Partridge in any depth, she would have known that would be virtually impossible for Edward to make any such statement. In the first place, Partridge was a hatter and businessman who knew next to nothing about soil or a poor land. Second, he never had any doubts about Zion or Joseph Smith, as can be readily seen in his many writings, letters, songs, and poems about these two subjects until his death in 1840. Partridge was totally dutiful to the Prophet and every other LDS ecclesiastical authority. Even in 1838 when things looked darkest as the Saints worked to establish a Zion in Missouri, Partridge did not murmur against Joseph or the concept of Zion. He wrote a letter to Joseph in November 1833, after the expulsion from Jackson County, expressing a hope that God would somehow allow the Saints to return to Zion. He later wrote a prayer in Far West, Missouri, that God might redeem the Saints' Zion in Missouri. He never gave up hope for that idea to his dying day in Nauvoo.[27]

My years of research in writing a biography of Edward Partridge, including an in-depth analysis of his letters and journals, plus interviewing many family members regarding all that Partridge wrote, dictate that it was just not in Edward's nature to criticize or question Joseph's authority as prophet. Edward believed in and followed his instructions implicitly. The only remotely critical thing the bishop ever said about Zion was in a letter to his wife, Lydia, in which he conjectured they would "suffer many privations [we] have not been used to," on the Missouri frontier.

Brodie's statement, if true, is not one that can be taken lightly, for she is declaring that one of Smith's most trusted followers, the first bishop of his church, tells Joseph to his face that he is not an inspired prophet. She could not find a more powerful statement in which to lay Joseph Smith open in this early period of Church history. But it would seem, with her exhaustive research, that she knows she is misleading readers. Or she is doing so out of ignorance.

Booth's allegations haven't been taken too seriously since the nineteenth century, says B. H. Roberts, but they created a great hindrance to missionary work in the early 1830s.[28] Booth comes across as rather well educated and sincerely disillusioned after walking to the promised land of Missouri, something he said he wasn't accustomed to doing. Apparently, he expected more miracles like the one performed on Mrs. Johnson. Instead, he saw no church built up as Cowdery had promised, few friendly residents, no guidance by the Spirit as expected, and a prophet who "joked and laughed too much," failed in faith healings (historian John Whitmer did not agree; see chapter 10), and suffered "diabolical depravity." In addition, he heard empty prophecies about Zion being a land worthy of the Saints' settlement. Finally, Booth proves his diatribe totally ridiculous by stating that Joseph's Book of Mormon made the Bible obsolete. Booth does not provide any details on the above points, other than to complain.

Joseph Smith says this of Booth: "When he actually learned that faith, humility, patience and tribulation go before blessing . . . as was the case in the days of Jesus—he was disappointed. He has left a monument to his own shame."[29]

Booth also aims a broadside at Sidney Rigdon, stating that Rigdon tells Smith his revelation on Zion is a bad thing. Brodie picks up Booth's statement in saying that Rigdon never had a spirit of vision and couldn't wait to return to Kirtland. What Brodie means by this is not clear. Nothing can be found that would support Rigdon's statement against Zion in Missouri. Brodie seems to be the only one who makes that claim.

This is a stark contradiction of John Whitmer's history of the early Church that quotes Rigdon as saying this about Zion: "This land, with an exceeding fertile soil, bespeaks the goodness of our God in providing so goodly a heritage . . . and truly it is a good land . . . suited for all the saints . . . [those] who have faith and confidence in God, who have ever seen this land, will bear the same testimony. Brethren, pray for me that I may be counted worthy to obtain an inheritance in the land of Zion."

Rigdon refers to the bounties of God in the new Zion. It is a "goodly . . . climate . . . for if it were unhealthy, He could make it healthy and if barren, He could make it fruitful."[30] There is nothing, as Booth charges, to indicate antipathy to the promised land being in Missouri.

Needless to say, Brodie doesn't include Whitmer's remarks. She doesn't even include them as balance to what she quotes Booth as saying. It would be acceptable to say that Rigdon's assessment was a peaches-and-cream assumption that proved exaggerated. Instead, she insists Sidney did not agree with Joseph that Zion might be found in Missouri. Rigdon here says otherwise in most emphatic terms. After a while, we wonder how Brodie can be taken seriously as an objective historian.

But back to Booth. After he was in the Church for a few weeks, Booth says the missionaries squandered Church money, were reduced to beggars, and failed to preach as they were commanded by Smith, although adding that adverse circumstances didn't allow it. Just what the adverse circumstances were is not mentioned. Booth calls Smith weak-minded and lacking courage.

"Neither need they fear that the Mormonites will obtain the possession of their lands by shedding of blood until the Spirit selects more courageous leaders than Smith or Rigdon." Further, "They must vote [as Smith directs] or they will be cast off for rebelling against the commandments of the Lord. Or that the

Church shall build him an elegant house and give him $1,000."[31] Booth then alleges several times that if Smith would have a husband killed to get the man's wife, members would comply. He gives no example or details. It has to be obvious to any mind that Booth's allegations are more than exaggerations. Most, if not all, appear upon the evidence to be fabrications.

But before she is through with Booth, Brodie uses him to give the impression that the Church conference of 1831 in Missouri was a complete fiasco. Booth says attempted faith healings didn't work, and a child died because the elders didn't call in a doctor; word spread that healings couldn't work in Ohio because "it isn't consecrated ground" like Missouri; the Missourians "had never quite forgiven their prophet for returning to undedicated and unconsecrated" Kirtland; and all of the members in Missouri were "in rebellion" against Joseph.[32]

To quell the awful rebellion, however, was rather simple. Joseph shows up. Brodie says that Smith "on his arrival, quickly relieved the major tensions." How so? He held an election "and was unanimously elected president of the Church by open ballot."[33] Apparently, it wasn't much of a rebellion.

You would hardly know that John Whitmer recorded the same event as Booth. Whitmer says: "During this conference, many stated their desire to consecrate all they possessed to the Lord. Many apostatized, but many have returned again to the fold from whence they strayed . . . many mighty miracles were wrought by the elders . . . and thus the churches again prospered and the work of the Lord spread." Then, "Twelve of us assembled ourselves together . . . and Ezra Booth who denied the faith."[34]

Quoting Booth as the final authority on Partridge, Rigdon, Smith, and their church wrests from Brodie the last vestige of hope that she will honor the tradition of trustworthy historicity. We should not be so concerned about a vengeful Booth misleading us as Brodie, for she purports in her preface to carry no bias against Joseph Smith. Booth does not make such a promise.

Brodie now has, if not earlier, a full-scale novel on her hands. Her biography has turned from a veto of Joseph Smith to a personal vendetta. If historians such as Nibley find her methods outrageous, it is understandable.

But Brodie can't decide in what manner to vilify Mormondom's prophet. All the while contending Joseph was a clever fellow capable of conjuring up visions and the Book of Mormon, she remembers she wants to put him down; so she quotes neighbors who said that he was really too "feeble of intellect" to ever amount to anything on his own.[35] Pretty much what the Mormon Church has been saying all along—Smith couldn't do it by himself.

Another problem arises for those seeking to evoke pity for the "deluded" followers of Smith or his religious program. Parley P. Pratt, in the midst of the Missouri afflictions, says: "Great blessings had been poured out upon the saints. Many great and marvelous things were manifested. . . . There was much sweet communion concerning the things of God." Pratt adds, "I received many admonitions and instructions which I shall not forget. We had not a single dollar but lacked for nothing."[36]

Edward Partridge also wrote in his journal during the barbaric abuse and persecutions of 1833 in Missouri: "Since . . . I have been willing to love and serve God with all my heart, and be led by the Holy Spirit, my mind has been as it were continually expanding—receiving the things of God until glories indescribable present themselves before my mind. Why is it that . . . rational men will suffer themselves to be led in darkness while such glories lamp up the pathway of the saints?"[37]

Thrust into a Missouri prison, Hyrum wrote, "However, I felt a determination to die rather than deny the things which my eyes have seen [he was one of the Eight Witnesses], which my hands had handled and which I had borne testimony to."[38]

Maybe some things are going on that Brodie and her anti-Mormon detractors know nothing about. The fence-sitting reader should examine these statements carefully. If these souls were misled, it must have been a glorious delusion. They are not talking about a brief moment of euphoria quickly dissipated but about a source of lasting enrichment and insight providing strength to meet life's challenges under the most adverse circumstances.

It appears most forcefully that they felt a peace of mind that comes from knowing they were in harmony with a power greater than themselves. Brodie mentions a few of these testimonies, but she utterly fails to comprehend their significance. Referring to Oliver Cowdery's rejoicing of an inspirational experience, she passes it off with, "No one can walk in the woods in May without an exultation of spirit."[39] But Cowdery is speaking of much more than "an exultation of spirit." A careful analysis of his statement indicates that he is speaking of something too precious to him to be simply palmed off as a stroll in the flowery woods of May. It was an experience that totally changed his life.

There are those, of course, who think any mention of anything that can't be explained in humanistic terms is unscientific or unreal. We must believe only that which can be demonstrated with consistency in the laboratory. Yet many scientists have a faith in God based on what can be demonstrated in the laboratory of life. One is Dr. Henry Eyring, a Latter-day Saint who advocates only one thing: an honest seeking after knowledge. He says this has led him to a firm belief in Jesus Christ.[40]

It is unfortunate that some anti-Mormon writers, such as Bernard DeVoto, take the attitude that belief in something not fully explainable or greater and more important than Homo sapiens is lacking in intellectual insight. At the core of this attitude is the concept of visions. Can a thing be declared invalid because it is not fully understood?

But even if one cannot believe in divine guidance outright, it is no reason to preclude an honest search for possible truth in a spiritual realm. By that is meant visions. Perhaps visions are, indeed, not fully explainable to human understanding. But it would seem that Brodie, and many of Joseph Smith's detractors, strain to explain the unexplainable by saying it did not happen because they don't understand it.

Nor does failure to explain something in human terms mean it couldn't have happened. I once asked an optometrist if he really understood how eyesight works. He said, "To be honest with you, and I've been in this business for forty years, I can say the iris or the pupil does this or that. But I can't really explain it. Maybe in another life."

The most refreshing statement by Brodie comes when she says this: "For some reason . . ." But such moments of wonder, not knowing the answers, are rather rare.

7
Brodie's Bainbridge Bungle

Fawn Brodie declares she hit a gold mine when describing the trial of Joseph Smith at South Bainbridge, New York, given as 20 March 1826. She says Smith is charged before a justice of the peace with being a disorderly person and an impostor. There were other allegations that he was a vagrant, a shiftless lad who preyed on the wealth of Josiah Stoal by deception. Brodie says that at Palmyra, Joseph admitted he pretended to tell, by looking at a stone, where coined money was buried, and that he could see two Indians fighting over a trunk, one killing the other, but the trunk kept settling away from under them while digging.[1] Several people testify that Joseph did such pretending for personal gain, but his crude attempts at magic fooled no one. His pretensions were obvious and disgusting.

Brodie then says that Josiah Stoal, under oath, tells the court that his friend and employee, Joseph Smith, pretended to have such skill. Being found guilty of all charges disgraced the money digger from Palmyra. It looks bad, indeed, for Joseph's character and honesty.

Brodie repeats the claims made by Philastus Hurlbut and E. D. Howe that Smith is a vile and wretched person, a crook and a fraud, as exposed in *Mormonism Unvailed* [sic]. Then Brodie adds, "This behavior is confirmed by the most coldly objective description of young Joseph that remains which historians have hitherto overlooked or ignored."[2] Enter the Bainbridge trial as proof.

Justice has finally caught up with Joe Smith for being a treasure hunter, a ne'er-do-well trying to defraud the family of Josiah Stoal out of its money. With Smith's reputation for lying, Brodie avers, how can Joseph's story of the Book of Mormon possibly deserve further credibility?

The trial of 1826 was the crown jewel in Brodie's case against Joseph Smith. But Joseph was acquitted in that trial, and information on it is sketchy; there is no trial transcript. What we have is tainted because a Presbyterian minister illegally pirated away what record there was, and by the time he returned it to Chenango County under sheriff's order, there is no way of knowing what he might have altered.

But to start from the beginning, here is Brodie's charge:

> The earliest and most important account of Joseph Smith's money-digging is the following court record, first unearthed in southern New York by Daniel S. Tuttle, Episcopal Bishop of Salt Lake City and published in his article on "Mormonism" in the *New Schaff-Herzog Encyclopedia of Religious Knowledge* published in 1883. The trial was held before a justice of the peace in Bainbridge, Chenango County, New York, March 20, 1826.[3]

Claims that Joseph was a fraud at this time were fueled by a magazine article that fanned considerable prejudice against Smith and the Church by saying, "There is in the Mormon system itself an almost lack of any moral standard. The gospel they preach is a gospel of hate. . . . The true spirit of loyalty to the flag has no place in their concept of utterances."[4]

Further prejudice against the Mormons can be seen in an article appearing in the *Chenango Telegraph* in 1845: "The Mormons are in a deplorable state. This abject body of deluded creatures . . . are starving. Subscriptions [are] passing through the city [Nauvoo] for the relief of the poor and every day baskets are carried round to collect provisions for the starving."[5]

As even anti-Mormon historians know from the date, the

Mormons were being besieged at gunpoint in Nauvoo in early 1845. There were no relief baskets being passed around for these creatures by non-Mormons. The entire point of the forced exodus was to exile an unpopular sect from Nauvoo, the sooner the better. With such information floating about, as historian Francis Kirkham puts it, anything might be said or written, and believed, at the time about this unpopular sect.

If printed, it must be true, seems the kind of bias rampant in western New York in the mid-1800s. Such falsehoods spawned many spurious articles about the Church, as will be seen.[6]

Hugh Nibley says that Tuttle, an Episcopalian minister, printed the articles in the *Encyclopedia of Religious Knowledge* in 1889 and 1891, which included claims that Smith was found guilty in the 1826 trial. But in subsequent editions, says Nibley, those articles do not appear.[7] The encyclopedia had, indeed, picked up the erroneous data from Daniel Tuttle in 1891 and then apparently, after further research, expunged it. Tuttle's lament against the Mormon Church vanished after 1891.

Where did Bishop Tuttle get his information? He says from a torn page from a book that was given to him from a Miss Pearsall, who had been in New York and removed it from a court record fifty years earlier. Red flags should have started popping up for Brodie, but she goes blithely on. It is enough for her that Tuttle says the woman who brought the torn page from an old court record is a reliable friend who found the record in New York at the house of her father, who was the judge at Joseph's trial.

How accurate that page, or record, might be is up for speculation. Shortly after Brodie's book appeared, Francis W. Kirkham visited Irving D. Tillman, county clerk of Chenango County, and could find no record as claimed by Tuttle.

However, in 1971 Presbyterian minister Wesley P. Walters did discover a partial record (some was illegible) of an 1826 trial involving Joseph Smith. This record was found in the basement of the Chenango County Jail in Norwich, New York.[8] Walters's assessment was that, while there was no precise record of Joseph being found guilty of the charges of being a disorderly person and a vagrant, he must have been. He was likely allowed to go free, conjectures Walters, because Joseph was then a minor, less than twenty-one years old.[9]

Walters's recounting of this trial was analyzed by Gordon A. Madsen, an attorney at law in Salt Lake City, in a paper titled "Joseph Smith's 1826 Trial, the Legal Setting."[10] In this analysis, it is Madsen's opinion, based on his experience as an attorney, that Joseph was acquitted because there was a lack of evidence that anyone had been financially harmed.

The trial had been brought about on the complaint of Peter Bridgeman, acting for the sons of Josiah Stoal, who it will be remembered, had hired Joseph to dig for treasure.[11] Stoal's sons testified that Joseph was taking money from their father, or treasure hunting, under false pretenses. But Stoal, who was the owner of that money, testified that Joseph was only doing what he, Stoal, had hired him to do.

Smith does not mention the 1826 trial in his official Church history. Nor, strangely enough, was it mentioned by any of the many anti-Mormon factions of the time, including E. D. Howe, author of *Mormonism Unvailed*; Pomeroy Tucker; or Esquire Cole, author of the *Dogberry Papers*—all contemporaries of Smith who railed against him. More research is needed on why anti-Mormon writers such as Howe, Tucker, and Cole do not mention the 1826 trial. It would seem to be a splendid opportunity to further list grievances against Palmyra's prophet.

Two trials in 1830 were covered by Joseph in detail but mentioned only briefly by anti-Mormon writers such as Brodie, perhaps because Smith was acquitted for a second and third time. Why the trial in 1826 was not recorded by Joseph is not known, other than it might have been so much like the two 1830 trials that Joseph did not feel it was necessary. This has, however, caused some consternation among historians, for it was thought until 1971 that there were no charges brought against Smith in 1826. Francis Kirkham and Hugh Nibley wrote extensively about whether there actually was a trial in 1826 charging Joseph with anything.[12]

Madsen's conclusions were (1) that while Smith was identified in the court docket as a glass looker, that was an appellation of identification, not a charge. Stories had been circulated about Joseph using a seer stone. But there was no mention of glass looker as a chargeable offense. (2) The word "impostor" was also used but did not describe any criminal offense on the misdemeanor charge. This left the only two charges as disorderly person and vagrant, or an individuals with no visible means of financial support. (3) Walters erroneously links Smith with a verdict of guilty as charged. Madsen says if Smith had been found guilty, a record of conviction would have been filed with the county clerk within forty days. No such record has to date been found in the office of the clerk of Chenango County.

Walters had based some of his conclusions about the 1826 trial on papers written by A. W. Benton and William Purple. Little is known about A. W. Benton, who wrote his article about the 1826 trial five years later. Purple, who did not write anything about the trial until forty-one years later, claimed that he was asked by Judge Albert Neely to take notes at the trial. In 1877 Purple wrote an article for the *Chenango Union* saying Smith was not only guilty but was also a charlatan and fraud.[13] Madsen says Purple provides no testimony from the trial but alludes to Smith as "bilking" Stoal out of his money.

Purple's allegations also include the following: Joseph took his peep stone far away to Lake Erie to find treasure but found none. Smith was "the hallucination of deseased [*sic*] minds, that drew all their philosophy from the Arabian nights."[14] This story totally contradicted Brodie's picture of Joseph, however, a man alert and intelligent enough to write the Book of Mormon with sources strictly from the United States frontier, not from any Arabian nights.

Brodie quoted extensively from Tuttle's account as if it were evidence per se of Joseph deceiving and defrauding Mr. Stoal.[15] The biggest problem with Brodie's account of the 1826 trial is that she uses it as a showcase to include all the stories of magic and necromancy about Smith. The stories are vividly told (digging for treasure and finding only a feather; a toad watched over the golden plates) by people under oath in a court of law. Yet Joseph was acquitted. How true were these stories in the first place?

Madsen concludes:

> There was no testimony that any of them [witnesses] parted with any money or other thing of value to Joseph Smith. Only Josiah Stoal did so and . . . he emphatically denied that he had been deceived or defrauded. . . . In short, only Josiah Stoal had any legal basis to complain, and he was not complaining. Even Purple surmised that, "As the testimony of Deacon Stowell could not be impeached, the prisoner was allowed to leave town."[16]

Madsen leaves Walters derelict of any grounds that Smith was found guilty and then allowed to go free because he was a minor.

Yet even the foregoing information given on the 1826 court document is suspect because, as mentioned earlier, Walters stole the document and did not return the same until ordered by Chenango County Attorney James Haynes on 16 September 1971. At first, Walters sent only a copy of the document. Then when told that the original must be returned by order of the sheriff's office, Walters finally did so. According to a letter from the County of Chenago Office of History, Sheriff Joseph Benenati was angry enough with Walters that he told him to "leave his office and not return."[17]

Walters tried to smooth over his theft of the court document by saying he was only going to improve the legibility of the papers (they had been stored in a wet place) and planned all along to return it. But in so doing, the integrity of both the document and Mr. Walters's reputation had been compromised. Walters insisted he made no alterations in the 1826 papers, but he had already committed one dishonest act. No one could ever know if a second one followed.

Imagine the hue and cry that would follow if anyone connected to the Mormon Church had illegally taken the document.

The perpetrator would be accused of trying to doctor the pages to make the record look better for The Church of Jesus Christ of Latter-day Saints.

Curiously, Brodie published her second edition of *No Man Knows My History* in 1971 but makes no mention of Walters's findings. She died in January 1981, allowing still more time for an addendum or third edition of her book on Joseph Smith to include Walters's find, had she so willed. (Walters had widely distributed his comments on the 1826 trial of Joseph Smith by 1974.)

Before leaving Brodie's dramatic invective in the 1826 trial wherein a "coldly objective" court found Smith guilty, a question arises: Even if found guilt, what is there so coldly objective" about a charge of disturbing the peace? It can happen to anyone who is "different." Jesus Christ could have been found guilty of disturbing the peace many times, as could Mahatma Gandhi or Henry Thoreau. All Joseph needed to face such a charge in Bainbridge, New York, or anywhere, anytime, was an enemy. Smith never denied having those. Brodie's claims are hollow in that anyone can be charged, but are they guilty? It seems a strange way to win awards for detached objectivity.

Let us also look at how Brodie builds her case based on a false premise. After saying Joseph "deceived" Josiah Stoal and that he only "pretended" to have the skill to find treasure, she then tosses out a straw man for "positive" history by saying Stoal defended Joseph "with great vigor." But it did the prisoner "more harm than good," for some of Stoal's relatives were convinced Joseph was draining off the family's money reserve. Brodie says Stoal testified that Joseph "told him to dig at the roots of an old stump, promising that he (Stoal) would find a chest of money and a tail-feather. At a depth of five feet he had uncovered the tail-feather only to discover that the money had 'moved down.'"[18] Even with the townspeople prejudiced (many had by then attempted to disrupt baptisms conducted by Joseph), no convicting evidence against Smith was ever presented.

Brodie quotes from the Rev. Tuttle's account regarding a torn page from court records brought forth by Pearsall, with much lurid testimony, including the feather story quoted above, but Madsen finds no mention of those accusations in the official record.

Brodie says the 1826 court pronounced Joseph guilty, although what sentence was finally passed "the record does not say." Does this not strike Brodie as odd? Could it be there was no sentence to be found because there was no conviction?

Of all the charges of being a vagrant and having no visible means of support, Nibley points out that if Smith was gainfully employed by Josiah Stoal in money digging for him, then he wasn't a vagrant as charged.[19] Stoal's sons could complain that their father was spending their inheritance foolishly, but whose business was that but Mr. Stoal's? In other words, the entire charge of vagrancy was a trumped-up allegation with no foundation whatsoever. An objective bystander must wonder what all the fuss is about.

But Brodie is insistent: "It would seem this trial . . . shocked Joseph into a sense of the futility of his avocation, for he now gave up his money digging altogether, although he retained his peep stone and some of the psychological artifices of the rural diviner. It may be that this renunciation came in part from disillusionment with his own magic."[20]

Let us now examine the 1830 trials involving Joseph, which Brodie wants to gloss over. As recorded in *History of the Church*, a neighbor of the Smiths lodges a complaint that Joseph is a disorderly person.[21] Questions are put to Josiah Stoal that are meant to prove Smith dishonest. However, the prosecution chose the wrong witness. Stoal testified that he was not told by Joseph that an angel told him (Stoal) that he was to give his horse to Joseph. Stoal says he was given a note for the horse, and "I know him [Joseph] to be an honest man; and if he [Joseph] wishes, I am willing to give him another horse on the same terms."

Unable to get anywhere with Stoal, the court put his two daughters on the witness stand. The results were the same. "But," says Joseph, "a warrant was served upon me at the very moment that I was acquitted by this [Bainbridge] court."[22]

Without being allowed any food during the entire day, Smith was taken to neighboring Broome County. Here, Joseph says, onlookers spit upon him and chanted for him to "Prophesy! Prophesy!" He was held all night in an armlock by a constable who, the next day when Joseph was acquitted a second time, apologized for the inconvenience. People were called to testify, "but all they could do was tell something that somebody else had told them."

The folly of the second trial came when Newell Knight was asked if Joseph had cast the devil out of him, and Knight frustrated the court by testifying that it was not Joseph but Christ who did so. There being no substance to any of the charges, said Joseph, he was allowed to go free.[23]

From Oliver Cowdery and Joseph Smith, we also have record of the trial in Bainbridge in 1830, in which Joseph was acquitted. The anti-Mormon writers have little to say about it, and as previously mentioned, Brodie gives it little mention. What has been recorded destroys Brodie's contention that Joseph was found guilty in court of anything, anywhere. She includes a few quick paragraphs about the 1830 acquittal in Bainbridge (now known as Afton) and the court acquittal in adjoining Broome County.[24]

It should be noted that with all the affidavits gathered by Hurlbut about a dishonest Smith family, there were no other court trials against Joseph. We would think that if anyone had any proof of any kind about any of the Smiths being a thief or a fraud, someone would have taken them to court more often. Perhaps the dismissals in 1826 and 1830 discouraged any more trials.

Years later, one of Joseph's defense attorneys, John Reid, a non-Mormon, totally corroborated Smith's account. Reid said in a lengthy statement that the prosecution searched for people in grog shops to testify against Smith, but nothing whatsoever could be proven against him. Reid gives the words of the court's verdict:

"Mr. Smith . . . we have examined the testimony and find nothing to condemn you, and therefore you are discharged."

However, to please the assembly, the court "reprimanded Smith severely" before releasing him.[25]

Reid added this, which Brodie didn't bother to include: "Joseph's character was irreproachable. . . . He was well known for truth and uprightness . . . intelligence and good morals. . . . I early discovered that his mind was constantly in search of truth, expressing an anxious desire to know the will of God."[26] Reid's lengthy eyewitness account of the trial at Bainbridge, New York, has, so far as is known, never been refuted. Brodie doesn't try.

Kirkham gives us further enlightenment about the steps some of Joseph's peers would go to in order to link Smith to fraud in the Book of Mormon. Two of them insist the book is a plagiarism of the Solomon Spaulding manuscript. A John Miller says, "I have recently examined the Book of Mormon and find in it the writings of Solomon Spaulding from beginning to end."[27]

Says one Oliver Smith: "On reading [the Spaulding manuscript], I found much of it the same as Spaulding had written, more than twenty years before."

But the idea that the Book of Mormon sprang from the writings of Solomon Spaulding is a non sequitur. Non-LDS scholars of Ohio's Oberlin College, where the manuscript ended up in 1881, declared soberly after examination that there was no similarity. The world "will have to look elsewhere for the source of the Book of Mormon"[28] stated the president of Oberlin College.

How, then, can one avoid the obvious errors of John Miller and Oliver Smith? How do we know who is telling the truth, either at the time or as a historian perhaps a century and a half later? Secondary and tertiary statements can't be taken at face value without further research and corroboration. Statements may be no more than careless gossip. Are the announced sources actual eyewitnesses? Is there an obvious ax to grind? A hidden one?

One might say that Joseph Smith had a crusade to promote. Yet in comparing Smith's detractors to the statement by say, John Reid, one finds a common denominator. Finding fault is easier and occurs far more often than rendering tribute. The former uses adjectives such as "wretched" and "vile," while the latter omits loose adjectives. A person can find honest fault, of course, but it would be more descriptive to say a person has been known to lie, citing place and time. The charges must be specific and relevant.

No sure guarantees exist, but one thing for is certain: we can select whatever testimony we desire, and, with Joseph Smith, it more than likely will be polarized. Read a few pages of Ezra Booth's letter and a few pages of Parley P. Pratt, who says, "Thus mightily grew the word of God . . . sown by that extraordinary personage, the Prophet [Joseph Smith] and Seer of the 19th Century."[29]

Are Booth and Pratt talking about the same church, the same man? In all his 471 pages, Pratt never wrote of Joseph Smith as anything other than devoutly sincere and divinely inspired. Amazingly, Booth and Pratt are also speaking of the same troubled times in Missouri.

The point here is not whether Booth or Pratt is right. They could both be right within their own sphere of expectations. Pratt found rich reward; Booth did not. It seems to depend on what we are looking for and how we go about obtaining it.

Thus, it would appear, as mentioned previously, that the only scholarly history must be one that presents evidence of (1) Joseph being an impostor and (2) Joseph being what he says he is—a prophet. Brodie's trouble is that she must, at all odds, prove only one side—the exposé.

Two interpretations are often given of the same set of facts. Brodie's brother, Thomas, reached different conclusions than did his sister, though both examined the same data. Vardis Fisher and his younger sister, Irene (Diane in Fisher's autobiographical tetralogy beginning with *In Tragic Life*) lived in the same home, with the same parents, facing the same demanding frontier challenges. For Vardis, these challenges drove him to despair—and away from organized religion. Irene, however, emerged as a temple-attending Mormon. She was also, said Vardis, free of his fears and anguish.

When asked about his own lack of religious faith, Fisher

answered that Irene had enough religion for the entire clan. In *Tiger on the Road*, Fisher biographer Tim Woodward labels Irene a "devout Mormon," a striking anomaly to Vardis despite identical upbringing.[30] It is obvious that many decipher religious truth with their own litmus test—a sound reason that it is folly to tell only one side of a story.

But to be entirely fair with Brodie on the Bainbridge issue, she may not have surmised she was using spurious sources. Yet as a sleuth for truth, she must do as the great London detective Sherlock Holmes did. She must look at evidence objectively. She must also examine motivation. What causes people to do what they do?

What would Reid, Stoal, and Knight gain from attesting to the sterling character of Joseph Smith, especially if requiring courage to buck the tide? Why did people such as Brigham Young, Wilford Woodruff, and Lyman Wight make great sacrifices for what Joseph Smith taught? Why is it the Whitmers, Cowderys, and Harrises never deviated from their story that Joseph is a good and righteous man? Brodie treats them as wooden figures with no purpose or logic to their actions of devotion and loyalty to Smith's announced teachings. But they must have felt some kind of motivation.

Detractors? It is easier to go along with the masses. Give the average man in a local pub a beer to agree with the crowd, and why shouldn't he say what you want him to? How committed is he to tell the truth? We have Hurlbut: was he driven by vengeance? Howe: bias? Tuttle: jealousy? Some media editors: laziness or ignorance? Or knowing that sensationalism sells newspapers.

Those who write history are expected to ferret out truth. Or if that is impossible, at least to present both sides. There is Vardis's side, and this is Irene's side. It is a great tragedy that Irene's side was never fully told by Vardis. We might have learned much about why she differed so much in religious philosophy from her brother.

Likewise, Brodie found a driving agenda to disprove, while her brother Thomas believed. Therein is a clue that giving only one side of a story is not only unscholarly but also, in this case, fatal.

8
Polygamy and Promiscuity

Brodie aims some of her sharpest darts at Joseph Smith's character when she accuses him of introducing not only polygamy into "his" church but promiscuity as well. In her chapter "If a Man Entice a Maid," she implies that Joseph Smith did not cease to love Emma but tired of his intolerably "circumscribed" life with but one wife. "Nothing was so sacred that it could not be recast."[1] Thus, she has Joseph saying to a friend, "Whenever I see a pretty woman, I have to pray for grace."[2]

A footnote says, "As reported to W. Wyl by J. W. C., 'Mormon Portraits,' page 55." Sounds like solid evidence. But we must know more about the circumstances and, above all, the source, Mr. Wyl. Hugh Nibley, whose curiosity often leads to identifying such mysterious people, traces Wyl (or Wyle) to a Wilhelm Wyl from Germany, who is unknown to the world other than as a man who in 1886 passed on a "thin volume of unauthenticated and lurid stories" published in the *Salt Lake Tribune*—at that time a highly critical anti-Mormon newspaper.[3] Where did Wyl obtain the remark? He said he got it from "someone who told him that someone had said that Joseph Smith had made that remark to an unnamed friend."[4] Brodie doesn't tell us this with her "painstaking" research.

She sets out, clear and simple, to prove Smith a womanizer. But all too often, she leads the gullible reader down a primrose path of historical poverty.

It doesn't mean that Joseph is entirely out of the woods of sensual suspicion. Brodie has many aspersions to cast, and a few (if you toss enough muck, some will stick) have sufficient surface sizzle that they must be sorted through, chaff from wheat.

David Whitmer to his dying day testified that he knew Joseph Smith to be a prophet of God in translating and bringing forth the Book of Mormon, but he said Joseph lost his humility and grew worldly during the Nauvoo period, becoming like King David of the Old Testament, a prophet falling into trespass.[5] Did Joseph, during the latter part of his ecclesiastical career, take on habits of promiscuity as did David and Solomon?

Brodie does not take Whitmer's stance, of course, because she never did believe Joseph to be a prophet in the first place. But she does reach a zenith of assault posture just prior to and during the Nauvoo period Whitmer is talking about. She introduces the plural marriage factor, stating that Joseph spoke of it as early as 1831—a fact known to LDS leaders today—but didn't publicly announce it until 1835.[6] Apparently, Joseph didn't feel the world was ready for it, and certainly not the bitterly anti-Mormon mobs of Missouri in the 1830s. Yes, Brodie was right; he did not want it to get out that plural marriage was being practiced in Nauvoo, ostensibly because persecution was hindering him from completing his many duties.

Brodie asserts that Joseph had hushed affairs with many women, not only those acknowledged by LDS Church officials as plural wives but also those he didn't bother to marry. Brodie also asserts that he romanced women married to other men, not just for a hereafter but also in this life.

The sanitized Saint may want to forego this chapter, for indeed, the accusations are not always pretty; but they must be addressed, for sooner or later someone somewhere will take them as proof the Mormon prophet was a licentious hypocrite in preaching chastity and doing otherwise. Let us see exactly where the truth is found.

Brodie starts off with Fanny Alger, a young woman Emma took into her home. The charitable Emma took in many new converts to her home and most anyone who had a need, if any room remained.

But much of Brodie's research relies on one John C. Bennett—a man so devoted to getting even with Joseph after being first welcomed but then excommunicated for fraud and adultery that even the anti-Mormon media learned to avoid printing anything he had to say. As Brodie confesses, the following newspapers refused to consider Bennett credible or publish anything with his name linked to it: *New York Herald*, *Illinois State Register*, and *Sangamo Journal*. (The *Journal* called Bennett's own *History of the Saints* "obscene and licentious in the highest degree.") The *Quincy Whig* said, "We can hardly put reliance on the statements of Bennett."[7] There were probably others she didn't list after Bennett became legend for his sensuous accusations throughout Illinois and environs. But the fact that others won't take Bennett's word for anything doesn't stop Brodie.

Historian N. B. Lundwall sheds this light on Bennett: On 17 May 1842, John C. Bennett made an affidavit before Daniel H. Wells "that he never was taught anything in the least contrary to the strictest principles of the gospel, or of virtue, or of the laws of God or man . . . by Joseph Smith. . . . He cried like a child [when Church leaders threatened to expose him for the pervert he was] and didn't want his mother to know."[8] Lundwall says that Bennett had secretly deserted a wife and family in the East.

Lundwall writes that Bennett promised to repent, but as soon as he was excommunicated, he began to slander both Joseph and the Church. Simply put, Bennett was an unstable and angry man who could be, and was, dangerous to anyone who opposed him. Lundwall says that Joseph patiently tried to persuade Bennett to repent but finally gave up.

While being careful to say Bennett was known to be passionately vengeful, Brodie nevertheless extracts lurid mileage. She sometimes states in footnotes that there were several differing LDS views. She cannot resist, however, in first including all that is colorful and titillating in any peccadillo related to Joseph Smith.

Where Brodie draws blood is when she points out that Oliver Cowdery accused Joseph of an affair with Fanny Alger, mutually considered by most historians to be Smith's first polygamous wife.[9] This is true. Not the Alger story necessarily, but that Cowdery made the accusation and was never known specifically to recant it.

LDS historians agree that Oliver, not knowing about the introduction of polygamy, connected Joseph, who was married to Emma at the time, to a "dirty, nasty, filthy affair" with the Alger girl. As one historian says, marriages were sometimes poorly documented in those days.[10] But while Brodie implies that Joseph never married Fanny, there is ample proof he did. First, however, let us examine Cowdery's charge.

For this allegation and other transgressions enumerated by one Seymour Brunson in Missouri, Church leaders excommunicated Oliver in April 1838.[11] Interestingly, it was not Joseph who initiated the proceedings against Oliver. It is also noteworthy that no one but Oliver ever raised this charge against Joseph. It was an impartial jury of Cowdery's peers that held him guilty of speaking "against the prophet's good name" and "falsely accusing him [Joseph] of adultery." Cowdery was the only one who ever disagreed with Brunson's charges. Thus, Cowdery was voted out.

The second elder had been estranged from Joseph for some time. Did Oliver seek to do something to bring down his leader?[12] Oliver confessed that he felt wicked and wanted to rebel against authority. Something else to be considered is that about the same time that Cowdery was excommunicated, someone impersonated Oliver both in person and in writing, claiming that he, Cowdery, doubted his previous testimonies.[13] That he didn't is borne out clearly when Oliver sought to clear his name with a lengthy letter affirming the divinity of the Book of Mormon and his role as a witness. He answered his critics by saying, "These were days never to be forgotten—to sit under the sound of a voice dictated by the inspiration of heaven. . . . Day after day I continued, uninterrupted, to write from his mouth, as he [Joseph Smith] translated."[14] This does not sound as if Cowdery considered Joseph a man who had never received divine communication.

As is well known, Cowdery had, just prior to his death, sought forgiveness of sins (1848) in order to rejoin the Church. Clearly, he was ready to go west and join the Saints in Utah but grew ill and died later that year. His sincerity can be seen in his traveling hundreds of miles from Ohio in inclement weather to Council Bluffs, Iowa, to rejoin the Church from which he was separated. Just to join old friends? It would seem more than that.

The reader can find much on Cowdery falsely accusing Joseph of adultery in Stephen LeSueur's *Mormon War in Missouri*.[15] There are many other sources among LDS histories. If the skeptics won't accept them, they are invited to study the entire setting: What was Oliver's mood at the time, and why was it no one else ever accused Joseph of an illicit affair with Fanny Alger, even enemies of the troublesome Missouri period, of whom there were many? Surely they would pounce on such a golden opportunity to assail Joseph if they could find a fact in their favor.

Church members say a dissident spirit took over Oliver's life after he was accused of renouncing the faith and selling his lands in Jackson County, contrary to Joseph's counsel. The result seemed to cloud Oliver's judgment, as witnessed by the rambling defense of "my rights to dispose of property and manage temporal affairs" as he saw fit.[16] It was Oliver in a new mind-set from the days of helping Joseph translate the Book of Mormon.

Cowdery did appear to have a practical point, however, in that there was no hope to redeem his property in Jackson County. Oliver's defense was economical, not ecclesiastical. But the Church was just not ready to give up yet on Zion—Jackson County. In the end, Oliver swallowed his pride and put his ego aside to seek readmittance to the faith earlier espoused. Yet why would Cowdery relinquish that stubborn pride and ego—not an easy thing to do—if he didn't believe in Joseph's teachings?

With or without Cowdery, Brodie wrote that Emma drove Fanny out of the house upon learning the pair were romantically involved. It must not have been quite as licentious as Brodie asserts, for Fanny's parents considered it an honor that Joseph was interested in their daughter. They moved with the Saints to Utah and remained active in the Church. Fanny herself divorced Joseph and left the Church to marry and raise a family elsewhere. Yet when asked, she never complained of her relationship with Joseph or complained that he failed to provide for her.[17]

The best research on Alger and Smith's other plural wives has clearly been done by Todd Compton in his comprehensive *In Sacred Loneliness*. After noting Brodie's pioneer attempts to fill a void left by LDS historians over the years, Compton nevertheless concludes that Brodie committed many errors of research. Among them are the following[18]:

• Appendix: the discerning reader will use it with great caution. Brodie made significant mistakes in her first survey and evaluation.

• Brodie frequently used sources biased against Mormonism that "were not firsthand and were both extreme and unreliable." One source used by Brodie, the *Abominations of Mormonism Exposed*, contained major factual errors. Joseph is accused of getting a beautiful woman pregnant while the husband served a mission in 1846–47. Joseph died in 1844.

• Brodie says that when Joseph was tarred and feathered in Kirtland, Marinda Johnson's brother Eli demanded that Joseph be castrated as well because he had been intimate with Eli's sister. In fact, Marinda had no brother named Eli, says Compton.

• An Ettie Smith quotes Presendia Buell, who says she had a child and didn't know if the father was her husband, Norman Buell, or Joseph Smith. An unnamed anti-Mormon writer says Ettie "so mixed up her fiction with what was true that she didn't know where one ended and the other began." Concludes Compton: "Brodie opens with a weak link."

• Brodie insists on an "unmistakable likeness" of Presendia's son, Oliver, to Joseph Smith. Brodie explains how a liaison could have taken place nine months before Oliver was born, but Brodie has the baby born in 1839, while Compton's evidence shows 1840. Meantime, Smith was incarcerated at the Liberty Jail. Compton notes that "this is not the strongest scholarship." Every link "is implausible, improbable, or impossible."

Compton says it is typical for Brodie to use unreliable anti-Mormon sources as a point upon which to build an implication and then follow it up with mistakes in assessment of historical events. He adds that Brodie interprets facts imprecisely in order to arrive at her desired perspective.

Speaking of Brodie's highly publicized, documented list of wives, Compton sends up this warning: "It is somewhat inflated." There are "some double listings." Brodie also lists a Mrs. Edward Blossom, who was married to an apostle as a plural wife, but Brodie admits there was never an apostle by that name. Says Compton: "But Brodie leaves her on the list to be padded by a source which even she admits is unreliable."

Compton also wonders why Joseph would have dangerous affairs when he could have marriages under the new polygamous structure. Of Fanny Alger, Compton says she "was married in approximately early 1833, at age sixteen, not an uncommon age for marriage in those days. At first she lived in Joseph's house as a maid, but was expelled from the house by Emma when Fanny became pregnant, according to one source." The source, however, is not given. No one knows what became of the child, but it was possibly raised under another name. Fanny married a non-Mormon from Dublin, Indiana, in 1836 and had nine children. Compton says she declined comment when asked about her experience with Joseph as a polygamous wife.

Expelled from the house sounds as if Joseph married Fanny without Emma's knowledge. But not necessarily.

Research by this writer into the unpublished diaries of Eliza and Emily Partridge (dated 4 March 1843) indicates that Emma initially approved of the sealings of the sisters to Joseph for time and eternity in the morning, but by evening she would not allow either Emily or her sister to remain in the house or spend the night with Joseph. The diaries reveal the following: "Emma not only approved the marriages but chose my sister and I. We were sealed in her presence with her full and free consent."[19] But before nightfall, according to Emily's diary, Emma would not allow Joseph to live with either wife long enough to consummate the marriage. "Emma said some hard things . . . or blood would flow."[20] There was to be no further mention of the Partridges's sacred marriage vows to the Prophet outside the Smith home. Neither Emily nor Eliza complained about being mistreated by Joseph, but it appears he did not take sides against Emma.

Brodie quotes *Historical Record* 1:240 in noting that Emily and Eliza were married secretly to Joseph two months before the above diary account, and when Emma gave her open consent, the sisters were then married in Emma's presence. In either case, the point is that Emma approved and then changed her mind.

The following is from my own research: "This was a terrible time for both Eliza and Emily, as they described it, for they considered their marriage vows sacred. 'The understanding was that all was ended between us.'"[21] The thing that stung the most, according to Emily, was that Emma allowed two other women, Sarah and Maria Laurence, to live in the Smith household as his wives, "but my sister and I were cast off."

This statement, of course, directly refutes those once made by leaders of the Reorganized Church of Jesus Christ of Latter Day Saints (now known as the Community of Christ), that Smith was not a polygamist. Emily provides indication of at least four plural marriages.

The tragedy deepened, according to Emily's diaries, when Joseph was martyred and she, with her sister, was not even allowed to mourn openly as his wives. When Joseph was dead, Emily wrote, "Emma was now most gracious, for there was no Joseph to be jealous of then." In 1883, looking back on it, Emily wrote, "Poor Emma. She could not stand polygamy. I hope the Lord will be merciful to her. Let the Lord be the judge."[22]

Emily suffered not only as Joseph's wife but again in the expulsion from Nauvoo when she was married to Brigham Young. She had to fend for herself, seeking a friendly fire, while her husband was busy elsewhere with the exodus. Emily wrote in 1833 that she did not pity Church members incarcerated under federal law for practicing polygamy. Instead, "I pity the ignorance of our enemies."[23] Thus, Emily did not condemn or find anything wrong with the practice of polygamy as a principle. If her husband, Joseph, was promiscuous with various women in Nauvoo, wouldn't Emily have taken offense? She takes offense only with his wife, Emma.

Polygamy was not announced officially until 1843, as stated in the preface to Doctrine and Covenants 132. Here we find: "It is evident from the historical records that the doctrines and principles involved in this revelation had been known by the Prophet since 1831." Yet when did the practice begin?

Brodie says Joseph was practicing polygamy by 1835 but lied about it. She does not help her cause by admitting that "there was no irrefutable evidence that it [polygamy] was actually practiced at this time [1835–36 period]."[24]

No irrefutable evidence? Then how did she know Joseph lied about it? But it happened, concluded Brodie, "because there was talk of it." No footnote.

Unhappiness in a plural marriage, of course, does not prove divine sanction or the lack thereof. Apparently, the situation was something Emma decided she could live with, for she never returned to her parents or left Joseph, and as far we know, she never threatened to leave him. Brodie even confirms that Emma "believed in him,"[25] and never quit doing so. Brodie puts it this way, "Whatever breach had opened up between Joseph and Emma was apparently closed. No hint of it crept into his journals. [But] a man of Joseph's physical charm scarcely needed to retire to his journal to relieve vague longings."[26]

No hint? This is award-winning history? Joseph is guilty if he does write anything in his journals about his marital troubles and guilty if he doesn't.

There is no other way to say it. The statement is totally ridiculous. By itself it casts doubt on any further attempt she makes at honest historicity.

But, of course, suspected abuses in polygamy were bound to draw complaint. How could a married man propose to a single woman and be turned down without a scandal resulting if the object of those affections resents any advances and tells all? No doubt some suitor might try to convince a prospective wife at times that she could better reach the celestial kingdom with his help, and it appears this happened in the LDS Church in the 1800s. The whole matter is an awkward situation even for the most sincere Latter-day Saint, man or woman.

If the woman is already married, of course, it is a different problem entirely. It is not only awkward but forbidden in Mormondom, and in most any other occidental religion. The question is: Did Joseph Smith participate in the latter?

Compton's *In Sacred Loneliness* documents Joseph's marriages to women who were married to other men. Polyandry was not particularly rare for the time. But the real research needed is to separate which ones were married posthumously, either after Joseph's death or the death of the husband.

It is known that in the early to mid-1800s divorce was not as rigidly fixed in law before taking on another spouse as it is today. There would be little argument that pioneer Jacob Hamblin was a righteous man who joined the Church just after the Nauvoo period. He married one Lucinda who disagreed with him on matters of religion almost "as soon as the ink was dry on the marriage contract." Lucinda told Jacob to take his "Mormon brats," go west, and join the Saints in Utah; she would be happier in Wisconsin. No divorce was sought by either party, nor was any insisted on by any government entity. Hamblin remarried in Iowa. There was never any need, it seemed, to file divorce papers. Both continued their lives amiably two thousand miles apart.[27] There was no governmental authority to declare any law had been broken.

A tangled web of women at the time apparently considered themselves unmarried because their husbands were not living their religion—the reverse of Jacob Hamblin's situation. This is a matter that should be more fully explored. But Compton, not Brodie, is the credible starting point.

Very early, we are told that the Book of Mormon teaches

against polygamy. Brodie quotes Jacob 2:27: "For there shall not any man among you have save it be one wife." But verse 30 opens the door to possible future polygamy: "For if I will . . . raise up seed unto me, I will command my people." It was a scripture conveniently overlooked by Brodie.

Yet there are complications in 1831, for Doctrine and Covenants 42:22 says, "Thou shalt love thy wife with all thy heart, and shalt cleave unto her and none else." The "love thy wife" part is reassuring to modern-day Mormons, but the "none else" makes it difficult to comprehend just how the process of plural marriage is going to work. Does a man who looks upon another woman after he is married "commit adultery in his heart"?

In trying to prove impropriety on Joseph's part as one who commits adultery in his heart, Brodie can get ugly. She depends almost entirely on the unreliable Bennett as her source, along with a fruitful imagination. She poses no worse accusation in all her writings than the one implicating both Brigham Young and Joseph Smith in sexual affronts. She first foists upon the reader an alleged conversation between Brigham and high-spirited Martha Brotherton, whom Young had set his heart on wooing and winning as a plural wife. To quote Brodie: "He took her to the famous rendezvous over Joseph's store, locked the door and proceeded with the curious bobtailed, hortatory [strong urging] courtship that was becoming so common in the city." What she means by bobtailed is up to conjecture. But the supposed conversation goes thusly: "If you will accept of me I will take you straight to the celestial kingdom. . . . Brother Joseph will marry us here today and you can go home this evening and your parents will not know anything about it." Brigham then calls in Joseph, who says, "Just go ahead and do as Brigham wants you to." He then added with a laugh, "He is the best man in the world, except me." Brodie then has Joseph urging her to try it for a month or two, but "if he turns you off, I will take you on."[28]

This "conversation," written by Brodie as occurring precisely word for word, and damning in a way that makes both men appear to have no scruples whatsoever—coupled with future preaching on the chastity of marriage vows—makes both Brigham and Joseph out to be unmitigated hypocrites. The entire LDS Church would be as well if it condoned such behavior. With such licentious leaders, it would be most difficult to continue gaining sincere converts and continue to grow as a church claiming Christ at its helm.

References? Brodie has one: A footnote that Martha later wrote about the incident in the *St. Louis Bulletin*, dated 15 July 1842. Brodie adds that Young called her story a base falsehood, as did Martha's two sisters and a brother. Church members, who knew her well and swore that she was a liar; but of course, they were coerced to do so, according to Brodie. She does not say who did the coercing. Thus, four are for the story being a lie, one against. But Brodie assures us that Martha, whom the two sisters and brother also called a harlot, is to be believed, and anyone saying otherwise is out of order.

Why should we accept Martha's version rather than the version of the other four, including Brigham, who was also there? Because Brodie says so. And in her index reference to *Brotherton, Martha,* Brodie says the LDS defense of the accusation is "slandered." She says the same elsewhere in the index about *Rigdon, Nancy.* Brodie does not even allow the LDS Church to defend itself against Nancy's or Martha's charges. This is a strange court of law, but it is possible, to be fair, that the editor did the indexing, not Brodie.

The woman is certainly within bounds to include any unflattering comments she wishes, but she has a duty to avoid presenting alleged quotes as actual conversation without documentation. She did not say, "Here is what might have happened." She passes it off as fact that it did happen.

But all of the above appears to be merely academic, for her referenced footnote to Martha was to the *Bulletin* of 15 July 1842, page 2. However, there was no *St. Louis Bulletin* in 1842, according to the paper's own records. The author was informed in researching Brodie's *St. Louis Bulletin* footnote that the *St. Louis Bulletin* did not begin publishing until 1859. No record whatsoever could be found of a *Bulletin* prior to that year. The author received this official response 29 November 2001 from Gayle Camarda, Web Reference Department, St. Louis (Missouri) Public Library, with reference to the State Historical Society of Missouri: "This title does not go back to 1842. . . . This publication began in 1859."[29] That's all there is to it. No 1842 *Bulletin*.

In Donna Hill's biography, *Joseph Smith, the First Mormon* (considered one of the more thorough histories of Joseph Smith by some LDS historians), Hill repeats Brodie's allegations by Brotherton without any reservations or notes. This is disappointing, for it appears Brodie made up at least part, if not all, of the Brotherton story. Whether she knowingly gave a wrong reference or not, it is nevertheless bogus.

Brodie also brings up the case of Sydney Rigdon's daughter, Nancy, nineteen. Brodie says that Joseph sought Nancy out romantically while married to Emma and then made the "mistake" of writing her a letter about the new order of celestial marriage.[30] What mistake? The letter simply talks of polygamy as the social order of the kingdom. To Brodie, it is proof that Joseph was unfaithful, or was trying to be. Perhaps the Rigdon girl asked about the doctrine. It is significant that the letter was not signed and is referred to six pages later in Brodie's book as "the alleged" letter. First a letter, then an "alleged" letter.

Brodie also has this, as related earlier: "But Nancy had been forewarned by Bennett, and met his [Joseph's] exhortations with tears . . . finally threatening to scream until the whole town came running unless he let her go home." We repeat: she provides no reference or footnote, and if the whole town came running, someone surely would know about it.

Incidentally, if Joseph was such a sexual libertine, why not keep Bennett around to set the tone? Why excommunicate a lustful fellow who breaks down the moral code and makes it all easier for those who follow? Bennett would fit right in with Brodie's perverted prophet.

Time and again Brodie purports to tell us what Joseph is thinking. In "If a Man Entice a Maid," we have: "Joseph could with a certain honesty inveigh against adultery in the same week he slept with another man's wife . . . or indeed several men's wives . . . because he had interposed a very special marriage ceremony."[31] Or this: "He stood proudly before his men, betraying nothing of the tumult and anxiety racking him from within."[32] Or: "Almost never in those days did Joseph step outside of himself to look with surprise and humility upon what he had become."[33] Next: "There is no record of her anger except in the dubious [not just normal but dubious] gossip of neighbors."[34] Or: Nauvoo was "abuzz."[35] None carries any reference to a source of any kind. All of Brodie's accusations rely on what Joseph or Emma were supposedly thinking. Somehow, Brodie, like the omniscient narrator in a Nancy Drew novel, knows the inside workings of the human heart, minus any overt clues.

Yet Brodie wrote in her preface: "The writing of biography that tries to explain motivation and character is an act of very great arrogance."[36] When does Brodie fail to tell us about Joseph's motivation and character? Such attempts are on almost every page. She announces what she will not do from the beginning and then proceeds to do it throughout. This is strange behavior for any historian, let alone one so decorated by such a prestigious publication as the *New York Times*. It is doubtful if the *Times*, priding itself on the masthead "All the news that's fit to print," would repeat this award today. In fact, the award should be repealed. After all, the *Washington Post* repealed a Pulitzer Prize given to one of its reporters after discovering that the reporter had made up several stories about a young drug user.

Lack of references in her book on key points is no anomaly. Consider where she says, "Joseph was a great favorite with the ladies."[37] The quote marks are apparently hers, but she doesn't say where she got them. Innuendoes are part of the process.

Many innuendoes seem there for no purpose, other than entertainment, such as, "Most attractive of all these women."[38] Even if Brodie was there, how would she select Zina Huntington Jacob as more attractive than someone else? What kind of nonsense is this? Then we have the "most famous woman in the Church." Many have never heard of her, but we are told she is William

Morgan's widow, Lucinda. "She is said to have admitted to Mrs. Pratt in 1842 that she had been the Prophet's mistress since four years."[39] Note the unsubstantiated words "She is said to," which is typical of Brodie's style. Also, there is no precise date—simply sometime in 1842. The reason she is the most famous woman in the Church? Because she was the Prophet's mistress. Only one of them? And of course, because she "had lost none of her blond beauty."

In implying that Oliver Buell was Joseph's son because he "bore an unmistakable likeness,"[40] we have the usual Brodie conclusion. But Todd Compton has already pointed out the improbability of it bearing any truth. Maybe Brodie missed her calling; she should have written the notorious novel, *Lady Chatterly's Lover*. Brodie could do it with impunity and skip the footnotes.

Some of Brodie's other famous assumptions scattered throughout *No Man* are "It is at least conjectural," "breath of scandal," and "it could have been that." She seems to be especially generous with suppositions in her supplement section.

Citing Bennett's accusations, Brodie slyly puts it this way in linking Sarah Pratt to Joseph: "Sarah is supposed to have replied . . ."[41] Here we go again. Supposed by whom?

Suppose Brodie alleges an affair by some man with your mother or sister or your wife and says, "So and so is supposed to have said . . ." No court of law would put up with it. Would any of us? Besides, Mrs. Pratt says she did not have any affair whatsoever with Joseph Smith. "He never said an improper word to me in his life. . . . There is no truth in the reports that have been circulated about him in this regard. He was always the Christian gentleman and a noble man."[42] After Brodie has had her way with Smith, she places this in a footnote. Obviously, she is more interested in manipulating the reader than presenting documented fact. If history accepts this, it has tunneled beneath its own lofty foundation for acceptable research.

It is difficult to understand why so many historians, some LDS, insist on a romantic liaison between Joseph and Sarah Pratt on the flimsy say-so of John C. Bennett. For a time, it must be said, Bennett's accusation caused a stir in the Nauvoo community and in the life of husband Orson Pratt, recently returned home from a mission to England. There might have been some initial ring of truth to it in the mind of Orson, or possibly Sarah may have held a romantic interest in Joseph. This would seem possible because word got around when Orson disappeared for a time that he was going to kill himself. But when Orson learned the origin of the liaison rumor to be John C. Bennett, the case was closed.[43] He knew Bennett to be an unmitigated liar. Pratt picked up his duties in the Quorum of the Twelve, and the matter never again seemed worthy of mention, at least by Orson or within the Church.

If Pratt was estranged from Joseph Smith by this alleged affair, it had no effect upon Orson's perception of Joseph as a prophet of God. This can be readily seen from *Orson Pratt's Works,* written after the above incident. "Was Joseph Smith Sent of God?" Pratt asks. "Here then, this great prophet has presented himself before the whole world with a bold, unequivocal message."[44] The entire chapter extols the virtue of learning from the feet of the Prophet Joseph Smith.

Outside the Church, Vardis Fisher picked up this innuendo about Sarah and Joseph, which had been passed along to the world courtesy of Bennett; but again, writing fiction, Fisher had license Brodie did not.

Author Will Bagley repeats the same innuendoes about Sarah Pratt and Nancy Rigdon. No new research into the allegations exists. Thus, when Brodie is answered, so is he.[45] It should be added, however, that Bagley claims early in his book that he entered the fray with an open mind. The claim is not an infrequent one.

Meantime, Brodie is quoted by William Mulder, rather proudly it would seem, as saying to her history students, "If he [the biographer] invents a single conversation he has become a novelist." On the same page, she is quoted by Mulder as saying that "if the story is of such consequence to me, why am I not a novelist?"[46] This is a strange comment, for it becomes obvious she is very much interested in making a novel of it if that makes for a more readable book. Why restrict yourself to rules, even if you have just announced them? It is easier to make things up. But a primary rule of making things up is that you've got to remember what you've said.

Brodie delivers the following remark in her preface: "The biographer cannot distort the truth without guilt."

Since Brodie brings it up, let's take a closer look at the whole problem of distortion. Researchers John R. Kirk and George D. Talbot list three types of distortion: stretch, fog, and mirage.[47] Stretch involves something as slight as rounding off a number such as 999 to 1,000. Fog is explained as observing a pond for several days and when an amphibian climbs onto the bank, concluding that life occurs spontaneously from water. Mirage is more serious. It is not seeing any water at all—it is a mirage.

Brodie frequently utilizes all three: stretch in insisting that Joseph looked upon women with a roving eye (how does a polygamist avoid looking at any prospective plural wife without looking away from the first?); fog in relating that Joseph may have had an affair with Fanny Alger minus marriage; and mirage in asserting that he was intimate with her, minus any proof.

Some of these incidents resemble news gathering at the *New York Daily News* in which Tom Goldstein says he and peers frequently made things up because they were "more concerned with writing interesting stories than factual ones."[48] Like Brodie, they were not reporters but novelists.

Perhaps Brodie can be forgiven for conjecturing that Emma was "wildly in love" with Joseph.[49] Credulity is stretched with such an insight, but no harm is done. Everyone likes to read about a good romance.

The following, however, is fog distortion: "It is quite likely [note the precision of the speculation] that Joseph had admired her [Eliza Snow] for a long time."[50] How does Brodie know? Because she must explain why Joseph will soon try to seduce Eliza. She must paint with a brush broad enough to be sure we know that Joseph, and the rest of the Mormon leaders, leaped into polygamy out of sheer lust. Interestingly, many of Brodie's non-Mormon colleagues who don't understand or condone polygamy see a difference between lust and polygamy. The latter includes a commitment to care for and love a woman and her progeny. If Brodie were more intellectually honest, she would include in her indictments of polygamy that it embraced more than mere physical attraction. Brodie has apparently forgotten that John C. Bennett and Philastus Hurlbut were excommunicated for adultery.

Eliza Snow did, in fact, later became a plural wife of Joseph. Snow's personal record book, in the possession of a family friend, shows that in Nauvoo Brigham Young married Eliza Roxey Snow to Joseph Smith on 29 June 1842. This record also shows Joseph's death "while under the protection of Gov. of the State, 27 June, 1844, Carthage Ill., murdered."[51]

Thus, Eliza was understandably angered when Emma declared late in life that she was the only wife Joseph ever had.[52] Emma had to knowingly lie when stating this, Snow concludes. The record backs up Eliza and leaves one to wonder if Emma was unwilling to face the fact, as once insisted by the Reorganized LDS Church she in time supported, that Joseph introduced polygamy into the church he led. No doubt exists that Smith took plural wives. We have a problem here. When can we believe Emma?

More fog distortion can be found by Brodie when she admits there are some marriage dates in her list of Joseph's wives "which must be guessed at."[53] How then, does she know Joseph married them?

Brodie likes to paint Joseph as one not only accepting polygamy but also quick to rationalize away Christian moral teachings in seeking to introduce adultery as an accepted practice. As Brodie says, "And who was to say him nay, since in the gentile world the simple pronouncement of a few time-worn phrases by any justice of the peace was all that was necessary to transform fornication into blessed matrimony."[54] To be sure, Brodie isn't saying she believes this, but she sets out to convince the reader it did happen because it might have happened.

The LDS point of view is this: Joseph was commanded to

restore all the principles of the early church to the latter days. Polygamy was one of them. The Lord apparently countenanced, even commanded, polygamy under certain prescribed conditions for Abraham and others, as attested in Genesis. He did so as well when restoring all that had been lost from the early Church.

But Brodie compares the Mormon practice of polygamy with that of the free-love community in Oneida, New York, under the libertine John Humphrey Noyes, who advocated that man ought to be able to enjoy different sex partners as he does food.[55] Brodie includes this for the purpose of titillation only, for she knows there is a huge difference between promiscuous sex and committing to marriage vows. How many of these men remained married to a plural wife? After children? If for lust only, desertion would surely follow. Yet the record shows there were few cases of husbands deserting plural wives.

Brodie quotes the Apostle Paul as saying there is no marriage or giving in marriage in heaven (actually it was Jesus who said it), and then in an entirely incongruous linkage says Smith contradicts this idea by "sealing on earth that which would be binding also in heaven."[56] Since it can't be done in heaven, it must be done on earth. What is contradictory here? How well does Brodie, for all her research, really understand the church she is writing about? Or the early Christian church? Has she done her homework here?

In one instance, Brodie includes an outright absurdity: "Emma's great hazel eyes, the only remnant of her once haunting beauty, had been full of reproach. He knew that she thought him a coward."[57] One of the most astute observations ever made in Mormon historicity is this by Hugh Nibley: "So, Brodie knows that Emma knew that Joseph knew what Emma thought."[58]

Give Brodie credit for pioneering research into a neglected art. But I must beg to differ with her "great service" to polygamous research in the early Mormon Church. How much true service has been rendered when indicting a man, or woman, for acts held by most of the Christian world as totally reprehensible without substantiating the facts?

For many it does not matter, but for thirteen million Latter-day Saints, it is a matter of integrity. No reverence should be tendered toward the charlatan Brodie has described, with much help from unreliable sources, even though he might be a prophet in the bringing forth of the Book of Mormon. Her unscholarly accusations, as presented above, stand as a beacon in how to commit character assassination. It is fine if you get the facts right. But with a loose cannon, more damage than good has been done.

Joseph's announcement about plural marriage received mixed reviews among the early Church hierarchy. It is easily the most controversial of all his teachings and, some would say, the main reason for most of the Church's persecution. However, there was considerable trouble, for whatever reasons, in Missouri well before polygamy was ever introduced. David Whitmer didn't like the idea, nor did Sidney Rigdon. Orson Pratt left the Church upon learning of polygamy but returned to write a series of articles proclaiming it to be God's will.[59] Parley P. Pratt welcomed the principle from the beginning with these words: "I received from him [Joseph] the first idea of eternal family organization and the eternal union of the sexes in those . . . endearing relationships which none but the highly intellectual, the refined and pure in heart know how to prize and which are the foundation of everything to be called happiness."[60]

The LDS response today is that sealing to spouse and family members in a temple ceremony is a great blessing, for while the world at large is marrying until death do us part, a bill of divorcement in the wedding ceremony, the Latter-day Saint seeks an eternal and lasting relationship with loved ones.

Polygamy has always shouldered social problems. If there was an unwritten rule in polygamous unions, or should have been, it was that contemporaneous wife, or wives, should be consulted beforehand and be in full agreement when choosing other wives.

Frankly, it would seem, judging from past problems pursuant to polygamy, that a smart man would not only get such permission in writing but also have it witnessed, stamped, and dated by a notary public.

But back to Brodie: Did she ever really understand polygamy from a biblical point of view? She says Joseph was fond of quoting Exodus 22:16: "And if a man entice a maid that is not betrothed and lie with her, he shall utterly endow her to be his wife." Adds Brodie: "The sin of adultery lay not in the act itself but in the subsequent desertion."[61]

Is she saying here there is no problem with adultery in the eyes of the Lord as long as the man marries the maid? Is she insisting God condones premarital sex? Elsewhere, God makes it plain a couple should be married before sexual union, as explained in 1 Corinthians 7:2: "To avoid fornication, let every man have his own wife, and let every woman have her own husband." But this would not serve Brodie's purpose, so of course she does not link Joseph Smith to it.

Does Brodie confuse adultery (one partner is married) with fornication? How does she know Joseph is fond of the scripture in Exodus? How does she know he thinks the way she says he does? How does she know?

But we've asked these questions before.

9
View of the Hebrews

Nothing is so vital in the history of Joseph Smith as this question: from whence sprang the Book of Mormon? Since the Solomon Spaulding theory has exploded, along with sequels, what else is left?

Non-Mormons have worked hard to find a substitute. No one works harder at it than Mrs. Brodie, who insists Joseph wrote much of the book on his own as a catharsis for a troubled home. For example, he is only portraying his family's domestic problems. Likening Joseph's brothers to Nephi's brothers, she suggests that Joseph's brothers threatened one another violently, just as Laman and Lemuel threatened Nephi and Sam.[1]

Her argument runs this way: Joseph's mother, Lucy Mack, thinks her son Alvin died from an overdose of calomel at the hands of a clumsy doctor. Brodie says it sounds more like appendicitis. Then, out of whole cloth, Brodie suggests that Alvin really died by violent means at the hands of his family, kept secret by them. After all, someone fired a shot in young Joseph's direction when he was entering the family home. Maybe Alvin or Hyrum or Samuel or one of the other siblings. First she confesses, "We do not know if Joseph Smith as a young boy was treated harshly by his older brothers . . . [but] one cannot help wondering if young Joseph harbored . . . fantasies about the would-be murderer being one of his brothers."

Who is wondering besides Brodie?

Then, she says, "The constantly recurring theme in the book about brothers killing brothers would thus seem to be more than a mere coincidence." What coincidence? The one she just made up? Under her imaginative mind, anything could be coincidence. What is her grudge against Joseph Smith that she must conjure up such a fantasy?

But even if true, what do these strained parallels have to do with producing the Book of Mormon? The sons of Lehi comprise a small portion of the book. She struggles to find similes in the other 99 percent of the volume.

But seemingly sensing that it is not really a plausible solution, Brodie, along with other detractors, comes up with the Ethan Smith theory; enter *View of the Hebrews*.[2] Brodie says this book, which suggests that the American Indian originated from the lost ten tribes of Israel, is not very scholarly, but she doesn't think the Book of Mormon is particularly so either. The view certainly does invite scrutiny, for even B. H. Roberts cites what he describes as striking similarities in the two works. (It is somewhat confusing to have two Smiths as protagonists, so I will refer to the one who wrote *View of the Hebrews* as Ethan and his book as *VH*.)

The Rev. Ethan Smith spent much time reading the Old Testament and conjecturing about what might have happened to the lost ten tribes of Israel. Ethan theorized that the Israelites came across the Bering Strait land bridge many centuries ago and found their way into South America via divine guidance.[3] The Book of Mormon says two tribes of Israelites came via divine guidance but in boats.

One main difference is that Ethan didn't write a narrative, which is what the Book of Mormon primarily is. Ethan wrote a lengthy essay on why and how he thought deity would bring Israelites to the New World. He supported his idea with many of Isaiah's prophecies concerning latter-day Israel. Since Ethan published his book in 1823 and 1825, some five years before the Mormon publication, the idea surfaced, at the final demise of the Spaulding theory, that the Book of Mormon could have been copied from Ethan's book.

The Book of Mormon didn't deal with the lost ten tribes, of course, but with a remnant of two of the twelve tribes of Israel, Judah and Joseph. Both *VH* and the Book of Mormon carry similar passages from Isaiah, wherein God promises the restoration of Israel. Quoting Jeremiah 16:16, "I will send for many fishers" to recover Israel, Ethan talks of an expulsion of Israel some 725 years before Christ (600 B.C. in the Book of Mormon). With his knowledge of Isaiah, Ethan speculates that Isaiah must have lived to see the expulsion of the ten tribes.

Ethan compared many similarities between words used by the American Indians and those in Hebrew or Chaldaic. "The hand of Providence is seen in this," he concluded.[4] The Book of Mormon doesn't say it in that language, but the concept is similar. Nine chapters of Isaiah appear in both *VH* and the Book of Mormon, but in a master's thesis, William Riley noted that only 13 percent of Isaiah's verses are actually carried in both books.[5]

One thing that caught the eye of critics was that Ethan's book was published in Poultney, Vermont, near Oliver Cowdery's birthplace, which is usually given as Poultney but sometimes as nearby Wells; both are near the border of New York. Thus, it is deduced that Cowdery could have taken the book to Joseph Smith. No evidence of any kind exists that Cowdery did so, or that Joseph ever saw *Views of the Hebrews*. Yet that possibility did exist.

Ethan is well versed in the writings of Josephus and the destruction of Jerusalem. He admonishes his audience that "if the Indians of our continent are of the 10 tribes of Israel who left at the destruction, then . . . we are the people . . . to bring them to a knowledge of the gospel."[6] In this, Ethan is saying that which is also emphasized in the preface of the Book of Mormon. How the Israelites got to America differs in the two accounts, and some argue the land-bridge theory is more credible. The Book of Mormon doesn't really explain how submarine-type ocean vessels could keep water out while en route across the Atlantic Ocean to America. But if we accept divine guidance, it seems a futile argument; with divine guidance, anything is possible.

In his *Studies of the Book of Mormon*, B. H. Roberts found two basic parallels between the books in question: (1) An overthrow of Jerusalem, the same event which caused Lehi to leave that land; and (2) reliance upon Isaiah's prophecies. Some speculated whether Roberts relegated the Book of Mormon to originate with *View of the Hebrews*, or in other words, lost his testimony of the Book of Mormon and was planning to leave the Church. Roberts submitted his list of similarities to LDS General Authorities, but they apparently saw no cause for reply. Receiving little feedback, Roberts stored the list away with his other belongings. Clearly, he never meant to have the list published. After Roberts's death, however, his papers were located by family members and published, with introductory remarks by Sterling McMurrin and Brigham Madsen.[7]

Truman Madsen, who later interviewed those associated with Roberts about the Ethan Smith matter, said Roberts strongly reaffirmed his testimony; he was merely playing devil's advocate in comparing the two books. He was seeking to strengthen missionary work by asking tough questions and seeking tough answers. Madsen said Roberts personally knew the Book of Mormon to be true, but he (Roberts) simply wanted to reach the fence sitters. Testifying of the truth of the Book of Mormon "is a simple, bigoted refrain," he said. "What about those for whom it is not enough? What about the many young men in the Church . . . what of the earnest inquirers in the world? The more thoroughly it is investigated, the greater shall be its eventual triumph."[8]

Roberts added: "I take the position that our faith is not only unshaken but unshakable in the Book of Mormon . . . therefore, we can look without fear upon all that can be said against it."[9] He served as mission president thereafter and continued faithfully as a General Authority to the end of his life. Thus, it does not appear that he lost his testimony in the Book of Mormon.

Bottom line: Roberts lists seventeen reasons that the Book of Mormon was not influenced by *View of the Hebrews*. He concluded, "Ethan Smith played no part in the formation of the Book of Mormon." Brodie does not mention this. Instead, she footnotes

Roberts in a way that ties him to an endorsement of the Ethan Smith-Book of Mormon origin hypothesis.[10]

Furthermore, in his book *An Unparallel*, historian John W. Welch produced a list of eighty-four unparallels between the two books. "The differences far outweigh the similarities," he wrote.[11]

An article in the *Encyclopedia of Mormonism* by Richard C. Roberts concludes, "There is little in common between the ideas and statements in *View of the Hebrews* and the Book of Mormon."[12] The encyclopedia, however, is an overtly favorable LDS history, a compendium basically written for a faithful LDS audience, as can be seen from the fact that scoundrels such as John C. Bennett do not enter its pages. In this, historians such as B. H. Roberts would enjoy greater credibility among skeptics; Roberts gives both sides.

A reading of both books reveals that while there are similarities in the concept of Israelites coming to America guided by Christ, as prophesied by Isaiah. But there is simply no likelihood that the Book of Mormon was based on *VH*. The Book of Mormon is much more complicated. *VH* is a list of conjectures, not connected by any narrative thread. Ethan ponders and writes down his speculations as they arise. The Book of Mormon unfolds a connecting narrative and, as such, must be internally consistent and logical not only in plot but also in characterization, theme, and point of view. It appears, as purported, to be the work of many writers, albeit edited by one man, Mormon.

In addition, the Book of Mormon gives specific instances and examples of man's relationship to God. It must be consistent throughout with known external events from the Bible. ("Other sheep I have, which are not of this fold" [John 10:16]), the Tower of Babel, parallels between the Old World and the American continent.) The only historical event mentioned in the Book of Mormon and also mentioned in *VH* is the destruction of Jerusalem, which is well known to Bible scholars, including the Rev. Smith.

As an author of thirteen books, hundreds of magazine articles, and thousands of newspaper stories over more than half a century,

I see no way anyone, let alone an unlettered youth, could, on his own, have written such a compendium as the Book of Mormon in any amount of time, let alone a few months. It is absolutely astounding that Fawn Brodie or anyone should claim to prove that such was the case. At least she saw the wisdom in not trying to foist it off on Sidney Rigdon. To his dying day, Rigdon said he never saw the Book of Mormon until it was brought to him by Parley P. Pratt.[13]

Interestingly, the LDS Church did not shy away from comparing *VH* to the Book of Mormon. In fact, the Church republished Ethan's *View of the Hebrews.* An introduction by editor Charles D. Tate says: "Since the Book of Mormon was first published in 1830, its critics have endeavored to find explanations for it other than the one given by Joseph Smith. Some have suggested the source was *View of the Hebrews.* Readers may find topics of interest for LDS history, but it is clear that they will need to look elsewhere to find the origin of the Book of Mormon." Also: "There is no direct evidence Joseph Smith had any knowledge of, or contact with, *View of the Hebrews* until possibly 1840 when the [LDS] *Times and Seasons* quoted several paragraphs from it that had been quoted in another book."[14] The facts seem to support Tate's conclusions.

No one has more extensively researched the mechanics of the Book of Mormon than J. M. Sjodahl. In his *An Introduction to the Book of Mormon*, he describes the golden plates, estimating size and weight. More important, he wonders how any writer could get so much message on alloyed metal plates about eight inches by eleven inches in size, weighing about sixty pounds, as witnesses testified.[15]

Sjodahl also says it is folly not to believe simply because you can't behold a thing in front of your eyes. "Who can see atoms and molecules that scientists tell us make up the universe? We accept them on authoritative testimony." Furthermore, "Just as there are light waves beyond our range of vision, so there must be . . . spirit beyond that which we generally recognize."[16] Today, we might say that when we make a cell phone call in our home to a long-distance location that sound waves are also circulating between the caller and receiver of the message—unseen sound waves.

No one today has seen the original of the Bible parchment. We don't wring our hands about it. We try to live by its precepts to see if they make a difference in our lives. For years, astronomers could not see the planet Pluto. It must be there, they theorized, because everything else was in harmony with this unseen planet. It was some fifteen years later that Pluto was actually observed by an improved technology in telescopes.[17] Yet science believed without seeing for a full fifteen years.

"In harmony" is an intriguing statement—in other words, acting "as if" based on existing knowledge, then expostulating. It is an argument that would seem valid in both scientific and religious inquiry.

Sjodahl also points out that there are words an impostor would almost surely have used in the Book of Mormon, thus betraying human origin. One is the word *Hebrew*. The word was not in use until about 130 B.C., says Sjodahl. "It would have been fatal for Nephi to use it in 600 B.C." Isaiah called it the "language of Canaan." Nephi called it "the language of my father" (1 Nephi 1:2).[18] Sjodahl says it was probably Josephus who first made use of the word *Hebrew*. a popular term for the Israelites and their language.

In addition, research that was unavailable to Brodie now utilizes modern language analysis. The publication *Book of Mormon Authorship, New Light on Ancient Origins* has a chapter by John W. Welch that includes studies on chiasms, or parallel word groupings found in both the Bible and the Book of Mormon.[19] The word comes from the Greek *Chi*, to mark with an X. Chiasms are described as ancient Hebrew literary forms that employ reverse parallel structure such as found in Proverbs 15:1. This scripture reads, "A soft answer turneth away wrath: but grievous words stir up anger." As a chiasm, it would read, "Grievous words stir up anger but a soft answer turneth away wrath." Examples from the Book of Mormon are found in 2 Nephi 29:13 and Mosiah 5:10–12.

Many chiasms have not survived the King James translation, says Welch, but were found in earlier Bibles. The value of this writing style is obvious. With such poetic quality and parallel construction inherent in chiasm structure, verses are easier to memorize and retain. Christians would call it inspired writing.

Another chapter in the same book by Wayne A. Larsen and Alvin C. Rencher describes a fascinating word-print analysis in which various words are compared from the Book of Mormon with prominent Mormon leaders of the 1830s, including Joseph Smith, Sidney Rigdon, Oliver Cowdery, and W. W. Phelps.[20] This study, albeit with some asterisks, concludes that the statistical odds of one author, any author, writing the Book of Mormon "are . . . less than one in a billion." The two researchers, statistics professors at Brigham Young University, compared the frequency of the following words: *and, the, of, that, to, unto, in, it, for, be.* Among the twenty-one authors studied in the Book of Mormon, only the word *in* was significantly repetitive. The probability that a single author would have such a relationship was listed at one in ten thousand.[21]

The study also focused on words infrequently used, such as *about*, appearing 262 times in the Book of Mormon, and *exceeding,* with 175 mentions. *With* occurs 1,520 times, and *should* occurs 1,188 times. (It would be interesting to research the word *remember,* which also shows up many times in both the Bible and the Book of Mormon.)

Another aspect of the study was termed MANOVA, or multi-variate analysis of variance. In this, none of the Book of Mormon selections resembled the writings of any of the nineteenth-century writers, including Joseph Smith. This was strong evidence, of course, that the Book of Mormon did not originate in the nineteenth century.

The authors advise some caution in that they need to do more research on word phraseology rather than single words only. A "quantification of evidence, followed by a rigorous and objective statistical analysis," is needed.[22] This is sometimes referred to as the science of stylometry, detailed by H. Q. Morris in the volume

Literary Detection.[23] The two researchers also came to the conclusion that the phrase *And it came to pass that* was one word in reformed Egyptian.[24]

One problem remaining is that LDS scholars such as Roberts and Sjodahl know that Joseph did not interpret the reformed Egyptian into English word for word. For instance, there is no word in the Egyptian language for *was*, commonly appearing in English sentence syntax.[25] Did Joseph Smith simply peer into the Urim and Thummim, see words there he read to scribes (most of the time Oliver Cowdery), and when read back correctly, those words vanished? That seemed to be the way described by David Whitmer.

But Whitmer saw only that something appeared in the "interpreters" and surmised what was happening. Since the words Cowdery wrote down were in Smith's vernacular of the time and in his understanding, the original copy of the Book of Mormon was not published in the polished English it might have been had Smith been an English scholar, says Sjodahl.[26] Anti-Mormon writers make much of this, saying God is "a poor linguist." But one explanation is that there would be little intellectual or spiritual growth in man if God did all his work for him.

From the explanation given by B. H. Roberts, Joseph looked into the "screen," saw the message of the ancient writers, and then put it into his own words. With almost no schooling, Joseph must have struggled, focusing on the meaning but required to express the thought in his own language. If written down word for word, the Book of Mormon would be difficult, indeed, for us to read today, says Roberts. He puts it this way: "Joseph saw the Nephite characters, and understood the thought they conveyed, then expressed that thought in such language as he was master of."[27]

Let us assume that we also have a fourth-grade education and that we are given the *1776 Dominguez-Escalante Journal* to translate from Spanish of that period to modern English. We must explain to others, in our native language, what was meant by these words penned by Escalante: *league, solemn high mass, thrice holy saints, bad going, rosettes, a tint between purple and white.* And these are only from page five.[28]

In addition, the translators of the *Escalante Journal*, Fray Angelico Chavez and editor Ted J. Warner, spend page after page explaining that some words just don't lend themselves well in being translated from 1776 (Catholic) Spanish of the frontier into modern English. When Escalante writes *gully* or *arroyo*, does he mean a small wash or a large canyon? When he uses Catholic words, what if we are not a Catholic?

Why then have an unschooled lad such as Joseph Smith do the translating of the Book of Mormon? Why not professor Charles Anthon or Sidney Rigdon? Anthon was out because he was an unbeliever. Rigdon was a pious man but wouldn't qualify because people would say he could do it by himself; he didn't need God's help. A schooled minister of divinity would be a poor choice because he'd have his own ingrained thoughts and procedures and would be difficult to retrain in the new work to be done as God wanted it.

The chosen prophet must be teachable, like young David of the Old Testament. No one is more teachable than one who is dedicated but knows he has a lot to learn. Christ often chose the poor and meek of the earth, saying to Peter and his associates, "Follow me, and I will make you fishers of men" (Matthew 4:19). He did not choose the elect high priests, scribes or Pharisees, or even learned rabbis, for they would have too much to unlearn. Would God not want someone who could show himself a beacon of divine light, where before there had been none? In this manner, unbelievers can see God's handiwork. It would seem to shine in the matter of selecting Christ's Twelve Apostles among rank and file, not Jewish hierarchy.

But let us examine another matter. Critics want tangible proof, such as evidence of Indian battles in the Hill Cumorah area. It is there, if it proves anything. Sjodahl tells of Susa Young Gates visiting the area near Palmyra in 1901 and conversing with a Mrs. Sampson, who owned the surrounding area. She and her husband had been for some time selling "bushels of arrowheads," found on the hill, to tourists.[29]

Incidentally, Brodie conjures this idea: "Joseph imagined the hill itself to be an ancient Indian mound."[30] The mound builders heaped large ones it is true, but as described by William E. Barrett in *The Restored Church*, Cumorah is huge, rising some 150 feet above surrounding terrain. "The hill, like the smaller ones in the same region, is a glacial deposit," explains Barrett, "the southernmost advance of the great ice cap" in western New York.[31] But as long as one is speculating, why check the facts?

There is another interesting thing to ponder about the coming forth of the Book of Mormon. On 20 June 1892, an inquiry to Dr. August LePlonger, a Mayan Indian language expert in Brooklyn, New York, from Elder D. M. McAllister of Salt Lake City, was answered this way: "I have carefully examined the characters [copied from the gold plates] from which the Mormon book was translated. The following are [also] found in the Mayan writings." He then lists many letters and words found on both the plate samples and in the Mayan language.[32] It will be recalled that Prof. Anthon once denied there were any similarities whatsoever.

Little has been said about the Book of Mormon's companion volume, the Pearl of Great Price. These two, along with the Bible and the Doctrine and Covenants, constitute the standard works for the LDS Church. Critics have panned Abraham in the Pearl of Great Price because Joseph said it was translated from Egyptian scrolls purchased in New York. There is less criticism of the book of Moses because Joseph said it originated as inspiration rather than translation. But in both Abraham and Moses, the reader will find richness of thought that would seem foreign to a man with so little education. Many questions about the Creation, Adam and the Fall, premortality, and the War in Heaven are answered in what would seem to be beyond man's mundane understanding.

But Roberts pointed out a knotty problem: in her history of Joseph Smith, his mother, Lucy Mack, said her son regaled the family with stories about the ancient Americans even before Joseph received the gold plates.[33] Did Moroni open up the past to

Joseph's view, that he might learn of the people he was to write about? Oliver Cowdery said as much in the *Messenger and Advocate* 1:80: "From a letter written by Oliver Cowdery, we learn that the angel [Moroni] gave a general account of the history of the aborigines of this country."[34] The reference is to the 21 September 1823 visit by the Angel Moroni.

Why didn't Joseph just share with the world what he did with his family? As Brodie tells us, there were many things Joseph didn't broadcast to the world. In that, there is little argument.

For believers, the Book of Mormon solves a problem about man's creation. How did the Indian get here—if from Asia? It seems certain the natives found here by Columbus got here somehow. The only other explanation, if not by God's will, is that evolution created two highly separate but identical races of homo sapiens. Said Marquis Nadaillac centuries ago: "Must we admit different centers of creation? Could evolution and natural selection [alone] . . . have produced a type of man resembling the European and Asiatic, alike in the structure of his frame and in intellectual development?"[35]

Sjodahl says, "The Book of Mormon furnishes this explanation of transcontinental migration without denying one single fact scientifically established."[36] He adds, "The great appeal of the Book of Mormon is that it answers [such] questions, and gave man a way to become closer to God."

So what if the Book of Mormon was ignored by most Palmyrans and disparaged by those who printed it, including critical newsmen such as Pomeroy Tucker?[37] It was also alleged by him and others that Martin Harris would never get back his three thousand dollars on the printing of the first five thousand copies of the Book of Mormon.

But if the book was ignored by some in 1830, history records that one of the greatest volumes of the Western World was *Plutarch's Lives of the Noble Grecians and Romans.*[38] Yet Plutarch and his book were never even mentioned by contemporaries Juvenal, Quintillian, or Martia.

It requires time to put some things in perspective. Thus, it would appear that the Book of Mormon, *View of the Hebrews*, and other religious books, including the so-called classics such as *Walden Pond* and *Leaves of Grass*, require time for reflection and proper assessment. Time is the test. Has the Book of Mormon passed it?

Historian Stephen LeSueur says, "The book cannot be easily dismissed as the work of an imaginative youth. It maintains a complex narrative, presents doctrinal themes, and answers questions not fully explained in the Bible."[39]

Then there is this dimension: Men who are incarcerated for long periods sometimes find that they are able to turn their lives around, gain control of their behavior, and become productive citizens by reading and following Christ's teachings as given in both the Bible and the Book of Mormon. That is the testimony of LaDell Andersen, who spent months working with prisoners at the federal prison located at the Point of the Mountain in Draper, Utah, in the 1980–90s.[40] Again, this does not prove a thing to be divinely inspired but simply points out that these two books have had a profound effect in changing the lives of those who studied them intently. They are not the ashes asserted by Brodie, at least for those people who testify that they have found strength beyond their own human capabilities to make needed changes in their lives.

Academia may not accept such personal research. But for Andersen and others who have taught from both the Bible and the Book of Mormon, the positive effects have been both measurable and real.

10
Detractors and Defectors

Brodie lined up a phalanx of hostile eyewitnesses against Joseph Smith in her appendix A. They are people who knew Joseph "intimately," such as Peter Cartwright, Pomeroy Tucker, Willard Chase, Peter Ingersoll, William Stafford, Joseph Capron, and of course, Joseph's father-in-law, Isaac Hale. Not to mention newspaper editors E. D. Howe and Obadiah Dogberry. None has a single positive thing to say about the prophet from Palmyra. And then there is Lucy Harris, who said she didn't know Joseph all that well, but after Martin Harris became acquainted with Joseph, Harris changed. He became "more cross, turbulent and abusive to me."[1]

P. Hurlbut rounded up most of these names for *Mormonism Unvailed* [sic], printed under the name E.D. Howe. Howe himself calls Smith "the vilest wretch on earth."[2] It will never be known what persuasion Hurlbut may have used to influence his affidavit signers; yet they are on record stating Joseph pretended his visions with Moroni.[3] LDS historian Richard L. Anderson says his research suggests that Hurlbut's affidavits "were written by a single hand," most likely Hurlbut himself, or Howe.[4]

We might also discredit Hurlbut by pointing out that the man was excluded from the Methodists "for immoralities."[5] This statement by historian Donna Hill, however, carries no footnote. Hill also says that Hurlbut confessed his sins in the Mormon Church but was excommunicated in 1833 "to his great indignation."

Hill adds, "Hurlbut declared himself an enemy of the Mormon Church from that day."[6]

Her research also shows that William Kelley of the Reorganized LDS Church (now Community of Christ) went to Palmyra in 1881 and did his own survey. While there was some controversy about his methods, and neither his nor Hurlbut's polls preserved specific questions or procedures for posterity, a "substantial refutation of Hurlbut's vindictive work" was made known.[7] The weakness in this argument, published in the *Saints Herald* on 1 June 1881, was that it likely didn't interview the same people as Hurlbut, or Robinson before him.

Yet if Mormons can rightfully claim that the eleven witnesses to the Book of Mormon, or even the Three Witnesses, are enough to obtain a conviction in court, it would seem the detractors named above might be enough to convince an impartial jury. These people charged Joseph primarily with attempting deception for private gain and shiftless loutery. They testified: "Joe was a lazy, good for nothing lout, chiefly noted for his capacity to hang around a corner grocery store and punish poor whiskey. He could wrestle pretty well but was not given to exerting his muscles in any practical way."[8]

However, Brodie's Smith was a more ambitious man; he must be so to write the Book of Mormon, make all those speeches, and hoodwink thousands of followers. Brodie does not launch into the worthless adjectives of many other detractors, although she includes their allegations, and thus we have two types of charges against Joseph. Was he really a lazy lout, or did he really write the Book of Mormon?

The lazy-lout description does not hold up for obvious reasons, looking at the man's accomplishments before the age of thirty-nine. In addition, the lazy-lout story has contradictions. It says Martin Harris refused to rejoin the Mormon Church because it was of the devil and that he died near his home without ever going west.[9] This is easily disproved from the records that show Harris migrated west, was rebaptized, and was later buried in Clarkston, Cache County, Utah.

Almost in the same category are the Tuckers and Chases. They testify that Joseph only pretended to have a gold Bible, or a book of any kind. It isn't worth wasting any time on this one. Joseph clearly produced a book in 1830, with some five thousand copies of the book coming off the E. B. Grandin Press. But others testified that Joseph spent much time searching via his unique magical means for buried treasure, leading to a whole chapter by Brodie on the subject, along with an appendix A listing most of Hurlbut's gallery of critics.

Brodie did form a starting point to ferret out the truth of these affidavits. Such research was Brodie's major contribution to the historicity of the Mormon story. Many allegations must be addressed.

Yet we must cast a pall on Brodie's rogues' gallery by pointing out easily discerned bias in many statements, such as Peter Ingersoll's, who said he was hired by Joseph to drive his belongings to Pennsylvania. Ingersoll said Joseph confided to him that he, Joseph, had duped his family. He did so, says Ingersoll, with a story about white sand he'd gathered being passed off to his family as the gold Bible.[10] Flags begin waving everywhere. First of all, Joseph never in his life used the term Gold Bible, as so many others did. He always referred to the Book of Mormon as a companion scripture to the Bible, another witness for Christ, not something in competition to it. Ingersoll might have simply thought that he would please the crowd with the Gold Bible story floating about.

Second, why would Joseph confide in a casual acquaintance that he had duped family members? It doesn't make sense. It especially doesn't make any sense if he is practicing to become an impostor, as Brodie maintains. Why give away your secrets? Why betray trust in a close-knit family circle to an outsider?

As with Ingersoll, and everyone mentioned in Hurlbut's affidavits, no other witness exists to tell the story. Chase is alone when Joseph confides in him, as usual. According to Chase, Joseph was halted from picking up the golden plates by a "toad that assumed the appearance of a man," who then struck Joseph on the side of the head. Next, this "spirit knocks Joseph several rods."[11] It is a story unique to Willard Chase, never mentioned anywhere else.

Chase's account also said Joseph "couldn't have the plates until he brought his older brother with him." Since Joseph never did so, it would be reason enough for Chase to speculate that Joseph never actually had any plates; yet eleven eyewitnesses said otherwise.

Chase then says that if Smith hadn't gotten a "peep stone" from him, Joseph couldn't have obtained the gold plates. This is the first time that anyone had ever heard of this story. Chase also says the peep stone, which was found while digging a well, should have been his; Joseph pirated it off and wouldn't give it back. Two accounts of this exist, one that the digging was done on the Smith property, in which case the stone would belong to the Smiths, not Chase. Another account says that "we" found the stone, but it was on Chase's property, so it belonged to the latter. It may be a trivial thing, yet Chase gets considerable mileage out of it. But if the rock possessed no special properties for translating, as Chase asserted, why would anyone want it anyway?

Chase's argument also has another, more serious deficiency. He said Smith did all this to translate the Gold Bible. These are Chase's words, dated April 1830: "I again asked him for the stone which he borrowed from me. He told me I should not have it, for 'I had use of it in translating the Bible.'"[12] Apparently, Chase is talking about the Book of Mormon, but the latter had at that time already been printed for nearly a year. Why would Joseph want to translate something already published?

One thing no one will ever know, including the most devout Latter-day Saint, is why Joseph needed a seer stone to interpret gold plates if he had the Urim and Thummim. The record indicates he used both, but it would be consistent to say that if we are working miracles, what does it matter whether the stone was made of granite, schist, or flint? Joseph says that when he looked into it, the stone assisted in translating the reformed Egyptian. It is a mystery Smith never clarified, and Brodie did not try.

As for Pomeroy Tucker, his main complaint in *Origin, Rise and*

Progress of the Mormon Church was that Smith had a remarkable and pretended vision. This is fair enough so far because Tucker has every right to give his opinion that the vision was pretended." But then he adds this: "Smith told a frightful story of the display of celestial pyrotechnics on the exposure to his view of the sacred book."[13] Since Tucker wasn't there, and Joseph says nothing about a frightful story of celestial pyrotechnics, where did the idea originate? Furthermore, since Tucker's *Origin, Rise and Progress* came out in 1867, Tucker is remembering back some forty years. This is not fatal, merely suspect. But non-Mormon John Gilbert, who printed the Book of Mormon for Grandin, has this to say about the above author: "Now, Tucker, in his work, he told many big things; nobody could believe his stories."[14]

The record shows that Tucker gave Howe a picture of Joseph "taking the plates from Mormon Hill" for use in his *Mormonism Unvailed*.[15] The picture shows a nearly nude female figure, yet Tucker described the angel Moroni as "a tall, slim, well-built, handsome man."[16]

More unkind words emanate from "intimate associate" Peter Cartwright: "Joseph Smith had a vast fund of low cunning." He was "Clumsy Joe," who was an "impudent desperado in morals."[17]

In 1830 there was no national association of editors and publishers to set ethical standards. Newspapers were in business to make money and to reflect the owner's views, with emphasis on the latter. The local newspapers in that day cared not a whit for impartial reporting.

The *Palmyra Reflector* was proof of that when it published what can only be called a parody (not a satire, for a satire comments on truth) titled *Pukei*. Not even the slightest attempt was made here to imitate objectivity.

As for the *Painesville Telegraph*, it printed a story sarcastically reviewing the Book of Mormon, with the title, "Its Divine Pretensions Exposed.[18]

But still, the casual reader has to wonder how so many nasty things can be said about one man; surely, there must be some thread of truth in it all. However, some of these concepts mentioned above originate not with the newspapers of the day but with Brodie herself. Let us see how she skillfully, or possibly ignorantly, uses all of the above to convince the reader she is going overboard to portray the scholarly and balanced truth. On a single page in her book, she makes the following assertions: (1) "Joseph's money digging is well established by the previous [1826] court record," and (2) "newspaper stories," and (3) "Hurlbut's affidavits . . . which can hardly be dismissed by the objective student."[19]

In another instance, Brodie admits that Hurlbut's affidavits were biased "but corroborated and supplemented"; yet she insists Joseph was an unsavory character based on Dogberry's editorials and Smith's own admissions in an 1826 court record.[20] She dismisses Lucy Mack Smith's *History of Joseph Smith* because everyone knows that Lucy was naive and protective of her special son.

Since the first two statements have been addressed, let us look at the idea that Lucy Mack Smith is naive. Brodie is entitled to any opinion she wishes but apparently she didn't read Lucy's chapter on traveling to Kirtland via the Lake Erie Canal. Lucy Mack's handling of teenagers becoming rowdy and out of control sounds rather sophisticated and, well, like the wisened mother of a large family.[21] But that is not the point. The point is that all Brodie has said on the subject is assertion based on misinformation. These statements parallel her "there is no record save gossip" statement.[22]

The reader can accept Brodie's allegations showing Smith to be a charlatan or, just as easily, trust a statement by Truman Madsen, who quotes a letter found in a Sevier County, Utah, attic. The letter expresses a family's great love for Joseph Smith because he was honest, upright, and such a hard worker. Madsen does not bother to give a footnote resource because he can't document its authenticity.[23] Yet it is precisely the sort of source Brodie seems willing to use if it serves her purpose. This isn't to say either source is correct, but we can obviously choose depending on our individual point of view.

While the many accounts of Joseph Smith's shiftless behavior might have been enough to convict him then or now in the court of public opinion in western New York, there were opposing testimonials from men who knew Joseph well, such as Brigham Young, Heber C. Kimball, Edward Partridge, Orson and Parley P. Pratt, and Wilford Woodruff. When Edward Partridge was investigating whether to join the Church that Joseph formed, the skeptical, highly successful hatter interviewed neighbors as to Smith's character and even examined the family's farm while they were gone to see if they employed habits of industry. The last thing the pious Partridge wanted was to be drawn into something disreputable or immoral. He said, as stated in his *Long Journal,* written in 1835, that there was no complaint from anyone "other than on the point of religion."[24]

Then, there are additional statements by others, which directly contradict the Chases, Tuckers, Cartwrights, and Ingersolls. One is by Thomas H. Taylor, an attorney who knew the Smiths in Palmyra: "They were very nice men. The only trouble was that they were ahead of people . . . they had the manhood to stand up for their convictions." Taylor said neighbors once dunked Joseph in a pond because they were so angry at him, but he would not rescind his story, presumably about religious beliefs. "Some way, he knew more than they did, and it made them mad."[25]

And there's this, from Orlando Saunders, another neighbor who knew the family in Palmyra: "They were very good people. He [Joseph] was a very good worker. They were the best family in the neighborhood in case of sickness." Saunders said that when his father died, the Smiths spent considerable time at the Saunders home trying to help them in time of need.[26]

From a non-Mormon writing to the *New York Herald* comes this: "Joseph Smith . . . is a man of the highest order of talent and great independence of character . . . firm in his integrity . . . devoted to his religion."[27]

A member of Congress writing to his wife after meeting Joseph Smith in Washington, D.C., said, "Everything he says is said in a manner to leave an impression that he is sincere. There is no levity, fanaticism, no want of dignity in his deportment."[28]

A writer to the *Weekly Bostonian* observed: "Joseph Smith knows no impediment . . . never halts in his course till he has accomplished his object. . . . He is a genius and a rare one."[29]

We also have this from William Smith, Joseph's brother: "In consequence of his vision, and his having the golden plates, and refusing to show them, a great persecution arose against the whole family, and he was compelled to remove into Pennsylvania with the plates, where he translated them by means of the Urim and Thummim (which he obtained with the plates) by the power of God. . . . We were all very much scoffed at and persecuted all the time while Joseph was receiving his visions and translating the plates. . . . Owing to the persecution of the religious world in consequence of Joseph's visions, his obtaining the plates and translating them, our neighbors conceived an antipathy against us, calling us all manner of names, such as 'money-diggers.'"[30]

Would not an objective Brodie have included these testimonial insights into the persecution suffered by the Smith family? This was the same William, incidentally, who Brodie accused of not believing in his brother's divine mission. William's statement does much to assist the reader in understanding why neighbors could hold the Smiths in high esteem prior to 1820 and then assail the family's character following Joseph's announced first vision.

Josiah Stoal and Martin Harris sought constantly for clues of dishonesty or laziness before committing time, money, and energy to Joseph's cause. The Smith family might be poor materially, as were many in the region—especially with a large family recently moved from Vermont—but the question is whether they were hard workers and morally upright citizens seeking to make an honest living. The answer seems to lie in whether you believed in Joseph's visions or not. If the answer is no, he is a fraud, and little good can be said about him. If the answer is yes, then he is tellng the truth and is a good citizen.

Historian Donna Hill suggests another slant: "It is puzzling why Joseph's claims of such a religious experience in his youth should arouse skepticism and hostility. An intense conversion experience is not uncommon during adolescence and this was recognized in Joseph's day."[31]

Apparently, some LDS historians can't even agree. Joseph's religious experience was unlike any other claimed since Stephen, who said he saw both God and Jesus Christ (Acts 7:55–56). Would Joseph have been railed on by local ministers had he only claimed inspiration? Isn't claiming to see God an entirely different matter?

In the pursuit of truth, it all depends on how it is presented. Joseph Smith did not stand on a downtown soapbox to convince the public he had witnessed visions, other than attesting to it in his official *History of the Church*. And that came about primarily to set the record straight, "owing to the many reports which have been put in circulation." Joseph adds, rather powerfully it would seem, that, "I had seen a vision; I knew it, and I knew that God knew it" (Joseph Smith–History 1:1, 25).

But contrast it with Dogberry's bombastic claim that the Book of Mormon was pirated from Solomon Spaulding: "A faithful account . . . undertaken with great reluctance . . . the truth, the whole truth."[32]

Of all Smith's detractors, however, perhaps the most objective account is by one who never knew him personally. Thomas Nelson, a minister of the Church of Scotland in 1946–47, well recognized the problems Mormon missionaries were causing among his native flock. At one point, Nelson postulated that Joseph Smith must be an epileptic, yet the minister had this to say: "The charge of his enemies is that it is merely a clever invention and fraud. But it does not touch the problem, for this charge does not explain how such an ill-educated man could produce so elaborate a system. This is a bigger problem than most people imagine. The elaborate system . . . still remains unexplained. . . . Perhaps the only theory that may explain the phenomenon is the psychological hypothesis of dissociated personality. It is suggested that people like Smith can absorb ideas they do not normally understand, and then in 'visions' or 'trances,' or under some self-hypnosis, can speak with apparent ease of ideas and expressions quite foreign to their usual intelligence."[33]

There is no conspicuous attempt to dissect Smith's religion or doctrine to examine its merits. Instead, going on the defensive, Nelson issues this warning: "If their missionaries should come here . . . we should remember their religion disregards the moral standards of the Christian gospel."[34]

This was late enough in the progress of Mormonism that polygamy is not an issue and Nelson does not elaborate on what moral standards are being disregarded by the Mormons. But he adds, "In the past, many gullible people have been induced to go out to Utah. . . . There is nothing wrong with Utah. I understand it is a well-doing and well-conducted state." But, cautions the minister, don't be gullible and go there. He gives it as his opinion that Joseph Smith couldn't have been a prophet because he was an unlearned boy. "God picks the best to do his best work," the minister proclaims.[35]

To be true, Nelson has an advantage over the Chases and Ingersolls, for Nelson could see the fruits of Joseph's claims. All Smith's detractors in Palmyra seemed certain that but a few scant fanatics would buy the Book of Mormon or follow those who preached it to Kirtland, Missouri, Nauvoo, and the Great Basin. Dogberry and Howe might be surprised today to see what has transpired from such humble trappings in Palmyra.

Nelson has also seen enough in the passion and intensity of the LDS missionary program to worry him about ecclesiastical competition. He did not dismiss its effectiveness, as had earlier detractors. By the early 1900s, the British Isles in particular were seeing thousands of Mormon missionaries reaping thousands of converts. Rev. Nelson had, of course, noticed.

But let's take a look at another kind of detractor, Illinois governor Thomas Ford. This man was placed in an admittedly difficult situation. He didn't want to bother with the Mormons, but his constituents demanded it. Abraham Lincoln, another Illinois product, would later say his answer to the Mormons was his father's way of handling an old stump on the landscape: Ignore it. Dig around it. Besides, Lincoln had the Civil War to worry about.

But Ford found himself in a civil war of his own. He was under heavy fire if he used his heart and tried to sympathize with the Mormons but was threatened by an angry bloc of non-Mormon voters if he didn't use his head and renounce them. Of course, with the Nauvoo Charter and Legion, and Joseph running for president, Joseph became too conspicuous to ignore. Ford did what many politicians did by trying to please both sides. Thus, he pleased neither.[36]

Indeed, in vacillating about trying not to anger one side any more than the other, Ford became afraid to do anything lest it was wrong. Few of any party or religious persuasion could find much bold or courageous leadership action in his game plan. He let the mob have its way, promising safety to Joseph and his captive cohorts in Carthage, and then let them be murdered in his absence. Ford then wrote a history of Illinois intended to vindicate himself, but he succeeded only in showing his impotence.[37] LDS historian George Q. Cannon put it this way: "Gov. Ford was an imbecile."[38]

Once the Mormon leader was not there to defend himself, Ford wrote: "It is not to be supposed that the pretended prophet practiced the tricks of a common impostor; that he was a dark and gloomy person, with a long beard." No, said Ford, Smith "dressed like a dandy, and at times drank like a sailor and swore like a pirate . . . he always quailed before power and was arrogant to weakness.

"His leaders . . . [those of the 'first division'] embraced a numerous class of broken-down, unprincipled men of talents, to be found in every country, who, bankrupt in character and fortune, had nothing to lose by deserting the known religions and carving out a new one of their own. They were mostly [not all?] infidels, who, holding all religions in derision, believed they had as good a right as Christ or Mahomet . . . to create one for themselves; and if they could impose it upon mankind, to live upon the labors of their dupes."[39]

Ford labels Smith's successor, Brigham Young, as "a cunning but vulgar man."[40] What is meant by either term is not known. Ford says nothing of Col. Thomas L. Kane, who praised the Mormons and their industry. A non-Mormon, Kane saw the Saints as a sincere and prayerful but downtrodden people to be admired.[41] It is difficult to realize that he and Ford are talking of the same cross-section of humanity.

Ford also gave his version of how the Eight Witnesses could have gained their testimonies by coercion from Smith "to use their faith"; but we can't fault Ford too much on this because he apparently had picked up some hearsay and earnestly wanted to believe Joseph's version couldn't be true.[42]

Gov. Ford knew what his constituents wanted to hear and he said it, at least to their faces. He sought public approval any way he could get it. The tragedy of it is that Ford knew better; he knew Joseph and the Mormon leaders were not as he described them in his history. A letter from John Bernhisel apprised Ford of how much Joseph meant to the Saints, but Ford apparently ignored it.[43] The governor was, at the least, morally feeble and, at worst, lacking in integrity when currying favor with anti-Mormons.

Ford could have easily made his point and avoided linking Joseph to deity, a thing apparently impossible in Ford's mind, by simply writing that he thought the self-styled prophet Joseph Smith to be a forceful but deluded leader who tried to improve the Church of Christ by claiming revelations for it. And he could have said that Joseph built Nauvoo by some sort of inner inspiration, but that his people were driven from their beautiful city due to the unpopularity of his newfound religion.[44]

The above would have sufficed. Many non-Mormons could have accepted it.

Enoch Bartlett Tripp, who came to Nauvoo in 1846 from Maine to take advantage of the imminent Mormon migration and buy up their furniture and goods at cheap prices, said he was warned in Carthage that a gentile would be shot on sight. He expected to see dead men lying in Nauvoo gutters. But after spending a few days in Nauvoo, he wrote in his diary that he thought the Mormons were "much lied about."[45] Their industrious character was much to be emulated. Tripp joined the Church two days before it was expelled from Nauvoo.

According to N. B. Lundwall's *Fate of the Persecutors of the Prophet Joseph Smith*, Ford's funeral was attended by almost no one, and his grave remained unkempt for decades. In other words, Ford died a lonely and forgotten man.[46] We can contrast that with the funeral of Joseph and Hyrum, wherein many wept openly.

Lundwall's book has many statements by people who had moved to Utah and told of confessions of people who had conspired to kill Joseph and Hyrum. Many of these conspirators suffered terrible deaths, according to Lundwall.

One such account may be accurate in every detail but contains no particular significance: Wolves dug up a named persecutor's grave, scattering his bones to the desert wind. The same happened to many good men and women buried in shallow graves between Winter Quarters and Great Salt Lake Valley. This is no indication of anything, save perhaps that someone needed to return and dig a deeper grave.

Anyone claiming as much as Joseph Smith is bound to invite harshly opposing forces. Consider Doctrine and Covenants 110. Here Joseph claims that in 1836 he and Oliver Cowdery saw the following heavenly messengers: Jesus Christ, Moses, Elias, and Elijah. An incredible epiphany indeed! What was the purpose for this glorious vision? Section 110 says Christ accepted and blessed the Kirtland Temple, the first temple in the claimed restoration of all things. Others brought the keys of their various dispensations so that the restoration might proceed in an orderly manner. All had a specific purpose in coming, as Smith explained it.

Little middle ground is possible. It becomes ever more obvious that Joseph is either a monumental fraud or a modern-day prophet like unto Paul of old. It is no wonder Joseph encountered enemies determined to explode his extraordinary claims. But since Joseph and Oliver were the only ones there in some cases, we must apply an after-the-fact objective test, as the Christian world did with Paul: determine where their claims led them. This question must also be asked: If Christ's true church were on the earth, could it be here without its leaders claiming so? Not likely. Thus, while the claims of Joseph and Oliver may be extraordinary, they could also be labeled internally consistent.

But Oliver Cowdery and most of the other witnesses were not detractors. They were defectors. It has been well documented that Oliver, Martin Harris, and David Whitmer firmly upheld their witness testimonies to their deaths. All of their reaffirmations are intriguing in that they could have smeared Joseph into annihilation. The question even non-Mormon historians are still asking is: Why didn't they? Only one hint of collusion, and the game is over.

Ponder the damage that could be done by any of the witnesses who might say: "We got together in the woods one day and decided that if we asserted to see a heavenly messenger, and claimed to put out a book this messenger helped us find, we could all get rich and famous." Or, "Joseph Smith thought it up himself, but now that Joseph has rejected and abused us so, we can let the cat (spirit, toad, or whatever) out of the bag."

It would all be over as quickly as it began. Some would say that admitting collusion or fraud would have hurt the witnesses as much as it hurt Joseph. Let's analyze that assumption. Take David Whitmer. All he had to do in Richmond, Missouri, was make one overture against Joseph Smith as a prophet or claim the Book of Mormon as fake, and Whitmer would have been an instant hero to the Missourians. David had left the Church and was associating with but few members by the late 1830s. His neighbors were not Mormons. He had estranged himself from most of his old associates. His peers now were the same Missourians who ran the Mormons out of their state. They naturally tried to get David to change his story but to no avail. Credit Whitmer with the courage of his convictions.

Yet David did associate with the church of James J. Strang, who claimed to be the successor to Joseph Smith. After Brigham Young led the Saints west in 1846, the record shows Whitmer sought spiritual meaning for a time with Strang's church, even as a leader in that sect. Did Whitmer claim revelations for Strang? Yes, and he later solemnly declared that he had made a mistake.[47]

When Oliver Cowdery went into law practice in Michigan, he would certainly anticipate clearer sailing if he disassociated himself with the gold plates. He did not do so.

Martin Harris vacillated into and out of many churches after the Mormons left him in Kirtland. Interestingly, the only thing he stuck to was his account of being a witness to the gold plates. Martin also went on a mission to England for the church James J. Strang founded, but Harris obviously did not find what he was looking for with Strang and ultimately chose to join the Saints in Utah.

So why did these men so close to Joseph choose to defect from him and his work? This will always be a matter of conjecture, but there are plausible answers. Thomas B. Marsh and Orson Hyde succumbed to the physical threat of Missouri mob violence in the 1837–38 period, and indeed, it was a time to try men's souls. Col. Thomas L. Kane, who befriended the Saints in their darkest hours after the expulsion from Nauvoo, told the Philadelphia Historical Society that the persecution of the Mormons had the effect of purging from them, before the trek to the Salt Lake Valley, all fence-sitters and lukewarm dissidents. If so, it rid the Church of mugwumps such as Marsh, once president of the Church's Quorum of the Twelve, and Hyde, an apostle who told Missouri governor Lilburn Boggs that the Mormons were seeking to overthrow, burn, or sack Independence and Richmond, among other Missouri cities.[48] There followed the governor's famed Extermination Order. Vilified for this clearly unconstitutional edict, Boggs might have some justification if thinking that Marsh and Hyde, two high-profile Mormons, were telling him the truth.

Both men later rejoined the Church, but the damage was done. There were other defectors, such as Ezra Booth from an earlier period, who did the Church a favor to leave it, for he would have done more damage as a member than as an announced enemy.

The defections of the Three Witnesses, and most of the Eight Witnesses, was different. All expressed love for, and defended, the

Restoration and its concept. They were not mad at the Church, just Joseph Smith. Take John Whitmer. After writing a history of the Church as commanded from 1831 to 1838, John was excommunicated for refusing to turn his history over to authorities for possible corrections, seemingly something any church would require. After all, it wasn't a history of John Whitmer but of the church he represented. Other charges included alleged embezzlement of Church funds. But Whitmer affirmed to his dying day, even among non-Mormon enemies, that he had seen and hefted the golden plates. In effect, this confirmed a belief in Joseph Smith as a prophet.[49]

Much speculation exists as to why men such as David Whitmer would leave the Church, but many of these men had unrealistic expectations. They appeared to anticipate not so much a repeat of the hardships experienced by the early Christians as they did rewards.

Martin Harris was all but forgotten, never holding any church position. Perhaps Joseph grew weary of Martin's importuning for special favors, such as his wife seeing the 116 pages, which later vanished. Maybe Smith simply wanted to build a broader base and bring in more brethren, give them positions of leadership to build their faith, and promote the Church's credibility in the eyes of the world. It is possible also that the Whitmers and Harrises were not willing to shoulder the particular duties Joseph had in mind for them.

Another matter that must be squarely addressed is that the language of the Doctrine and Covenants (see sections 57–59) was interpreted by the body of Saints to mean that Zion in Missouri was to be an imminent place of peace, a haven for the Saints, a refuge from the turmoil in New York and Ohio. It didn't happen, of course. Some have explained that the word *Zion* means all of America. Maybe so, but in this regard it seems a cop-out. Doctrine and Covenants 57:1–3 is explicit in pointing to Jackson County as site of the new Zion. Seeking much-needed refuge from persecution in Ohio, the Saints would naturally believe it meant within their own lifetimes.

While some historians blame the Saints themselves for their expulsion from Missouri (certainly they were not without blame in proclaiming themselves heaven-sent), Alexander Majors, who lived for a time in that state while the Mormons were there, saw the old residents as the main problem. "Missouri was settled by a poor and illiterate people. It was considered blasphemous . . . to claim one had met angels. I was there and the sole reason the Mormons were evicted was their religion. But whatever the Mormons obtained was by their own industry. No one found them guilty of committing any crime."[50]

From this it could be concluded that the Mormons were not going to fit in no matter what they did. Missouri was determined they could not stay, but some began to blame Joseph for bringing them there and for what they suffered.[51]

B. H. Roberts has a point when he explains how the Saints escaped the devastation wreaked on Jackson County during the Civil War of 1861–64 and afterward.[52] If the Saints had remained there, they'd have surely suffered terribly in the middle of a state caught midway between North and South. But that didn't change the dark hours of despair experienced by Church members in Missouri during the 1830s, climaxed with Boggs's extermination order.

When the Saints were driven out, convinced by 1838 that there was no hope in their lifetimes of any return to Zion, it caused a considerable loss of faith, a loss seemingly more so in Joseph than in the Church.[53] By this time, persecution was so rife that Sampson Avard and his Danites were threatening to drive out all bad apples in the ranks. Danites were also credited with secretly killing church enemies, although accusations were more rampant than any proof. Sidney Rigdon's salt sermon also forced many to decide once and for all whose side they were on.[54]

Confusion and indecision about where to turn for survival took its toll on many previously devoted members, including W. W. Phelps. He had been a stalwart during the burning of the Mormon press in Independence but decided he'd had enough. As history records, however, Phelps returned to the fold in a dark hour at Nauvoo, humbly seeking forgiveness; he lived a life of service thereafter in the Church.

Yet it was a difficult time while Joseph was incarcerated in the Liberty Jail, resulting in a lack of conspicuous earthly leadership to guide the Saints' troubled minds. It is not so surprising that many hearts quailed. Significantly, some did not, as witnessed by devoted members Parley P. Pratt and Hyrum Smith, who defended their beliefs.[55] Why not dwell on the fidelity of some rather than the infidelity of the others? Cowdery remained second elder in name for more than a decade but never held any official position in the hierarchy. Nevertheless, he did hold his peace until about 1838, when he began to find fault with Joseph as previously explained in his excommunication. How he returned to the Church, despite accusing Joseph of transgression, has been told herein; but it is interesting that many of Oliver's contemporaries faulted Cowdery, not Joseph. For example, George Hinkle said in 1838 that when he asked Oliver if the charge against Smith was true, "He gave me to understand that it was false. I bear this report for the good of Joseph Smith, Jr."[56] It was also reported that Cowdery "was unvirtuous and indulged in impurity." With no further details, is it possible Cowdery was involved in the very thing of which he accused Joseph?

Jacob Gates, in a sworn affidavit dated 3 December 1915, said that in an interview with Cowdery, the latter told him, "I felt wicked." He then reaffirmed his witness: "It was no dream, no vain imagination of the mind."[57]

Fawn Brodie never shows her agenda more clearly than when she says, "From the moment of his arrival in Missouri, he [Joseph] did not rest until he had seen Oliver Cowdery and John and David Whitmer cut off from the Church. Their expulsion left him with no rivals of any stature."[58] So, according to Brodie, Joseph's plan was to ruthlessly rule alone. The statement is not only untrue—Brigham Young, Edward Partridge, Sidney Rigdon, and many other men of stature yet remained—but also shallow. Joseph needed all the witnesses to the Book of Mormon at his side now just as much as ever, maybe more so with persecution closing in and with only two of the eleven witnesses remaining in the Church: his brother Hyrum and his father, Joseph Sr.

Enemies of the Church can say what they will about Cowdery, but his most enduring statement was this: "These were days never to be forgotten—to sit under the sound of a voice dictated by the inspiration of heaven."[59] The bottom line on Oliver Cowdery is simply that he came back to the Church he and Joseph were instrumental in founding.

Harris is accused of telling his wife that she should "shush up" because his association with Smith and the golden plates just might some day bring pecuniary advantage to them. (Maybe Martin wasn't so naive after all; it is probably the only answer he could give the woman to satisfy her objections.) It is recorded elsewhere how Harris rejoined the Church and, in Utah, reaffirmed to his death that his testimony was true about the angel and the golden plates.

David Whitmer did not rejoin the Mormon Church but reaffirmed that Joseph Smith was called of God to translate the Book of Mormon. He said Joseph drifted into error, although he never gave details, following the translation when "he took power unto himself."[60] Whitmer felt that Sidney Rigdon might have had an influence on Joseph in saying that Joseph was no longer as humble after the Kirtland period. Or could it be Whitmer was jealous of Rigdon, who, after all, had nothing to do with bringing forth the Book of Mormon? Nor was Rigdon called on to face the early ridicule and sufferings of the witnesses.

Let's look at something now that Brodie never did relate: the warnings Joseph gave two of the witnesses that they were about to lose their Church membership. Doesn't it seem strange, if there were a conspiracy of some sort among Joseph, David, and Oliver, that Joseph would tell them this:

> Dear Brethren—Oliver Cowdery has been in transgression . . . I trust that he will yet humble himself and magnify his calling, but if he should not, the Church will

> soon be under the necessity of raising their hands against him. . . .
>
> David Whitmer, Leonard Rich, and others have been in transgression, but we hope that they may be humble and ere long make satisfaction to the Church, otherwise, they cannot retain their standing. . . .
>
> Joseph Smith, Jun.[61]

Does this sound like something a man would do if he were afraid of angering a coconspirator? Obviously, Joseph Smith is standing on principle, just as we would expect a prophet to do. He seems to have no concern whether Cowdery or Whitmer might become angered against him. At least Joseph has nothing to fear if these witnesses bore an honest testimony in the first place. If not, he has everything to fear. As history records, Joseph never wavered at cutting anyone off from the Church who was not living up to its standards.

But we must also look at some hard facts: Harris, Whitmer, and Cowdery joined other churches after they were excommunicated.

Let's examine the facts. It is true that all three explored the claims of other leaders after becoming disaffected from Joseph. But as Brigham Young foresaw, William McLelland's church, as well as the churches created by others claiming authority, including James J. Strang, came to naught. "They will not prosper," Brigham had predicted.[62] Whitmer realized this within a year and then totally repudiated McLelland's claims as being in error. Note that Whitmer never did declare Joseph's claims to be in error; he simply had a falling out with the man.

Cowdery joined the Methodist Protestant Church in Tiffin, Ohio, and was listed for a time as a secretary; yet he spent most of his time there in contact with the Saints to determine how he might rejoin The Church of Jesus Christ of Latter-day Saints. Stanley Gunn's *Oliver Cowdery, Second Elder and Scribe* carries many pages of Cowdery's letters to Phineas Young about where he might find the Mormon Church on its march west in order to rejoin. It would appear in these letters that his pride, helped along by a feeling of guilt for separating from the Church in the first place, hindered Oliver for a time. Consider this letter to Phineas Young, of which the author has a copy in Cowdery's handwriting, obtained from a descendent of Young's. It was sent by Oliver in 1846 while in Ohio: "I have never asked to be excused . . . of my fault or wrong . . . for of these there are many. . . . I have been sensitive on this subject, I admit; but I ought to be so—you would be, under the circumstances, had you stood in the presence of John, with our departed Joseph, to receive the Lesser Priesthood—and in the presence of Peter, to receive the Greater."[63]

Where does Cowdery leave any doubt of his absolute and sincere testimony?

It is well known that Martin Harris followed McLelland and his claims for a time but, determining that they were empty, returned to the fold to which he originally belonged. Harris wrote to Hanna B. Emerson of Smithfield, Utah Territory, in January 1871: "No man ever heard me deny the truth of the Book of Mormon nor the organization of the Latter-day Saint Church under the administration of Joseph Smith, the prophet whom the Lord reared up."[64]

These men never denied their witness testimony and even when they had differences with Joseph, they declared that they knew him to be a prophet of God. They might have felt Joseph was growing too big for them, or that they were no longer important to him, or perhaps were even jealous of him, but they did not deny the only important fact: their testimonies of the divine origin of the Book of Mormon through the prophetic calling of Joseph Smith.

In a portrait in Brodie's book of Joseph in full-dress Nauvoo Legion uniform, it might be said that he looked proud. It would be extreme folly to judge him based upon an artist's interpretation. Further, in examining the speeches Joseph gave at Nauvoo, there is no charge of arrogance, although some enemies linked him with being a pretender. He acted as if he was in charge of the town, under God, and he ran it that way. He called followers to repentance without fear or favor; if a chastised follower was himself proud, he might feel hurt, resent Joseph, and say so. But even prominent non-Mormon visitors such as Josiah Quincy did not quibble about Joseph's ability to lead and rule his followers by unwavering principle.

There were some in Nauvoo who plotted against Joseph's life; some remained resentful about destruction of the *Nauvoo Expositor*.[65] This newspaper, of which there was only one edition, printed what church leaders termed lies; it was a public nuisance. But destroying it was clearly against the First Amendment, which protected freedom of the press. Joseph was called to task for this incident by Gov. Ford, and there is no doubt it stirred a nest of hornets against the Mormon prophet.

Yet it appears the assassination faction remained a small minority. Plots against his life in Nauvoo failed mainly because Joseph had so many loyal friends.

David Whitmer always emphasized that no one should discredit the Book of Mormon anymore than they would the Bible because of King David's transgressions. Whitmer didn't, of course, ever accuse Joseph of sins as serious as those committed by King David; Whitmer seemed to simply be making the point that he knew Joseph to be a prophet in translating the gold plates, whatever shortcomings came later.

Perhaps the most poignant thing Whitmer ever said about his leader in the early days of the Church was this: "Joseph was a religious and straightforward man. He had to be, for he was illiterate. He had to trust in God."[66]

Some have complained that Joseph was not illiterate if he was so eloquent in writing the Revised Version of the New Testament. However, that was in 1831, well after the period of receiving the gold plates and translating the Book of Mormon (1823–28) that Whitmer was talking about.

It was said in the *Palmyra Reflector* that Whitmer that admitted he saw the plates "but not the angel."[67] Did Whitmer himself make this statement? No. It was not only by a hearsay third party but also by "our informant," which could be anyone.[68] No sincere historian would dare touch the "our informant" statement as face-value truth. LDS historian Richard Anderson points out that Brodie's source is "an editor's version of his informant's version" of what Whitmer allegedly said. This isn't to say the *Sentinel* editor wasn't sincere, for anyone who plays the parlor whisper game knows how things like that work, particularly if the whisperers have a preconceived bias.

No one reaffirmed his testimony of the angel's visit more vigorously and often as did David Whitmer. In 1881 Whitmer bore his testimony of this event by writing in the March 25 *Richmond Conservator*, "I have always adhered to that testimony. That no man be misled . . . I do again affirm the truth of all my statements."[69]

Later, Whitmer was visited by Joseph F. Smith, Orson Pratt, and others and told them: "He [the angel] stood before us. Our testimony, as recorded in the Book of Mormon, is strictly and absolutely true."[70]

In August 1883, the much-traveled James H. Hart stopped in to see David Whitmer in Richmond and wrote an epic poem that he stated was read and approved by Whitmer. It is too long to repeat here, but an excerpt from it reads:

No tongue can tell the glory and power
That was revealed to us in that blest hour.
The plates of brass and gold the angel took
And placed them before us like an open book.
We saw the fine engravings on them too
And heard the voice declare the book is true.
No power on earth could from our minds efface
The glorious visions of this trysting place.
We've done, as then commanded we should do
And testified that the Mormon book is true.[71]

Fine poetry or no, the message is clear from still another testifier who talked with David Whitmer personally and found the man as firm in his testimony as ever.

In July 1885, James H. Moyle, who said David told him he believed as firmly as ever that Joseph Smith was a prophet of God, visited Whitmer. Whitmer confirmed to Moyle that he saw an angel and heard him say that the book "was translated correctly." David tells of being in the forest by a fallen log and that "it happened in the presence of Joseph Smith, Oliver Cowdery and myself."[72]

In 1886 Whitmer said to Church member Edward Stevenson, "As sure as the sun shines, and I live, just so surely did the angel appear unto me and Joseph Smith and I heard his voice and did see the angel standing before us."[73]

On his deathbed at 5:30 P.M. on 22 January 1888 and before many witnesses, including his family and his attending physician, a Dr. Buchanan, who affirmed that David was "of sound mind," as written in the January 25 *Richmond Democrat*, Whitmer said: "I want to say to you all that the Bible and the record of the Nephites are true, so you can say that you have heard me bear my testimony on my deathbed."[74]

While it would be difficult to imagine how anyone could refute this testimony, one tried, charging that Whitmer was a drinker. The *Richmond Conservator* of 25 March 1881, answered this way: "We the undersigned citizens of Richmond, Ray County, certify that we know him [David Whitmer] to be a man of the highest integrity and of undoubted truth and veracity."

Brodie has another charge. In her 1971 "Supplement," she says Joseph first called the messenger of the gold plates Nephi before later making it Moroni" in his 1838 history. This would be a serious mistake on Smith's part if he actually said it, for he claims the angel announced to him three times in one night that he was Moroni. Joseph couldn't forget this anymore than he could forget he had a vision in the first place. But Brodie claims Joseph first called the messenger of 21 September 1823 by the name of Nephi.[75]

Brodie also has a reference to Peter Ingersoll making a claim that Joseph used the wrong name, which she says is "found on page 411." Yet on page 411, there is no such reference. This might well have been an editing error, however, for which she was not responsible. There is a reference to Ingersoll on page 432 in appendix A, but there is nothing there about Nephi. Is this an oversight? Did Peter Ingersoll make such a statement, or didn't he? We can't tell from Brodie's reference.

Yet we find there was a mistake made in *Times and Seasons* referring to Joseph's nighttime messenger as Nephi, an error mentioned by B. H. Roberts in his *Comprehensive History of the Church.*[76]

Who was the editor of the *Times and Seasons* on that occasion? If it was Joseph, Brodie has a point. If not, it is a mistake anyone could carelessly make. Brodie also cites Lucy Mack Smith as referring to the angel as Nephi in her writings.[77] But a one-word error might happen in a book edited by someone else, as was Lucy Mack's *History of Joseph Smith.*[78] It could even be what is commonly called a typographical error, or typo.

Many embarrassing mistakes, or typos, occur in newspapers and advertisements despite seemingly meticulous proofreading. One occurred in an advertisement for a man who was to be the recipient of a benefit dinner. In explaining his need for financial help following an illness, the ad said he was the father of "your" children instead of the father of "four" children. The effect was not one desired by the fund-raising sponsors. This is a simple slip of the fingers. A more serious kind can occur when an editor is thinking one thing and writes another.

Chances are that it was not a writer or editor who made this mistake but a mechanical operator who allowed his fingers to slip on the keys and, in the process, crated a typo. The same could have easily happened in the *Times and Seasons* and *Millennial Star* articles. If so, it would be a serious error, yet the work of man, not God. An error in a periodical put out by Mormons is not the same as an error in the Book of Mormon itself.

Typos or errors could even exist in Brodie's book. She admits to inevitable errors in a letter to Dale Morgan, dated 24 March 1945.[79] From this it might be concluded that errors could happen to anyone, even those complaining about others making errors.

11
What Can We Believe?

Brodie provides clues time and again, even if she hadn't told us in the preface, that she didn't entertain with an open mind any possibility of Joseph Smith being a prophet. To reiterate, she could have gained a measure of credibility with the words, "This is in favor of Smith being a true prophet, this against." But such words do not appear. She takes the stand that she can prove he is not. As indicated, the best she can do is to prove herself an eloquent novelist and a bankrupt historian.

She won many awards from people who seemingly didn't want Smith to be a prophet anyway. One was from Bernard DeVoto, an announced atheist born, like Brodie, in Ogden, Utah, who noted that Brodie "has written as a detached, modern intelligence, grounded in naturalism, rejecting the supernatural." As Hugh Nibley suggests, who is better qualified to speak on religion than the one who never had any interest in learning about it?[1]

Most assuredly, Brodie rejected the supernatural. But in the process, she was necessarily forced into conjecture, which is not considered a legitimate tool of the historian. Jack Nash of Oakdale, California, says he studied Brodie's penchant for speculation while working on a Ph.D. in history at the University of California, Berkeley. "She was heavy into conjecture not only in her 'history' of Joseph Smith but Thomas Jefferson as well."[2] Nash said in a June 2002 interview that his research showed her biography of Jefferson to be strongly panned as creative history. Yet those critics "had little to say when she used the same creativity on Joseph Smith."[3]

I avoid bringing in Brodie's *Thomas Jefferson: An Intimate History* for the same reason a court judge won't allow testimony of a suspect's past life. Brodie's *Jefferson* is not on trial here. But Nash, an LDS historian, makes an interesting observation in comparing critiquing procedures. If it is wrong for a historian to use conjecture instead of documented fact with Jefferson, the same should also be true with Joseph Smith.

Granted, in moments of fictional fantasy, Brodie scintillated. Take, for example, this depiction of new Church members: "Converts would roll along the floor to the Church door and out onto the frozen ground in a masochistic frenzy. Some would mount stumps to preach to imaginary congregations in unknown tongues; others, making apish grimaces, would speed across the fields, returning with revelations that they swore they had copied from pieces of parchment hanging in the night sky."[4]

No evidence of the above exists in any LDS literature. But it is a nice touch, picturesque and easy to visualize. It could have even happened that way in an instance or two in the LDS Church, although Brodie adds that it was a hallmark primarily of other religions, particularly a few Pentecostals, not the Mormons. That it didn't happen in any account save Brodie's makes no difference to a writer with such a rich imagination.

There was such a thing in the early LDS Church as speaking in tongues, but Brodie does not understand this phenomenon referred to in the Book of Acts, and to be fair, most modern-day Mormons don't either. It is just as well to acknowledge that it occurred in the early church and try to understand that it had some purpose in communicating at that time.

As historian David Whittaker sums it up, Brodie's book *No Man Knows My History* does not succeed as a historical biography—it succeeds as art.[5] Brodie shows her fictional agenda even more clearly in the following statements:

- "He [Joseph] saw gold in every odd-shaped hill."[6] Was this meant to assert that he sought the gold plates only for money?

Cannot she even give him credit for trying to implement a new religion?

• Smith: "You have prayed me here."[7] Despite the fact that Joseph tells Newell K. Whitney what Newell has been doing for the past several days in praying for Joseph's presence, Brodie chooses to ignore the remark. It is a coincidence. It wholly disarms Whitney. That's it? The only explanation is there is no explanation? Merely naturalism at work?

• Brodie tells us, in effect, that Joseph knows nothing about the concept of the United Order, that it is the work of Rigdon; yet it is so important in the Book of Acts in the that people were struck dead for mocking it. She asserts that Joseph couldn't possibly be following the will of deity in the United Order because he got the idea from Sidney.[8] But even if Joseph made it up, he must be consistent in restoring all things that God wanted restored from biblical times. If this were the goal, why wouldn't Joseph want to include such a conspicuous commandment from the Bible?

It is true that the United Order failed in the Mormon Church several times, including in Utah, but neither did it last long in Christ's primitive Church. Under the concept of moral agency, not even God could make anyone live it who didn't want to. Certainly mere mortal Joseph Smith could not. If it didn't spring from within the human breast, it would be of no efficacy to a higher power.

• Jesus sought a higher kingdom, while "Joseph only sought one on Earth."[9] What does Fawn Brodie know about what Jesus sought? Is she an expert on Jesus Christ? And how does she know that Joseph definitely did not intend his teachings for a hereafter? What were all the commandments in the Doctrine and Covenants, even as fiction, if not hope for a better life in the next existence? Of course, Joseph had to be concerned about this life as well, or his teachings would fall on deaf ears. So would Christ's. In this, Brodie shows her ignorance of the Bible to which she, nevertheless, makes frequent reference.

• Joseph engaged in "crystal gazing, an old profession."[10] Seer stones, Urim and Thummim, crystal ball—they may all be the same to the anti-Christian, but they are not interchangeable among Christian followers. While there is an element of magic in Brodie's eyes, a crystal ball to Christians is the tool of a fraudulent seance medium; the Urim and Thummim is a tool of Christ. It is as plain as reading the Old Testament.

• One of Brodie's crowning research achievements seemed to be ferreting out a statement by Brigham Young that Joseph Smith "might get drunk every day of the week" but he "was still a prophet."[11] It does not apparently occur to Brodie that Young frequently used such language to emphasize a point. Here he was trying to point out that if Joseph was a prophet relaying the word of God, he should be listened to, regardless of whatever human weaknesses we might find in him. Obviously, even if he occasionally imbibed hard liquor, and there is no indication he did, Joseph didn't get drunk every day of the week.

One glaring act of omission in Brodie's thesis, and that of many critics, is how the teachings promulgated by Joseph Smith elevated the lives of his followers. Take this scenario as explained by Parley P. Pratt: After Missouri judge Austin King held trials in which Mormon witnesses were ignored, or even arrested on the spot, resulting in months of imprisonment for a host of innocent LDS leaders, King condescended to interview Pratt in jail. Apparently, King felt a need to calm a guilty conscience, said Pratt, for the judge could not look him (Pratt) in the eye, spoke in a voice barely audible, and repeatedly hung his head. Pratt said, "The looks of guilt and misery portrayed in his countenance . . . bespoke more misery than we had suffered during our confinement. I actually pitied him in my heart."[12]

Obviously, Joseph's teachings, with all the earmarks of being divinely inspired, gave his followers strength they had not previously possessed. Science may ignore this, as did Brodie, because it is a difficult thing to measure. But our entire justice system, with tradition-rooted centuries before the *Mayflower*, trusted in testimony of men who put their hand on the Bible and swore they were telling the truth. Many other testimonies besides Pratt's were given about gaining strength beyond earthly experience:

Brigham Young, Heber C. Kimball, Wilford Woodruff, Edward Partridge, and Lyman Wight likewise testified. How can they all be ignored?

Brodie makes monumental claims in many areas that she cannot possibly support, including the entire hypnotism business. And then there is this: "Joseph conjured up a vision they would never forget."[13] How is that done by a professional magician, let alone by a person in his early twenties who has never been known to practice magic, or even read books on the subject?

William Smith, as Joseph's brother living in the same house, is the perfect control factor. He was angry several times in his younger years at Joseph for trying to impose religion on him—angry enough to strike and injure Joseph. Yet he never tried to get back at his brother in a way that would have been the most destructive of all: expose Joseph's magic tricks to the world. Rather, William declared to the world shortly before his death that he believed from the beginning, as did the entire family, that Joseph was divinely inspired in bringing forth the Book of Mormon.[14]

In fact, Brodie's insistence that William didn't believe in Joseph because Joseph attacked him physically, causing great consternation in the family, is a perfect example of Brodie's agenda run amok. She is so blinded in trying to prove Joseph a charlatan that she cannot see how kindly and patiently, in a Christian manner, Joseph deals with his younger brother.

William admitted he had wild oats to sow; he confessed his mistakes; he sought humbly for Joseph's forgiveness. William said, "I was quite wild and inconsiderate, paying no attention to religion of any kind." But he added, "We [the entire family] believed all he [Joseph] said."[15]

Yet Brodie equates this family squabble with William, calling Joseph a false prophet.[16] To imply this is grossly misleading. Brodie tells us William said he hoped Joseph would never escape his enemies: "If I had the disposing of my brother . . . I would have hung him years ago."[17]

In a responsible newspaper, this in-family moment of anger,

later recanted, would have been considered a nonstory—certainly not what Brodie made of it. Joseph enters this in his *History of the Church*: "This day [18 December 1835] received the following from Brother William Smith; 'Brother Joseph: . . . I am unworthy to be called one [brother] . . . after coming to myself . . . I feel sorry for what I have done and humbly ask your forgiveness.'"

Joseph's reply was several pages long, but he finishes with a prayer of great compassion for his younger brother that "all blessings be restored, and the past be forgotten forever."[18] Rather than an indictment against Joseph as Brodie makes it out to be, the document emerges as a positive statement in behalf of Joseph's character.

William's writings in 1883 also reveal another side of the Smiths than that portrayed by the Hurlbut affidavits: a loving, close-knit farm household that, while not blessed with material wealth, was united often in a sincere worship of God. Family prayer was routine. The testimony given by William indicates strongly a family receiving rich spiritual blessings, exhibiting a strong faith in a higher power, and at one time seeking guidance to know which church to join.[19]

Other places exist where Brodie is plainly in serious error despite her "thorough" research and subsequent accolades for "detached objectivity." A few such places not mentioned previously include:

- She has Joseph not denying responsibility for the Danite actions led by Sampson Avard.[20] She says Joseph only mildly reprimanded Avard, as if Joseph condoned his actions generally. In reality, here is what Joseph said about this enemy of the Church: "Satan was no less busy in striving to stir up mischief in the camp of the Saints: and among the most conspicuous of his willing devotees was one Dr. Sampson Avard . . . to form a secret combination at the expense and the overthrow of the Church."[21] A mild reprimand? It is another case of Brodie seeking not only to distort the truth but also to turn it around 180 degrees to her own preconceived bias.
- She says that historians trying to endorse the Book of

Mormon didn't realize that the crucifix, or cross, originated with the Spaniards rather than the aborigines of South America.[22] She provides no valid evidence against the many archaeologists who are still trying to explain what a crucifix or cross was doing in ancient America. Or the expectations of the return of the white, bearded god the Indians called Quetzalcoatl.[23]

• Brodie says that when Joseph bestows the title of Melchizedek Priesthood upon his male followers, they are the only ones besides Jesus Christ and Melchizedek to ever hold that esteemed office. She says Joseph probably got his idea for a higher priesthood from a book written by James Gray, giving no title or footnotes. It is typical of Brodie to give an erudite answer when a simplistic one is more plausible. Prophet or phony, why not just get it from the Bible? The title of high priest is quite conspicuous there and, as explained by Joseph, is an office in the Melchizedek Priesthood and is part of the restoration of all things. The Jewish historian Josephus frequently mentions high priests.[24] Maybe the idea came from Josephus, who got it from the Old Testament.

• Brodie, along with many others of Joseph's detractors, insists without offering a single flotsam of evidence that the man must have some sort of psychic disorder that can be detected and measured by modern science. Brodie refers to a Dr. Phyllis Greenacre, psychiatrist, who had studied Oedipal conflicts, wherein the afflicted replaces an estranged father with the mother. But as Marvin Hill points out, "Brodie admits in her supplement that Joseph Jr. was very fond of his father."[25] Thus, this approach doesn't work, says Hill, and indeed, Brodie admits in her second edition preface that, "There is as yet no competent appraisal of Joseph Smith by a psychologist, psychiatrist, or psychoanalyst."

• If Brodie insists that W. D. Purple's story is true, saying that historian Francis Kirkham refuses to face its implications,[26] why does she not carry Purple's rambling narrative in her own history? The only conclusion plausible is that she doesn't believe it credible enough to share with her readers.

Then, there are areas where Brodie only borders on the

apocryphal. For instance, her statement that Joseph's appeal to the Green Mountain Boys of Vermont, Joseph's native state, avers that it was so terribly inaccurate on language translations that church leaders were embarrassed and withdrew it from pages of the Church's official history.[27] Joseph was running for president of the United States at the time and also encountering severe public prejudice. The Green Mountain appeal was not something claimed as a revelation intended as scripture for inclusion in the Doctrine and Covenants.

It was simply an appeal to human reason and public acceptance, one Vermonter to another. Since the Green Mountain Boys never responded to the letter, there was no particular reason to include it in an official history. It remains, however, in LDS literature as *The Voice of Truth*, containing the public writings, portrait, and last sermon of President Joseph Smith, given in Nauvoo, Illinois and printed by John Taylor in 1845. It included the King Follet funeral discourse, Joseph's final major sermon before Carthage. If LDS leaders have attempted to conceal Joseph's letter to the Green Mountain Boys, they didn't do a very good job of it. The entire Follett discourse, outlined in *The Voice of Truth*, is one of the most revered and quoted in LDS history.

• While Brodie is given credit for promulgating the fact that the Spaulding romance had nothing to do with the Book of Mormon, she didn't tell the rest of the story. When Philastus Hurlbut got hold of the manuscript, he turned it over to E. D. Howe, whose *Mormonism Unvailed* insisted that it was the true origin of the Book of Mormon. But Howe couldn't use it because upon examination, he realized that it had no connection whatsoever to the Book of Mormon.

Spaulding's novel about adventure-bound Roman sailors just didn't link up with a group of Israelites coming to America under religious commandment. Thus disappointed, Howe stored the book in a back corner to emerge decades later when L. L. Rice of Honolulu bought the contents of Howe's print shop, put the manuscript away, and didn't look at it until requested by Oberlin College to examine it for any mention of the Civil War.[28] Rice located nothing on the Civil War but, in the process, did find the long-lost Spaulding manuscript.

Officials of the college scrutinized the Spaulding papers carefully and declared to the world in 1888, and since, that the latter bore no resemblance to the Mormon book. Oberlin College president James H. Fairchild put it this way after comparing the two works: "Some other explanation for the Book of Mormon must be found."[29]

It is clear that Howe deceived the public by never printing a retraction to his Spaulding theory. Brodie had to know this, yet she borrowed quotes from Howe whenever it served her purpose.

• Brodie could also have pointed out, while disposing of the Spaulding manuscript, the fact that the learned Sidney Rigdon did not in any way help write the Book of Mormon. Sidney testified before many witnesses, including his own son, to his dying day that he never met Joseph Smith until after the Book of Mormon was printed. "My first look at it [the Book of Mormon] was when Parley P. Pratt and Oliver Cowdery placed it in my hands."[30]

• Brodie particularly attacks the Book of Abraham in the Pearl of Great Price because Smith claimed it was translated from Egyptian papyrus. She concedes that the writing was Egyptian but insists it was not from Abraham and, even if it was, the translation was not correct.[31] But there is much doctrine and wisdom in the book that correlates with Genesis. If it was the concoction of Smith in the year 1835, it was brilliant, along with the accompanying Book of Moses, in the depth of its religious instruction and wisdom concerning a scientific creation of Earth, a premortal life, and the fall of Adam. Brodie makes no attempt to explain how Smith could be the sole source of these spiritually wise and widely acclaimed gospel teachings.

• While Brodie makes out Smith to be a "fiendishly clever man,"[32] the evidence points out that Joseph is more of a naive and unschooled country boy—at least prior to publication of the Book of Mormon that Brodie insists he was clever enough to write on his own. After studying nearly two hundred letters written by

Smith to friends and family, Hill concludes that Joseph "never thought of himself other than a man called of God to perform a mission."

• If Brodie had been more conversant with the Bible, she might also have pointed out the many parallels, since she finds so many parallels everywhere else, between the experience of Joseph Smith and the Apostle Paul. Instead we are left with the impression on almost every early page that Joseph was a disturber of the peace and a charlatan because he encounters opposition. For example, if one is preaching only love and peace, how can one make so many enemies?[33]

But let's take a closer look at the life of Paul. He received much the same reception as Joseph: Acts 14:19, stoned until the Jews thought he was dead; Acts 17:5, "lewd fellows of the baser sort" put the city in an uproar after hearing Paul speak; Acts 17:13, he stirred up the people; Acts 17:18, "what will this babbler say?"; 17:32, mocked for teaching a resurrection; and Acts 19:24–30, acted contrary to law. When on Mars Hill, Paul chastised the Greeks for putting up a sign to the Unknown God, and an angry crowd nearly killed him. He was jailed numerous times for being disorderly and was nearly annihilated on the spot by silversmiths making idols to the Greek god Diana when Paul preached that man should not worship gods made by man's hands. Paul was also told that "much learning doth make thee mad" (Acts 26:24).

You get the idea. He met opposition, as did Joseph Smith. There must be something in the water, or perhaps in teachings about a divine power.

In short, the fearless and resolute apostle told people what they didn't want to hear. He wouldn't have made enemies if preaching benign doctrine such as "Have a nice day." Instead, Paul preached that the law of Moses—a law his hearers had been living for centuries—was no longer valid. Smith also preached that new creeds were replacing old creeds. No wonder nonmember ministers were often at the head of persecuting mobs. Joseph with his lay member church was taking away livelihoods. It was not surprising rival clergymen were upset.

Many believed that Paul received a vision from Christ; many did not—same with Smith. But the greatest similarity between their lives was that many refused to follow their instructions to see if they bore fruit as promised.[34]

As Paul said, the majority of the people would not hear the truth, "lest they should . . . understand with their heart" (Acts 28:27). Christ explained why, after telling the parable of the seed planted in barren ground: "He that hath ears to hear, let him hear" (Luke 8:8).

Clearly, not all had ears to hear. They rejected the testimony of Christ and his disciples because they hated the truth, as Christ explained: "I have chosen you out of the world, therefore the world hateth you" (John 15:19).

The above does not prove Joseph Smith a prophet or Paul an apostle, for that matter, at least on an intellectual basis. But it does indicate that the problems encountered by Smith are not that far amiss from biblical tradition. Apparently, anyone claiming to convey the word of God is subject not only to passive disdain but also to hate and ridicule.

Paul did get zapped in unexpected fashion. But normally, we must put forth our own effort to be spiritually instructed. Yet there is no way of knowing if Paul did not pray in secret beforehand to know more about this new Christian religion.

As for Brodie asking why Smith did not return to his enemies in the media, asking them to publish his words, it would have been as efficacious as Jesus' followers seeking an audience with Pilate after the crucifixion to testify they had seen the living Christ. What would be accomplished?

It is interesting that many people, even avowed scientists, will not countenance anything they cannot explain. Dr. Raymond Moody tried to conduct scientific experiments recording testimonies of those who seemed to die but who recovered on the operating table. An associate of Dr. Moody, Dr. Elisabeth Kubler-Ross, wrote this in the preface of Moody's book about out-of-body experiences: "I recommend this book to everyone with an open mind."[35] But the problem, she said, is that people stopped telling of near-death experiences when others began ridiculing them. Human nature was at work, and for a time Dr. Moody's work was stifled. But what could be more scientific than systematically recording what people say about an unknown matter?

Apparently, the public does not agree with the general scientific view that we can believe only what is empirically measurable. A poll conducted by *Newsweek* magazine, appearing in the October 2000 *Reader's Digest*, found that 84 percent of adult readers believe there is a God who performs miracles; 43 percent of those who say they have no faith at all nevertheless stated they had prayed for miracles.[36]

Even pagan cultures such as the idol-worshiping pharaohs of ancient Egypt held out hope of an afterlife, else why the attempt to preserve their remains for a future time?

Yet enemies of the Mormon Church began to spread such vicious rumors for decades following the death of Joseph Smith that in the Parliament of Religions held in Chicago in 1893, The Church of Jesus Christ of Latter-day Saints was officially denied admittance to the World's Fair of Religions.[37] The Mormons were told they did not believe in Christ; they only carried His name in their name. This isn't saying one way or the other whether their religion is within deity's cognizance. But if they claim to worship Christ, admittedly in an unorthodox manner compared to Catholic and Protestant faiths, why deny them that right?

Joseph Smith was truly an enigmatic figure, as indicated by his statement, "No man knows my history." Many have tried to explain him, says Brodie in her preface, yet the "results have been fantastically dissimilar."

Brodie then confided to a colleague that "Smith's career continues to astonish me—as does the stubborn survival of the Church."[38] Also, "the more I work with the man, the more of a challenge he becomes."[39] But if she has any misgivings in asides to associates, they seem to all disappear in her book. Would that she had been as forthright in it as she was in letters to her chief mentor, Dale Morgan.

Brodie also states that, "There are few men who have written so much and told so little about themselves."[40] Especially if you don't believe what he did say about himself.

When finished with her treatise on Smith, Brodie tells a colleague that she has finally wrapped it up and "put five bullet holes" in the Mormon prophet.[41] Few Christians would say that about Mahomet. It hardly seems appropriate for a historian. But Brodie is consistent. The "five bullet holes" incident complements her announced theme from the beginning.

Brodie laments that her father's refusal to read her alleged biography was an "act of real hostility. . . . His refusal to discuss it hurt me more . . . than an angry argument about the contents would have done."[42]

The suggestion is that her father refused to look at facts. But maybe the "facts" seemed so twisted to the elder McKay, especially in the aspersions cast on Joseph for dishonesty, immorality, and lack of religious sincerity, that he could take it no longer.

If any of us were to write a history of the Seventh-Day Adventists or Jehovah's Witnesses or any other minority sect, we couldn't take at face value statements by avowed enemies. While Fawn Brodie did not appear to write with malice, the bottom line is that she was never able to write from the eyes of her subject's followers with as much zeal as she did from the eyes of his severest critics. That cripples her work from the first page.

Cloaked behind an aura of superior scholarship, Brodie not only affixed the barnacle of an occasional bias on the good ship *History* but also sank the entire vessel. Or rather, she tried to keep the ship from reaching water.

Brodie brands Joseph and his Mormonism a fable.[43] But by raising LDS hackles, she did manage to do one thing most LDS historians have not: stimulate more meaningful research. In her seminal approach, Brodie acted as a more effective catalyst than perhaps any anti-Mormon writer ever has.

Since Brodie is positive Smith must have been something other than what he claimed—and he claimed a great deal—she "doesn't quite know what to do with him."[44] What she did with him was to research him extensively without explaining him. It is an irony, at best, that she proves that no man knew his history—not even Fawn Brodie.

She claims an exposé but then provides a dartboard of speculation in which she frequently misses the board entirely. If Joseph Smith wasn't who he said he was, it remains for someone else to accomplish what Brodie did not.[45]

But let us move beyond Brodie to all who have tried to explain Joseph Smith: it would seem to require a greater leap of faith to believe the man's many detractors than his own explanation. As LDS Church President Joseph Fielding Smith once said, "Never before in recorded history do we have an account of truth passing through such a crucible and being put to such a test as has the truth known in the world as Mormonism."[46]

So far, those applying the test, such as Brodie, have fared worse than the object of their disdain, Joseph Smith. In their failure to prove the charges against Joseph Smith, his own claims emerge even more credible. It is Brodie who, despite the tarnished accolades, in promising a full exposé takes on the appearance of a charlatan.

Of course, questions remain. If there is a God who wants us to believe in him, why should those questions remain? Perhaps it is not meant that man mathematically prove deity anymore than he can disprove him. What would then be the test of man's mettle? The need for him to stretch forth in faith and trust, the vehicle by which he might reach upward?

The real question is, has enough hard data been provided, such as the Book of Mormon and eleven eyewitnesses to its divinity, that man may use them as a springboard to intelligently seek God through the means outlined in scripture: prayer, faith, trust, and obedience to the commandments?

One thing is for sure: Brodie and her associates have not successfully refuted those means as taught by Joseph Smith. Following her failed cannonade, they loom more meaningful than ever in the human experience.

Chapter Endnotes

Chapter 1

1. Bringhurst, *Reconsidering No Man Knows My History,* 60.
2. Ahlstrom, *A Religious History of the American People,* 504; see also *Reconsidering,* 60.
3. Bringhurst, 60.
4. Ibid., 40–41; Brodie, *No Man Knows My History,* back flyleaf cover.
5. Wixom, "Public Credibility Thresholds Toward Errors in Print Journalism."
6. Brodie, 1.
7. Brodie's initial demonstration on Smith's sincerity prompted Morgan to say, "You are positive beyond what the facts will support." Also, "His sincerity can hardly be questioned" (Bringhurst, 19–20, 28, 171; referenced from Dale L. Morgan to Fawn Brodie, 28 August 1944).
8. In Bringhurst, 76. Joseph's letter, dated 6 June 1831, is in the Mormon Manuscript Collection.
9. Bringhurst, 48.
10. Brooks, *The Mountain Meadows Massacre;* see also Wixom, *Hamblin: A Modern Look at the Frontier Life and Legend of Jacob Hamblin,* 77–166.
11. Hinckley, *What of the Mormons,* 203.
12. In *The Mormon Experience,* Leonard Arrington and Davis Bitton called the pioneer treck a heroic effort. To be fair, the authors also say snow piled up behind the pioneers made backtracking difficult.
13. Bringhurst, 45.

14. Ibid., 44–45 for a complete summary of many complaints made against Brodie personally.
15. Brodie, 91.
16. Ibid., acknowledgments.
17. Bringhurst, 43–45.
18. Ibid., 45–46
19. Ibid., 46.
20. Ibid., 47; Dean Brimhall to Fawn McKay, 16 June 1946; copy in Brodie papers. It is probably a faux pas here on the part of Brimhall when he calls Fawn's work "great creative writing," given that she claimed it be accurate historical documentation.
21. Juanita Brooks to Dale Morgan, 9 December 1945.

Chapter 2

1. Bringhurst, *Reconsidering No Man Knows My History,* 63.
2. Brodie, *No Man Knows My History;* see Martha Brotherton in the index.
3. In Brighurst, 160, 161. Todd Compton says, "But any student of rhetoric will agree that Cowdery's accusation is couched in extremist language"; see also Steven LeSueaur, *The Mormon War in Missouri*, 37–38.
4. In Brodie, back cover flyleaf; see also Brighurst, 40–41.
5. *New York Times,* 9 January 1946; see also Brighurst, 40–41.
6. *New York Herald-Tribune,* 16 December 1945; see also Brighurst, 40–41.
7. Brodie, back cover flyleaf. *Time,* 28 January 1946. Praise was also heaped on Brodie by *Newsweek* on 26 November 1946; see also Brighurst, 40–41.
8. Bringhurst, 29–30.
9. James Pratt, *The Last Valentine.* These are the opening lines of Pratt's best-selling novel. It would seem difficult to write more powerfully.
10. Brodie, 182.
11. Ibid., 310.
12. Ibid., 165–66.
13. Ibid., 166.
14. Ibid., ix.

15. Ibid.
16. Ibid., 16–22.
17. Lucy Mack Smith, *History of Joseph Smith,* 92–93.
18. Ronald W. Walker, "The Persisting Idea of American Treasure Hunting," *BYU Studies* 24, no. 4 (Fall 1984): 429–52.
19. Roberts, *A Comprehensive History of the Church,* 1:98. The primary source is a letter from Mrs. Martha Campbell to Joseph Smith, now on file in the LDS Church Historian's Office, Salt Lake City, Package iv.
20. Smith, *History of the Church,* 1:89–94.
21. Brodie, 90.
22. Smith, *History of Joseph Smith,* 96–97.
23. Wixom, "Public Credibility Tolerance Thresholds Towards Errors in Print Journalism."
24. Brooks, *News Reporting and Writing,* 20–21.
25. *World Book Encyclopedia,* s.v. "Abraham Lincoln."
26. Ibid.
27. Smith, *History of Joseph Smith,* 82.

Chapter 3

1. Brigham Young, in *Journal of Discourses,* 3:51.
2. Edward Partridge, "Long Journal," comp. Edward Partridge Jr., 1878, LDS Church Archives; see also Smith, *History of the Church,* 1:390–91.
3. Joseph Smith, *History of the Church,* 3:446.
4. Bringhurst, *Reconsidering No Man Knows My History,* 28; referenced from a letter, Dale Morgan to Fawn Brodie, 28 August 1944.
5. Brodie, *No Man Knows My History;* this is a theme of nearly every chapter (see particularly 168–93; 405).
6. *The Saints' Herald* 34 (February 1887): 89; for discussion, see Brighurst, 70.
7. Brodie, 3.
8. Ibid., 397.
9. Wilford Woodruff, *Leaves from My Journal,* 83–85.
10. Brodie, 256–74; many Saints made the sacrifice to come to Nauvoo without ever meeting Smith.
11. Bringhurst, 129.

12. Nibley, *Tinkling Cymbals and Sounding Brass.*
13. Nibley, *No Ma'm, That's Not History,* 26.
14. There should be little debate on this given the millions of copies sold around the world and the various languages into which the book has been translated.
15. Bringhurst, 211.
16. Brodie, 366.
17. Ibid., 378.
18. Brighurst, 84.
19. Ibid., 116.
20. Darrick Evenson, *The Gainsayers.*
21. Bringhurst, 158; see also 12, 188. Bringhurst said that some of Morgan's criticisms may have been directed at an early Brodie draft. He added, "In my judgment, many of Morgan's early criticisms of *No Man Knows My History* are strikingly appropriate to the finished product wherein Morgan says: 'You have an intellectual but not yet an emotional objectivity about Mormonism . . . you are still in a certain mood of rebellion.'" It is interesting that Bringhurst comes to this conclusion while Brodie is showered with honors by the news media for "objective reporting." One must also ask if Morgan grew weary of counseling Brodie, deciding to simply approve her final draft.
22. Brodie refers to Wesley Waters's *New Light on Mormon Origins from the Palmyra Period;* see also Brodie, 410.
23. Lucy Mack Smith, *History of Joseph Smith.*
24. Porter, "Reinventing Mormonism: To Remake or Redo," *The FARMS Review* 7, no. 2 (1995): 128–30.
25. Bringhurst, 66.
26. Backman, *Joseph Smith's First Vision,* 86–87.
27. Joseph Smith, *History of the Church*, 155.
28. Brodie, 410–11. Whatever records of the Palmyra Presbyterian Church show, there is other evidence that the family believed Joseph's words that a new church was to be born. Evidence also exists that Latter-day Saints remained members of record long after they had left the Church.
29. Lucy Mack Smith, *History of Joseph Smith,* 82–83.
30. See Porter, 123–43.

31. Brodie, 41.
32. *Deseret News,* 20 January 1894.
33. *Amboy Journal,* 2 July 1879.
34. Orasmus Turner, *History of the Pioneer Settlements of Phelps and Gorham's Purchase,* 214–16.

Chapter 4

1. Brodie, *No Man Knows My History,* 74.
2. Bringhurst, *Reconsidering No Man Knows My History,* 207.
3. Ibid., 74, 83–97.
4. Brodie, 79–80. Brodie here repeats statements made by Illinois governor Thomas Ford, who said someone told him the Eight Witnesses looked at an "empty box." Although Brodie labels Ford as "weak," one who leaned whichever way political winds blew him, Brodie leaves us with the impression that she agrees with him by offering no other explanation than his.
5. Bringhurst, 208.
6. Anderson, *Investigating the Book of Mormon Witnesses,* 112–13.
7. Roberts, *A Comprehensive History of the Church,* 1:137–47; Anderson, *Investigating the Book of Mormon Witnesses,* 107–122; Barrett, *The Restored Church,* 72–76.
8. Ibid. The testimonies of the witnesses were never of a passive nature. The more challenged they were in their older ages, the more vigorously they seemed to defend them. For example, even though David Whitmer never rejoined the Church and was often questioned about his role, he told James H. Hart just prior to his death that he approved of Hart's poem declaring him a witness as testified in the forefront of the Book of Mormon (copy of poem in possession of Edward Hart, grandson of James H. Hart, Provo, Utah.
9. Anderson, 51–66, 79–94, 107–122.
10. "Near Death Experiences," *Provo Daily Herald,* 7 November 1993, D-2. The story says Dr. Moody records in *Life after Life* the statements of three thousand people who had near-death experiences. The story says Moody's book has sold more than ten million copies in thirty-eight languages.
11. Grant, *Kingdom of God Restored* (theme of book).

12. *World Book Encyclopedia,* s.v. "hypnotism."

13. Brodie, 33, 61, 74.

14. Ibid., 80.

15. Brooks, *News Reporting and Writing,* 20. "Fairness requires, above all, that you make every effort to avoid following your own biases. . . . The goals of accuracy and fairness are summed up as journalistic objectivity." One can ask if these standards were observed in 1945 when Fawn Brodie received her awards from several prominent newspapers of the period for "detached objectivity."

16. Kennedy, *Early Days of Mormonism,* appendix.

17. Roberts, 1:108–9.

18. Ibid.

19. Smith, *History of the Church,* 1:20.

20. Roberts, 1:108.

21. Arrington, *The Mormon Experience,* 13.

22. Nibley, *Three Mormon Classics,* 74–79.

23. Sperry, *Our Book of Mormon,* 39–55; Nibley, *Since Cumorah,* 169–96.

24. Smith, 1:1–11.

25. See Bringhurst, *Mormonism's Lost Generation,* 16. Letter to Fawn Brodie, 28 August 1944; see also Bringhurst, 193.

26. Ibid., 49, 148.

27. Bringhurst, *A Biographer's Life,* 105.

28. DeVoto, quote from Brodie, flyleaf; see also Brighurst, 41.

29. Brodie, 281.

30. Ibid., 283.

31. Ibid.

32. "I will not live until I am 40 years old. . . . I heard Joseph Smith say it many times" (Young, *Discourses of Brigham Young,* 467).

33. Smith, 6:47 (letter to Thomas Ford); Ford, of course, was not satisfied.

34. Fawn Brodie to Dean R. Brimhall, 14 June 1939; original in Dean Brimhall papers. For further comment, see Bringhurst, *Reconsidering,* 8.

35. *Saints Advocate,* Independence, Missouri, October 1879 (published by the Reorganized Church of Jesus Christ of Latter Day Saints, now

known as the Community of Christ).

36. Nibley, *Since Cumorah,* 144–45.
37. Ibid., 129.
38. Tad R. Callister, "Prophet of the Restoration," *Ensign,* June 2002, 64.
39. Ludlow, *A Companion to Your Study of the Book of Mormon,* 5–24.
40. Brodie, 69.
41. During the past ten years, 51 million copies of the Book of Mormon have been distributed. Today the book is available in 106 languages (Gordon B. Hinckley, "Opening Remarks," *Ensign,* May 2005, 5).
42. Brodie, 169.
43. Sperry, *Our Book of Mormon,* 77–78.
44. *Since Cumorah,* 137–52.
45. Brodie, 61.
46. Brodie, 91, 20; reference to "A memo from Dale Morgan; original in Dale Morgan papers."

Chapter 5

1. Reynolds, *Book of Mormon Authorship, New Light on Ancient Origins,* 185.
2. Nibley, *Since Cumorah,* 169–96.
3. Brodie, *No Man Knows My History,* 50.
4. Ibid., 54.
5. Interview with J. H. Gilbert, *Post and Tribune,* Detroit, Michigan, 3 December 1877, 3; for comment, see Nibley, *Since Cumorah,* 4.
6. Nibley, *Since Cumorah,* 4–5.
7. Roberts, *Defense of the Faith and the Saints,* 268–69, 305.
8. *Saints Advocate,* Independence, Missouri, October 1879 (published by the Reorganized Church of Jesus Christ of Latter Day Saints, now known as the Community of Christ).
9. Ibid.
10. Brodie, 39–40, 55.
11. Ibid, 69. In a letter to Dean Brimhall dated 14 June 1939, Fawn Brodie confided that she "was able to trace nearly every idea in it [the Book of Mormon] down to Ontario County, New York" (the original letter is in Brimhall collection). However, by 1971 Brodie apparently

widened the book's parameters "to the frontier of New York."

12. Called by the Emperor Constantine in 325 A.D. at Nicea, Asia Minor, "to settle the Trinity question." The council decided that God and Christ "are of one substance" and that God "came down and was made flesh" (*World Book Encyclopedia,* s.v. "Nicene Council."). By contrast, Joseph Smith taught that God and Christ appeared to him in 1820 as two separate beings. Smith's explanation of deity was also simple—there were no vagaries such as "Light of Light, God of God, very God of very God," and so forth.

13. See tenth article of faith; Smith, *History of the Church,* 4:535–41. For a summary of LDS beliefs on the Apostasy and the Restoration, see Bruce R. McConkie, *Mormon Doctrine,* 43–46, 633–34.

14. Dyer, *The Meaning of Truth,* 123.

15. This classification "Restored" was for years rejected by the U.S. Military but seems to be slowly gaining acceptance.

16. Smith, 1:396.

17. Bringhurst, *Reconsidering No Man Knows My History,* 61. On 9 September 1943, Brodie told Dale Morgan that she didn't feel welcome in LDS Church archives, so she did most of her research in New York and Chicago, where she completed a master's degree.

18. Brodie to Dale Morgan, 19 November 1943; Brodie to Dean Brimhall, 18 June 1942 and 3 November 1942.

19. Bringhurst, 61 (referenced from a paper delivered to the Mormon History Association, New Haven, Connecticut, October 1972).

20. Arrington, *The Mormon Experience.* Arrington said he was approached by Knopf to write the book in 1967, well before Brodie's 1971 book was published.

21. *Saints Advocate,* 1879.

22. Brodie, 80.

23. Ibid., 116.

24. Ibid., 283.

25. West, *Trial of the Stick of Joseph.*

26. The stick of Joseph and the stick of Ephraim (Joseph's son) are one and the same, according to the Doctrine and Covenants reference; see also Ezekiel 37:15–19; D&C 27:5.

27. Brodie, 377–400

28. Ibid., 294.
29. Ibid., 54.
30. Ibid., 75. Brodie again betrays her lack of objectivity (after describing a vision reported by Mrs. Whitmer), by stating, "It is probable that there was no one more surprised at this than Joseph Smith. . . . Joseph doubtless pondered the miracle in his heart with wonder." She can get by with probably, but the word doubtless is a conclusion she is in no position to make. The entire purpose, of course, is to substantiate her conjecture that no one could receive inspiration if Joseph was not there to hypnotize them. As for miracles, she refers to them as a "contagion."
31. Josephus, *Complete Works, Antiquities of the Jews,* 379.
32. Brodie, 83–97.
33. Richard L. Bushman, "The Visionary World of Joseph Smith," *BYU Studies* 37, no. 1 (1997–98): 183–204. Bushman discusses Smith's "visionary world" in detail.
34. Bringhurst, 71–73.
35. Ibid. It should be remembered that a Dr. Robinson obtained sixty signatures in Palmyra attesting to the sterling reputation of the Smith family just a few years before Hurlbut obtained his (Lucy Mack Smith, *History of Joseph Smith,* 96.) It is possible, depending on how the questions were worded, that neighbors gave Hurlbut the information they perceived he wanted.
36. Brodie, vii. Brodie has Smith saying the words of her book title with "a wanton moment of self-searching" and "a kind of wonder."
37. Ibid., 411–12.
38. *Zion's Ensign,* Independence, Missouri, 1893; interview at Bradtville, Wisconsin, with William Smith.
39. Ibid., 63–65.
40. Ibid., 27.
41. Nibley, *Tinkling Cymbals and Sounding Brass,* 77–78.
42. Brodie, 7.
43. Bringhurst, 62.
44. Fisher, *Children of God* (theme of entire book)
45. Frank Gruber, *Zane Grey: Man of the West* (Cleveland, Ohio: Greenberg, 1949), 65. Herein Grey says, "You ought to see the Mormons I'm

going with. If they aren't a tough bunch I never saw one. They all pack guns. But they are nice fellows." This is but one comment by Grey about the few Mormons he actually met.

46. *World Book Encylopedia,* s.v. "Zane Grey." "Grey wrote 60 book titles which sold millions of copies." Anti-Mormon themes were prevalent but perhaps harshest in *Riders of the Purple Sage,* considered by many to be Grey's most popular novel. At the same time he was known in several books and interviews to say he admired the few Mormon men he had met (see note 45 above).

47. Brodie, 398.

48. Brodie admits as much when she says on page 406 that stories in the *Palmyra Reflector* mocked Joseph's reported visions as early as 1831. As Hugh Nibley says in *Tinkling Cymbals,* what good would it have done then to report them earlier? Smith's account was further mocked by the media after he told it in his official *History of the Church* (*Tinkling Cymbals,* 76–77).

Chapter 6

1. Nibley, *Tinkling Cymbals and Sounding Brass,* xiii.
2. Ibid., 69–103.
3. Howe, E. D., *Mormonism Unvailed,* theme of introduction.
4. Brodie, *No Man Knows My History,* 22–25, 406.
5. Richard L. Anderson, "Circumstantial Confirmation of the First Vision through Reminiscence," *BYU Studies* 9, no. 3 (Spring 1969): 374.
6. Dean C. Jesse, "Early Accounts of the First Vision," *BYU Studies* 9, no. 3 (Spring 1969): 275–94. There are other well-researched accounts, but Jesse's listings will suffice for purposes of comparison.
7. Brodie, 14. "In the 16th year of my age," or fifteen, going on sixteen.
8. Jesse, "Early Accounts of the First Vision," 275–94.
9. Ibid., 278–80.
10. Ibid., 280.
11. Ibid., 286.
12. Ibid., 284.

13. Smith, *History of the Church,* 4:535–41; see also William Smith's testimony, given in 1883, of Joseph's first vision. It strongly affirms Joseph's experience but also includes some words Joseph did not record: "A light descended . . . it appeared like fire" (see William Smith, *Origin of the Book of Mormon* [Lamoni, Iowa: Harold Steam Book and Job Office, 1883], starting on page 6).
14. Roberts, *A Comprehensive History of the Church,* 1:83.
15. One angel in Matthew 28:2, 5; two angels in John 20:12. Note also that Peter "and the disciple Jesus loved" are mentioned as being present in John's account but not in Matthew's account. Here Mary Magdalene is told to go tell the apostles.
16. Brodie, 24.
17. Smith, *History of the Church,* 1:6.
18. Lucy Mack Smith, *History of Joseph Smith,* 74.
19. See Brodie, Appendix A.
20. Brodie, 405. Brodie also implies here that there was no mention of visions at all until 1831. Appendix A is full of people she relies on to tell the reader of many alleged visions regarding the coming forth of the Book of Mormon.
21. Bringhurst, *Reconsidering No Man Knows My History,* 67.
22. Anderson, 390–91.
23. Smith, *History of the Church,* 1:6; for comment, see Jesse, "Early Accounts of the First Vision," 275–77. Smith admits some negligence in not getting the history written earlier, for reasons given in the text.
24. Brodie, 376.
25. Ibid., 115. Brodie is quoting Ezra Booth in the nine memeographed letters (unnumbered pages,) which are now combined in a single cover. Listed as "Booth Letters, Nelson, Portage Co., 1831" (L. Tom Perry Special Collections, Harold B. Lee Library, BYU. Provo, Utah). Booth's letter to Edward Partridge is relatively easy to find, although some of the writing is dimmed by time. Booth begins with generalities and tends to include details in later letters.
26. Smith, *History of the Church,* 1:128.
27. For a complete reproduction of Partridge's letters, songs, and poems concerning Zion in Missouri, see Wixom, *Edward Partridge,* appendices B, C, F, H; see also Edward Partridge, "Long Journal," comp.

Edward Partridge Jr., 1878, LDS Church Archives.

28. Roberts, 1:265–66.

29. Smith, *History of the Church*, 1:215–16.

30. In Whitmer, *History of the Early Church*, 77–83. Whitmer recorded the official early history of the Church, by commandment, from 8 March 1831 to 1838. He was excommunicatred in 1838 when he refused to turn his history over to Church authorities for possible corrections. The book is a sympathetic account of LDS history until the last two chapters, when Whitmer appears to grow bitter against Joseph. Whitmer was also accused of using Church funds for private use. Yet he continued to affirm his testimony of the gold plates, even in the presence of Church enemies. See also *Times and Seasons* 5: 482.

31. Brodie, 115. Ezra Booth letters.

32. Ibid. While Brodie is quoting Booth's letters, she has strained beyond history by adding her own speculations about Rigdon's views of Zion.

33. Brodie, 20.

34. Smith, *History of the Church*, 1:77–83.

35. Brodie, appendix A.

36. Pratt, *Autobiography of Parley P. Pratt,* 110, 117.

37. Edward Partridge, "Long Journal."

38. *Times and Seasons* 1:23.

39. Brodie, 74. Writing of claimed visions, Brodie often treats her subjects as robots, without intelligence or feelings. She does so particularly in this instance.

40. Eyring, *The Faith of a Scientist* (Salt Lake City: Bookcraft, 1969); this is the theme of entire book.

Chapter 7

1. Brodie, *No Man Knows My History,* 30–31, 427–29.

2. Brodie, 16. Brodie adds that Joseph Smith admitted indulging in magic arts, but this was attributed to an alleged court trial that will be examined herein.

3. *The Schaff Herzog Encyclopedia of Religious Knowledge,* 2: 1577. It might be asked why this Funk and Wagnall-published encyclopedia would ask an Episcopalian minister to write an article about the Mor-

mons. Perhaps it was because Tuttle, working in Utah and Idaho, had written a book earlier titled *Reminiscences of a Missionary Bishop.* It included much Mormon apocrypha, even beyond the usual negative rumors of the times. One example: "In 1857 the Mormons were particularly vain, glorious, and arrogant," minus any footnotes or further explanation. For further comment, see Kirkham's *A New Witness for Christ in America,* 2:354. One of Tuttle's problems is that he wrote in favor of Spaulding's Book of Mormon theory, later disproved.

4. *Eclectic* magazine, New York, 1873; *Fraser* magazine, London, 1873; and *Utah Christian Advocate,* 1886, published such stories (see Kirkham, 1:491–92.

5. Kirkham, 1:473–74. This statement in the *Chenango Telegraph* is one of the most biased in the annals of ecclesiastical history. It speaks of material conditions only, not belief, resolve for a cause, or a willingness to sacrifice toward it. The same could be said of the children of Israel "starving" or in a "deplorable" condition as they wandered in the wilderness, as depicted in the book of Exodus. It could also be said of the disciples of Christ or of Christ himself.

6. Some are included in Brodie's appendix A. She builds on articles like those that appeared in *Eclectic* magazine, with no foundation in fact, to make her point.

7. Nibley quotes from Kirkham's *A New Witness to Christ in America,* 1:386; 2:480.

8. Bringhurst, *Fawn M. Brodie: A Biographer's Life,* 120–21. Bringhurst quoted Brodie that the court records had been destroyed by fire. See also the chapter titled "A Compelling Piece of Detective Work," 71–115. They had not been destroyed by fire but were located in 1971 by Wesley Walters.

9. Walters, *Inventing Mormonism* (theme of book).

10. Gordon A. Madsen, "Joseph Smith's 1826 Trial: the Legal Setting" *BYU Studies* 30, no. 2 (1990): 91.

11. Smith, *History of the Church,* 1:17, 89–93. Herein, Joseph explains the setting in working for Josiah Stoal, although there is no mention of the 1826 trial.

12. Kirkham, *A New Witness for Christ;* Nibley, *Tinkling Cymbals and Sounding Brass.* The authors' questions regarding the existence of an

1826 trial against Joseph Smith were raised before Walters's discovery of court documents in 1971.

13. Extensive references to Purple are found in Bringhurst's *A Biographer's Life,* wherein she drives to Chenango County, New York, to find the articles allegedly written by Purple about the 1826 trial. Brodie includes no reference to Purple in her index of *No Man Knows My History.*

14. Kirkham, 1:473–75.

15. Brodie, appendix A.

16. Madsen, "Joseph Smith's 1826 Trial: A Legal Setting."

17. Porter, *Reinventing Mormonism.*

18. Brodie, 29–31.

19. Nibley, *Tinkling Cymbals,* 250–54.

20. Brodie, 31.

21. Smith, *History of the Church,* 1:90–94.

22. Ibid., 1:91.

23. Ibid., 1:96.

24. Brodie, 87–88.

25. See also Smith, *History of the Church,* 1:94–96.

26. Ibid. Reid also credits deity with protecting Joseph from harm in rescuing him from an angry mob. Brodie never mentions Reid's name.

27. Brodie, 445 (Miller); referenced from an affidavit obtained from Solomon Spaulding's brother, John, in 1813. Also from Nahum Howard: "I have lately read the Book of Mormon and believe it to be the same as Spaulding wrote, except the religious part" (446).

28. Bringhurst, 207, footnoted to Lester E. Bush Jr., "The Spaulding Theory: Then and Now," *Dialogue: A Journal of Mormon Thought* 10 (Autumn 1977): 70–73; see also Brodie, 34–68, 168–80, 442–54.

29. Pratt, *Autobiography of Parley P. Pratt,* 110.

30. This is the theme of Fisher's book. It is Vardis Fisher against the world of organized religion, including his sister.

Chapter 8

1. Brodie, *No Man Knows My History,* 297.

2. Ibid. This is a particularly misleading assertion that sets the tone for

all Brodie has to say on this subject. The quote is there, but her source, W. Wyl, is (as Vardis Fisher warned) a clearly venomous anti-Mormon source, much like Ezra Booth, but more subtle.

3. Nibley, *Tinkling Cymbals and Sounding Brass,* 589, 659.

4. Ibid., 527; referenced to W. Wyl, "Mormon Portraits: or the Truth about the Mormon Leaders from 1830 to 1886," S*alt Lake Tribune,* 1886, 56.

5. *Saints' Herald* 34 (February 1887): 89.

6. Smith, *History of the Church,* 2:47; 6:46; for comment, see Brodie, 185; see headnote to Doctrine and Covenants, section 132.

7. Brodie, 317.

8. Lundwall, *Fate of the Persecutors of the Prophet Joseph Smith,* 326.

9. Letter from Oliver Cowdery to his brother, Warren A. Cowdery, from Far West, Missouri, 21 January 1838; original in Huntington Library, San Marino, California.

10. Brodie, 112.

11. Smith, *History of the Church*, 3:16–18.

12. Letter from Oliver Cowdery to his brother, Warren A. Cowdery, from Far West, Missouri, 21 January 1838.

13. Richard L. Anderson, "I Have a Question," *Ensign,* April 1987; see also *Salt Lake City Messenger* 73 (October 1989), 5–15. A letter from David Whittaker, curator of Western Manuscripts at BYU's Harold B. Lee Library, says, "The general consensus among those of us who have studied this ["Confessions of Oliver Cowdery"] is that the pamphlet is a forgery." The full essay, titled "Confessions," can be found in L. Tom Perry Special Collections, Harold B. Lee Library, BYU.

14. For more details, see Richard L. Anderson's *Investigating the Book of Mormon Witnesses,* 52–53, 60–61.

15. LeSueur, *Mormon War in Missouri,* 37–38.

16. Smith, *History of the Church,* 3:17–18.

17. Brodie, 458; the reference is from John C. Bennett's *History of the Saints,* 85–86.

18. Bringhurst, *Reconsidering No Man Knows My History,* 154–94.

19. The unpublished diaries of Emily and Eliza Partridge, unnumbered pages, can be found in the LDS Church Archives, microfilm access no. 3887.

20. This unpublished diary of Emily Partridge was begun in 1874.
21. Wixom, *Edward Partridge,* 110.
22. "I went with the rest [to Joseph's funeral] as a stranger, no one suspecting the extra sorrow that was in my heart" (Emily Partridge, unpublished diary).
23. Emily Partridge, unpublished diary.
24. Brodie, 186.
25. Ibid., 90.
26. Ibid., 186.
27. Wixom, *Jacob Hamblin,* 21–23.
28. Brodie, 306–7.
29. E-mail response in possession of the author. The help of Dr. Rafael Del Vecchio, Kayenta, Utah, is acknowledged in the search for this nonexistent newspaper document.
30. Brodie, 310.
31. Ibid., 308.
32. Ibid., 378.
33. Ibid., 366.
34. Ibid., 182.
35. Ibid., 291.
36. William Mulder emphasizes this point in Bringhurst, *Reconsidering No Man Knows My History,* xi.
37. Brodie, 29.
38. Ibid., 302.
39. Ibid., 301.
40. Ibid., 460.
41. Ibid., 316.
42. Ibid., 316.
43. Hill, *Joseph Smith, The First Prophet,* 301. To Parley P. Pratt's letter to his cousin John Van Cortt, dated 7 May 1843 from New York, was attached a letter from Orson Pratt, written 20 January 1843, in which he said: "J. C. Bennett has published lies about myself. . . . His book [*History of the Saints*] I have read with the greatest disgust. No candid man will ever believe it." Another source states, "Joseph Smith III said that Sarah denied to him that his father [Joseph Smith Jr.] had ever said an improper word to her" ("Memoirs of Joseph Smith," *The Saints'*

Herald, 22 January 1935; see also Smith, *History of the Church*, 5:138).
44. Pratt, *Orson Pratt's Works*, 27.
45. Bagley, *Blood of the Prophets*, 1–20.
46. Bringhurst, xii.
47. "Distortion of Information, ETC," 17:5–27, 1959. This pamphlet is available in most large university communication departments; see also Wixom, "Public Credibility Tolerance Thresholds Toward Errors in Print Journalism," 58.
48. Goldstein, *News at any Cost;* see also Wixom, 15.
49. Brodie, 32.
50. Ibid., 321.
51. This personal record book, in possession of Donna Hansen Woodward, was received from Eliza Small, a friend of the Eliza Snow family. The entry appears to be in Eliza Snow's handwriting (personal interview, 11 March 2001, Ivins, Utah.
52. *Women's Exponent*, 1 November 1879, 85; see also "Last Testament of Emma Smith," *Saints Advocate*, October 1879, 50. 53. Brodie, 335.
54. Ibid., 308.
55. Ibid., 186.
56. Ibid., 299.
57. Ibid., 384.
58. Brodie, 384; Nibley, *No Ma'am, That's Not history*, 54. Nibley asks, "Is this history?" It is only one example of Brodie's talent of creative writing.
59. Orson Pratt rejected plural marriage in 1841, was excommunicated in 1842, and was reinstated shortly thereafter. In 1883 he wrote a series of articles in defense of plural marriage. He was a man of diverse talents, publishing in 1886 *A New and Easy Method of Solution of the Cubic and Biquadratic Equations*.
60. Pratt, *Autobiography*, 329
61. Brodie, 298.

Chapter 9

1. Brodie, *No Man Knows My History*, 414–15.
2. *View of the Hebrews* was published in 1823 and republished in 1825, five years before the Book of Mormon. Ethan's book shows a deep rev-

erence and respect for God's dealings with the children of Israel.

3. Ibid., 177. The lost ten tribes would, of course, be those descended from Israel other than from Joseph and Judah, of which we have ample record.

4. Ibid., 64–65

5. William Riley, *Isaiah Comparisons,* master's thesis, Brigham Young University, 1971.

6. Ibid., 177.

7. Roberts's papers were retained by his family until 1946 when a son, Ben, gave a copy to the Timpanogos Club in Salt Lake City, which subsequently had it published under the title *Studies of the Book of Mormon.*

8. Roberts, *Defense of the Faith and the Saints,* 288; in Reynolds, *Book of Mormon Authorship, New Light on Ancient Origins,* 24.

9. Reynolds, referring to a March 1923 letter, 22.

10. Brodie, 47. She says, "Roberts once made a careful and impressive list of parallels between *View of the Hebrews* and the Book of Mormon, but for obvious reasons it was never published. After his death, copies were made which circulated among a limited circle in Utah."

11. Welch, *An Unparallel.*

12. Richard C. Roberts, in *Encyclopedia of Mormonism,* 1:509–10.

13. Rigdon, *Life of Sidney Rigdon,* 188–95; Roberts, *A Comprehensive History of the Church,* 1:234–45; Smith, *History of the Church,* 1:122–23. For comment, see Kirkham, *New Witness for Christ in America* 1:326–27.

14. Smith, *View of the Hebrews,* flyleaf, preface. This book, originally published by Ethan Smith, was republished by the BYU Religious Study Center in 1996. It is Tate who is quoted.

15. Sjodahl, *An Introduction to the Book of Mormon,* 35–46.

16. Ibid.

17. *World Book Encyclopedia,* s.v. "Pluto." "Pluto is a planet that was discovered in 1930. . . . As far back as 1915 an astronomer . . . had proven the existence of this planet by studying the behavior of Uranus and Neptune. Finally in 1930. . . ." It is interesting that a scientific explanation uses the word "proven" in 1915 even though Pluto was not actually seen for fifteen more years.

18. Sjodahl, 199–200.
19. Reynolds, *Book of Mormon Authorship,* 34–35.
20. Ibid., 163–66.
21. Ibid., 165.
22. Ibid., 158.
23. A. Q. Morris, *Literary Detection,* 1979.
24. See Reynolds, 34–35.
25. Sjodahl, 199–200.
26. B. H. Roberts makes the same point in *A Comprehensive History of the Church,* 1:130–31.
27. Ibid., 1:305.
28. S. V. Escalante and F. A. Dominguez, journal, 1776. The real question is, what were the actual words and their meaning as intended by Escalante before his journal was translated into English?
29. Sjodahl, 7–8.
30. Brodie, 36–37.
31. Barrett, *The Restored Church,* 30–31.
32. Sjodahl, 12.
33. Lucy Mack Smith, *History of Joseph Smith,* 82–83. Lucy also says, "From this time forth [22 September 1823], Joseph continued to receive instructions from the Lord."
34. Sjodahl, 21–22.
35. Ibid., 489.
36. Ibid. The statement might be argued by some that vessels can't stay out of water as explained in the Book of Mormon. But it is not known exactly how these vessels worked, nor how much engineering was needed with divine guidance
37. Tucker, *Origin, Rise, and Progress of Mormonism,* 1867. The theme of Tucker's book, of course, was that Joseph was a consummate fraud. An employee of the *Wayne Sentinel,* Tucker was in a position to write many anti-Mormon articles. For comments by Hugh Nibley, see *Tinkling Cymbals and Sounding Brass,* 69–70.
38. As judged by *Encyclopedia Britannica,* s.v. "Plutarch."
39. LeSueur, *Mormon War in Missouri,* 10.
40. Interview, LaDell Andersen, Las Vegas, Nevada, 7 March 2002.

Chapter 10

1. Brodie, *No Man Knows My History*, appendix A.
2. Howe, *Mormonism Unvailed*, 74.
3. Ibid., 74.
4. Bringhurst, *Reconsidering No Man Knows My History*, 72. Historian B. H. Roberts spells Hurlbut as "Hurlburt," but most historians write it as the author has spelled it.
5. Hill, *Joseph Smith, The First Mormon*, 156.
6. Ibid., 156.
7. Ibid., 157
8. *Detroit Michigan Post and Tribune*, 3 December 1877, 3. Still another detractor, not listed by Brodie, is Addison Austin (see Nibley, *Tinkling Cymbals and Sounding Brass*, 260).
9. The author has seen the monument marking Harris's grave in the Clarkston cemetery. The assertion is a strange one.
10. Brodie, 412.
11. Ibid., appendix A.
12. Ibid.
13. Tucker, *Origin, Rise, and Progress of the Mormon Church*, 30.
14. *Deseret News*, 20 January 1894, 166; for comment, see Hill, *Joseph Smith, The First Mormon*, 46.
15. Hill, 46.
16. Tucker, 30; reprinted in Howe, *Mormonism Unvailed*, 187; for comment, see Nibley, *Tinkling Cymbals*, 236.
17. Brodie, appendix A; for comment, see Nibley, *Tinkling Cymbals*, 141–42.
18. *Painesville Telegraph*, 15 March 1831, 1–2. The story is linked to Alexander Campbell, a bitter enemy of Joseph Smith.
19. Brodie, 432.
20. Ibid., 16–17.
21. Lucy Mack Smith, *History of Joseph Smith*, 195–205.
22. Brodie, 182.
23. Truman Madsen, *BYU Studies* (Spring 1969): 235.
24. Edward Partridge, "Long Journal," comp. Edward Partridge Jr., 1878, LDS Church Archives. See also Hartt Wixom, *Edward Partridge*, 153–55.

25. Hill, 157
26. Ibid., 157.
27. *The Millennial Star* 3 (May 1842).
28. Hill, 351.
29. *The Millennial Star* 3 (August 1842): 65.
30. William Smith, *Origin of the Book of Mormon.*
31. Hill, 53.
32. Obidiah Dogberry (Abner Cole), *Book of Pukei,* opening pages.
33. *New Forms of the Old Faith,* also given as a sermon in Edinburgh to the Church of Scotland; for comment, see Kirkham, *A New Witness for Christ in America,* 1:300–01,
34. Kirkham, *A New Witness for Christ in America,* 1:300–01
35. Ibid.
36. See Smith, *History of the Church,* 7:1–31. Brodie depicts Ford as one who "hoped Joseph would escape jail and take his followers with him."
37. Ibid.; see also Brodie, 388: "Ford was weak."
38. "Ford was deaf to all reason" (Lundwall, *Fate of the Persecutors,* 302).
39. Ford, *Ford's History of Illinois,* 329–54 (reprinted in Smith, *History of the Church,* 7:36–39). Ford also opines here that Joseph's followers "expected him to rise from the dead" (39).
40. See Smith, *History of the Church,* 7:38; pages 2–43 contain the major part of Ford's *History of Illinois* as it pertains to the Mormons.
41. "Discourses Delivered to the Pennsylvania Historical Society," 26 March 1850; see also Kane Diary for January 1858 (L. Tom Perry Special Collections, Harold B. Lee Library, BYU). Kane was questioned so often on his sympathetic portrayal of the Mormons that he issued a postscript to his second edition, saying that he "meant what I said," praising the Mormons a second time.
42. As explained by Brodie, 79–80.
43. Smith, *History of the Church,* 6:467–78.
44. The entire paragraph is conjecture by the author.
45. E. B. Tripp, unpublished diaries, typescript, 1-10, l. Tom Perry Special Collections, Harold B. Lee Library, BYU.
46. Lundwall, 301–2; it is difficult to find any sympathetic words for

Governor Ford.

47. *Ensign of Liberty* 1 (1849), 99–100.
48. Wixom, *Edward Partridge,* 92.
49. This is the theme of *An Early History of the Church,* by John Whitmer, except for the last two chapters; see also *Messenger and Advocate* 1 (June 1835): 144; 11 (March 1836): 287.
50. Majors, *My Seventy Years on the Frontier,* 44–63. This is the same Alexander Majors who was part owner of the Pony Express, which was headquartered in St. Joseph, Missouri.
51. The author's conclusion based on research for *Edward Partridge* (43–68).
52. Roberts, *A Comprehensive History of the Church,* 1:532–59.
53. See Brodie, 217–20. Reports carried to the Missouri legislature blamed the Mormons and, of course, Joseph Smith for not halting abuses on both sides (see Pech and Reed report, "Documents, Correspondence Orders in Relation to the Disturbance with the Mormons," published by order of the Missouri Legislature, December 1838, 103.
54. Smith, *History of the Church,* 3:179–82, 192–93, 209–10.
55. Related in the *Times and Seasons,* 1:23.
56. *Millennial Star* 60: 164–65.
57. Gunn, *Oliver Cowdery, Second Elder and Scribe,* 160.
58. Brodie, 217.
59. *Times and Seasons* 2: 201.
60. "To All Believers in Christ," Richmond, Missouri, 1887, L. Tom Perry Special Collections, Harold B. Lee Library, BYU.
61. Smith, *History of the Church,* 2:511.
62. Ibid., 7:232.
63. Ibid., 7:232.
64. *The Saints' Herald* 22 (1875): 630.
65. However few were involved, the plot to kill Joseph was a serious one (see Barrett, *The Restored Church,* 228–33).
66. Statement made by William H. Kelly and G. A. Blakeslee, 15 September 1882, Gallen, Michigan; for comment, see Roberts, *A Comprehensive History of the Church,* 1:130.
67. Brodie, 77–78.
68. Anderson, *Investigating the Book of Mormon Witnesses,* 152.

69. Ibid. Anderson points out an allegation that David Whitmer felt the need to refute.
70. Sjodahl, *An Introduction to the Book of Mormon,* 61.
71. A copy of this interview via James H. Hart with David Whitmer is in the hands of the author.
72. Interview, July 1885, Whitmer home in Richmond, Missouri. Moyle gave this account on 24 April 1927 in Salt Lake City. See also Sjodahl, *An Introduction to the Book of Mormon,* 66. "He believed as firmly as ever that Joseph was a prophet of God. He testified [that] he [Whitmer] saw an angel and heard him say that the plates were translated correctly."
73. Edward Stephenson, letter to Daniel H. Wells, Salt Lake City, 1886; for comment, see Sjodahl, *An Introduction to the Book of Mormon,* 61.
74. For comment, see Sjodahl, *An Introduction to the Book of Mormon,* 62.
75. Brodie, 411–12, 267, 432.
76. See Roberts, 1:11, footnote. "In the original publication of the History of the Church [in the] *Times and Seasons* in Nauvoo, the name appears as 'Nephi.' It was repeated in the *Millennial Star.*"
77. Perhaps Lucy or someone edited out the offensive word Nephi in a later edition. Page 81 of *History of Joseph Smith,* published in 1901, simply refers to the messenger as "the angel." For Brodie's comments, see 411; see also Lucy Mack Smith, *Biographical Sketches of Joseph Smith,* 78.
78 Lucy Mack Smith's *History of Joseph Smith* was edited by Preston Nibley. Lucy's words were dictated to Mrs. Martha Jane Knowlton Coray. It is not known if Brodie saw an earlier edition than the one issued in 1901.
79. Bringhurst, 31, referenced to a letter from Fawn Brodie to Dale Morgan, 24 March 1945. "There will be errors in the book in its final form. . . . I might as well reconcile myself to that fact."

Chapter 11

1. Nibley's precise words are, "Who is better qualified to speak on religion than one who totally rejects all religion?" (see *Tinkling Cymbals*

and Sounding Brass, 516).

2. Interview with Nash, 2 June 2002.

3. Ibid. Compare *World Book Encyclopedia,* s.v. "Thomas Jefferson," with Brodie's *Thomas Jefferson: An Intimate History* (New York: Norton: 1974).

4. Brodie, *No Man Knows My History,* 99.

5. Whittaker, *Mormon History,* 123.

6. Brodie, 27.

7. Ibid., 99–100.

8. Ibid., 118.

9. Ibid., 142.

10. Ibid., 21.

11. In *Journal of Discourses,* 9:77–79.

12. Pratt, *Autobiography*, 239.

13. Brodie, 78.

14. William Smith, *Origin of the Book of Mormon,* 1883 (theme of entire book).

15. Ibid.

16. Brodie, 164.

17. Ibid., 246.

18. Ibid., 246. See also Smith, *History of the Church,* 2:338–39, in which William apologizes for abusing Joseph. "Do not cast me off for what I have done," he says. For Joseph's reply, see pages 340–43.

19. Testimony given by William Smith in Bradtville, Wisconsin (*Zion's Ensign,* Independence, Missouri, 1893; interviewed by E. C. Briggs, written by J. W. Peterson, copied in the *Deseret News* 20 January 1894).

20. Brodie, 247.

21. Smith, *History of the Church,* 3:178–89.

22. Brodie, 48.

23. Warren and Ferguson, *The Messiah in Ancient America,* 2–4.

24. Josephus, *Antiquities of the Jews,* index.

25. Bringhurst, *Reconsidering No Man Knows My History,* 72.

26. Brodie, 441. "Kirkham faces the reality but not the implications of this document." She refers to *A New Witness for Christ in America,* 475n. The Purple document is excluded, and

Brodie does not even refer to Purple in her otherwise thorough index; nor does the name Kirkham appear in her index.

27. Brodie, 292. The King Follet Discourse was delivered at April conference 1844. It was added to *The Voice of Truth* as an appendix (edited by John Taylor). It also appeared in *Times and Seasons,* no. 60, December 1843.

28. Kirkham's *New Witness for Christ in America,* Vol. 2, carries this account as Spaulding wrote it (2:124–25). Hurlbut signed his name on the Spaulding papers certifying it was the long-lost Spaulding manuscript.

29. Roberts, *Defense of the Faith and the Saints,* 36

30. Rigdon, *Life of Sidney Rigdon,* 185–56; Roberts, *A Comprehensive History of the Church,* 234–35.

31. Brodie, 170–74.

32. Ibid.; author's conclusion.

33. This is a constant theme with Brodie (see 83–97, appendix, affidavits, and comments).

34. By this is meant the usual scriptural test—reading the teachings of a prophet and applying them in one's life.

35. Moody, *Life after Life,* preface, 17. "There will be many who find the claims made in this book incredible and whose first reaction will be to dismiss them out of hand." Nevertheless, Moody affirms that the research was scientifically conducted.

36. Reader's Digest, 136. A more recent poll since 11 September 2001 might show a higher percentage.

37. As reported by Roberts in *Defense of the Faith and the Saints,* foreword.

38. Bringhurst, 11; referenced from a letter, Fawn Brodie to Dean R. Brimhall, 18 June 1942.

39. Letter, Fawn Brodie to Dean R. Brimhall, 3 November 1942.

40. This thought is expressed in Brodie's preface, but it is also a theme of her entire book. Brodie then proceeds to tell us what she thinks Joseph Smith should have told us; see also Nibley, *No Ma'am, That's Not History,* 60.

41. Bringhurst, 26. Brodie is in a celebrating mood because, she says, "I finally succeeded in putting five bullet holes in the prophet" (referenced

from a letter, Fawn Brodie to Dale L. Morgan, 1 April 1944).

42. Bringhurst, 48 (referenced from a letter, Fawn Brodie to Dean Brimhall, 4 November 1959; see also Bringhurst, 26–27. Brodie said her revisions were going "badly" and "what I rewrite doesn't satisfy me either" (letter, Brodie to Morgan, 6 May 1944).

43. Brodie, preface, conclusioin (2d edition, 1971).

44. Bringhurst, 25; referenced from a letter, Fawn Brodie to Dale Morgan, 19 November 1943.

45. This is the author's conclusion on the basis of empirical appraisal alone. Those seeking to know spiritual truth can, of course, follow scriptural injunction.

46. Smith, *Doctrines of Salvation,* 1:190.

Sources

Adams, John Q. *The Birth of Mormonism.* Boston: Gorham, 1916.

Ahlstrom, Sydney E. *A Religious History of the American People.* New Haven, Conn.: Yale University Press, 1972.

Anderson, Richard L. *Investigating the Book of Mormon Witnesses.* Salt Lake City: Deseret Book, 1981.

Arrington, Leonard J. and Davis Bitton. *The Mormon Experience.* New York: Alfred Knopf, 1980.

Backman, Milton V. *Joseph Smith's First Vision.* Salt Lake City: Bookcraft, 1980.

Bagley, Will. *Blood of the Prophets—Brigham Young and the Massacre at Mountain Meadows.* Stillwater, Okla.: University of Oklahoma Press, 2002.

Barrett, William E. *The Restored Church.* Salt Lake City: Deseret Book, 1958.

Bennett, John C. *The History of the Saints.* Boston: Leland and Whiting, 1842.

Bringhurst, Newell, ed. *Reconsidering No Man Knows My History.* Logan, Utah: Utah State University Press, 1996.

———. *Fawn McKay Brodie: Biographer's Life.* Norman, Okla.: University of Oklahoma, 1999.

Brodie, Fawn. *No Man Knows My History,* 2d ed. New York: Alfred Knopf, 1982 (listed herein as 1971 edition at time Brodie completed her research).

Brooks, Brian S., et al. *News Reporting and Writing.* New York: St. Martin's Press, 1988.

Brooks, Juanita. *The Mountain Meadows Massacre.* Norman, Okla.: University of Oklahoma Press, 1991.

Compton, Todd. *In Sacred Loneliness.* Salt Lake City: Signature Books, 2001.

Cowdery, Oliver. Letterbook. 21 January 21 1838 (located at Huntington Library, San Marino, California).

Crawley, Peter. *A Descriptive Bibliography of the Mormon Church—Volume 1: 1830–1847.* L. Tom Perry Special Collections, Harold B. Lee Library, Brigham Young University.

Dogberry, Obadiah (Cole, Abner). *Book of Pukei.* New York: Abner Cole, 1830.

Dyer, Alvin R. *The Meaning of Truth.* Salt Lake City: Alvin R. Dyer, 1973.

Evenson, Darrick. *The Gainsayers.* Bountiful, Utah: Horizon, 1989.

Fisher, Vardis. *Children of God.* New York: Harpers, 1939.

———. *In Tragic Life.* New York: Cardinal/Pocket Books, 1952.

Givens, George. *In Old Nauvoo.* Salt Lake City: Deseret Book, 1990.

Goldstein, John. *The News at Any Cost.* New York: Simon and Schuster, 1985.

Grant, Carter E. *Kingdom of God Restored.* Salt Lake City: Deseret Book, 1955.

Gunn, Stanley. *Oliver Cowdery, Second Elder and Scribe.* Salt Lake City: Bookcraft, 1962.

Hill, Donna. *Joseph Smith, The First Mormon.* Garden City, N.Y.: Doubleday, 1977.

Hinckley, Gordon B. *What of the Mormons?* Salt Lake City: The Church of Jesus Christ of Latter-day Saints, 1982.

Howe, E. D. *Mormonism Unvailed* [sic]. Painesville, Ohio: E. D. Howe, 1834.

Josephus, Flavius. *Antiquities of the Jews.* Grand Rapids, Mich.: Kregel Publishers, 1978.

Kennedy, J. H. *Early Days of Mormonism.* New York: Charles Scribners & Sons, 1888.

Kirk, John R., and George D. Talbot. *Distortion of Information.* N.p.: John R. Kirk and George D. Talbot, 1959.

Kirkham, Francis W. *A New Witness for Christ in America.* 3d ed., 2 vols. Independence, Mo.: Zions Printing and Publishing, 1951.

The Latter Day Saints' Messenger and Advocate. Kirtland, Ohio, 1834–37.

LeSueur, Stephen. *The Mormon War in Missouri.* Columbia, Mo.: University of Missouri Press, 1987.

Ludlow, Daniel. *A Companion to Your Study of the Book of Mormon.* Salt Lake City: Deseret Book, 1976.

Lundwall, N. B. *Fate of the Persecutors of the Prophet Joseph Smith.* Salt Lake City: Bookcraft, 1952.

Madsen, Truman. *Did B. H. Roberts Lose Faith in the Book of Mormon?* Provo, Utah: Foundation for Ancient Research and Mormon Studies, 1986.

Majors, Alexander. *My Seventy Years on the Frontier.* 1893.

McConkie, Bruce, R. *Mormon Doctrine.* 2d ed. Salt Lake City: Bookcraft, 1979.

Moody, Raymond. *Life after Life.* Mechanicsburgh, Penn.: Stackpole Books, 1976.

Nibley, Hugh. *Tinkling Cymbals and Sounding Brass.* Edited by David J. Whittaker. Salt Lake City: Deseret Book and Provo, Utah: Foundation for Ancient Research and Mormon Studies, 1991.

———. *Since Cumorah.* Salt Lake City: Deseret Book, 1973.

———. *The Myth Makers.* Salt Lake City: Bookcraft, 1961.

———. *No, Ma'am, That's Not History.* Salt Lake City: Bookcraft, 1946.

———. *An Approach to the Book of Mormon.* Salt Lake City: Deseret Book, 1957.

Nibley, Preston. *Three Mormon Classics: Lives of Wilford Woodruff, George Q. Cannon, Jacob Hamblin*. Salt Lake City: Bookcraft, 1988.

Palmer, Grant. *An Insider's View of Mormon Origins*. Salt Lake City: Signature Books, 2002.

Partridge, Edward. "Long Journal." Compiled by Edward Partridge Jr. 1878. LDS Church Archives.

Poll, Richard. *Utah's History*. Provo, Utah: BYU Press, 1978.

Pratt, James M. *The Last Valentine*. New York: St. Martin's Press, 1966.

Pratt, Parley P. *Autobiography of Parley P. Pratt*. Salt Lake City: Deseret Book, 1938.

Pratt, Orson. *Orson Pratt's Works*. Salt Lake City: Deseret News Press, 1945.

Peterson, Levi S. *Juanita Brooks*. Salt Lake City: University of Utah Press, 1988.

Reynolds, Noel B. *Book of Mormon Authorship, New Light on Ancient Origins*. Provo, Utah: Religious Study Center, 1982.

———. *Book of Mormon Authorship Revisited, the Evidence of Ancient Origin*. Provo, Utah: Foundation for Ancient Research and Mormon Studies, 1997.

Rigdon, John W. *Life of Sidney Rigdon*. N.p., n.d. LDS Church Archives.

Riley, William. "Isaiah Comparisons." Master's thesis, Brigham Young University, 1971.

Roberts, B. H. *A Comprehensive History of the Church*. 6 vols. Provo, Utah: Brigham Young University Press, 1965.

———. *Book of Mormon Studies*. Chicago: University of Illinois, 1985.

———. *Defense of the Faith and the Saints*. 2 vols. Salt Lake City: Deseret News, 1907.

The Saints' Herald. Published by the Reorganized Church of Jesus Christ of Latter Day Saints, Lamoni, Iowa; and Independence, Mo., Janurary 1860–.

Sjodahl, Janne M. *An Introduction to the Book of Mormon.* Salt Lake City: Deseret News Press, 1927.

Smith, Ethan. *View of the Hebrews.* Provo, Utah: BYU Religious Studies Center, 1996. Originally published in Poultney, Vermont, in 1823 by Smith and Shute.

Smith, Joseph. *History of The Church of Jesus Christ of Latter-day Saints.* Edited by B. H. Roberts. 2d ed. rev., 7 vols. Salt Lake City: The Church of Jesus Christ of Latter-day Saints, 1932–51.

Smith, Joseph Fielding. *Doctrines of Salvation.* Compiled by Bruce R. McConkie. 3 vols. Salt Lake City: Bookcraft, 1954–56.

———. *Essentials in Church History.* Salt Lake City: Deseret Book, 1972.

Smith, Lucy Mack. *Biographical Sketches of Joseph Smith the Prophet and His Progenitors.* Lamoni, Iowa: RLDS Church, 1912.

———. *History of Joseph Smith.* Salt Lake City: Bookcraft, 1901.

Smith, William. *William Smith on Mormonism.* Lamoni, Iowa: Herald Steam Book and Job Office, 1883.

Sperry, Sidney. *Origin of the Book of Mormon.* Salt Lake City: Stevens and Wallis, 1883.

———. *Paul's Life and Letters.* Salt Lake City: Bookcraft, 1953.

Taylor, John. *Voice of Truth.* Nauvoo, Ill.: John Taylor, 1845.

Three Mormon Classics: Leaves from My Journal, My First Mission, Jacob Hamblin. Edited by James A. Little. Salt Lake City: Bookcraft, 1990.

Times and Seasons. Commerce (later Nauvoo), Illinois, 1839–46.

Tucker, Pomeroy. *Origin, Rise, and Progress of the Mormon Church.* Palmyra, N.Y., 1867.

Turner, Orasmus. *History of the Pioneer Settlement of Phelps and Gorham's Purchase.* Rochester, N.Y.: William Alling, 1851.

Walters, Wesley P. *Joseph Smith's Bainbridge, N.Y., Court Trials.* Salt Lake City: Utah Lighthouse Ministry, 1997.

Walters, Wesley P. and H. Michael Marquardt. *Inventing Mormonism: Tradition and the Historical Record.* Salt Lake City: Signature Books, 1994.

Warren, Bruce, and Thomas S. Ferguson. *The Messiah in Ancient America.* Provo, Utah: Book of Mormon Research Foundation, 1987.

West, Jack. *Trial of the Stick of Joseph.* Provo, Utah: Brigham Young University, 1954.

Welch, John. *An Unparallel.* Provo, Utah: Foundation for Ancient Research and Mormon Studies, 1985.

Whitmer, John. *An Early History of the Church.* Independence, Mo.: Herald House, 1980.

Whittaker, David, et al. *Mormon History.* Chicago: University of Illinois, 2001.

Wixom, Hartt. *Edward Partridge.* Springville, Utah: Cedar Fort, 1998.

———. *Hamblin: A Modern Look at the Frontier Life and Legend of Jacob Hamblin.* Springville, Utah: Cedar Fort, 1996.

———. "Public Credibility Tolerance Thresholds Toward Errors in Print Journalism." Master's thesis, Brigham Young University, 1991.

Woodward, Tim. *Tiger on the Road.* Caldwell, Idaho: Caxton Printers, 1989.

Young, Brigham. *Discourses of Brigham Young.* Selected by John A. Widtsoe. Salt Lake City: Deseret Book, 1946.

Index

O

P

Q

R

S

About the Author

Hartt Wixom has an extensive background in both academia and newspaper journalism. He taught reporting and editing at Brigham Young University for fourteen years and has worked as an investigative reporter.

He received a master's degree from BYU in 1994 and has done post-graduate work in English and history at the University of Utah, studying under such notable historians as Davis Bitton, Charles Peterson, and David Miller.

Brother Wixom, who has a reputation for not shying away from difficult and controversial subjects, has received several national and regional awards for telling it like it is. He is the author of fourteen books, including biographies of Jacob Hamblin and Edward Partridge, prominent figures in LDS history.

He and his wife, Judene, live in Ivins, Utah, and Cokeville, Wyoming. They have seven children and nineteen grandchildren.

0 26575 78340 7